Divided Borders: Essays on Puerto Rican Identity

Juan Flores

Arte Público Press
Houston
Texas
1993

This book is made possible through a grant from the National Endowment for the Arts, a federal agency.

Arte Público Press
University of Houston
Houston, Texas 77204-2090

Cover design by Mark Piñón

Juan Flores
    Divided borders: essays on Puerto Rican identity / by Juan Flores.
       p.   cm.
    ISBN 1-55885-046-5
    1. Puerto Ricans—United States. I. Title.
E184.P85F57 1992
305.8'687295073–dc20   91-37313

                                                               CIP

The paper used in this publication meets the requirements of the American National Standard for Permanence of Paper for Printed Library Materials Z39.48-1984. ∞

Contents

Author's Note   7

Introduction by Jean Franco   9

I

The Insular Vision: Pedreira and the Puerto Rican Misère . . . 13

II

The Puerto Rico that José Luis González Built 61

Refiguring *La Charca* 71

"Bumbún" and the Beginnings of *Plena* Music 85

Cortijo's Revenge: New Mappings of Puerto Rican Culture . . 92

III

National Culture and Migration: Perspectives from the Puerto
  Rican Working Class (with Ricardo Campos) 111

Puerto Rican Literature in the United States: Stages and
  Perspectives 142

IV

La Carreta Made a U-Turn: Puerto Rican Language and Culture
  in the United States (with John Attinasi and Pedro Pedraza) 157

"Qué assimilated, brother, yo soy asimilao": The Structuring
  of Puerto Rican Identity 182

V

Living Borders / *Buscando América*: Languages of Latino
  Self-Formation (with George Yúdice) 199

Notes 225

Divided Borders: Essays on Puerto Rican Identity

Davilita (Pedro Ortiz Dávila), Juan Boria, Luis Lebrón, Mirta Silva, Odilio González y los Hispanos arriving at New York City Airport, 1956. Photographer unknown. The Justo A. Martí Collection, Centro de Estudios Puertorriqueños, Hunter College, CUNY.

Author's Note

These essays were written over a span of about twelve years (1979–1991) for a range of different occasions and readers. Most were conceived and developed in the context of my association with the Centro de Estudios Puertorriqueños at Hunter College (CUNY). I have resisted the strong temptation to revise or re-write: aside from some editorial adjustments aimed at removing serious repetition, the versions included here are the same as in their initial publications. I have arranged the essays in a sequence that I thought might lend the collection a certain thematic coherence.

Introduction

On a recent visit to Sao Paulo I discovered a huge relief map of Latin America on the floor of the folk museum which was situated in a complex of meeting halls, theater and exhibition rooms that had been built as a tribute to Latin American solidarity. As I walked alongside the map tracing the waterways, cities and mountains from the Tierra del Fuego to Cuba I noticed something odd about the Caribbean—Puerto Rico was missing. It was not on the map of Latin America. At the time, that omission seemed to me shocking, even tragic. But after reading Juan Flores' book, *Divided Borders*, I began to understand that this very absence upsets the facile notions of Latin identity that the map was designed to promote. Both in Latin America and the United States, Puerto Rico stands for something which cannot be assimilated. It is island and continent, a colony and a nation, a community bound by a language that some Puerto Ricans do not speak.

Divided Borders: Essays on Puerto Rican Identity begins appropriately with a revisionary exploration of two classic interpretations of Puerto Rican identity—Antonio S. Pedreira's *Insularismo* (1934) and José Luis González's *País de cuatro pisos* (1980). Although based on very different assumptions—indeed González founded his edifice on the black Puerto Rican that Pedreira wanted to reform or whiten—these essays both privilege ethnicity over class and both of them enclose Puerto Rican culture within the boundaries of the island, severing it from the dynamic and culturally productive emigrant experience. The value of *Divided Borders* is that it extends the whole concept of Puerto Rican culture beyond the island to the working class communities in New York and the East Coast and their dynamic interaction with black Americans and with workers' movements. Flores brings into view what has been "hidden from history"—and certainly hidden from traditional literary and cultural histories.

In restoring the perspective of class to cultural history, Flores vigorously corrects the view so often conveyed by "high culture" that the immigrant experience was somehow impoverished, degraded and impure. For this reason, he shifts emphasis from island literature to popular music, especially the "plena," to the working class politics of the twenties and thirties, and to contemporary Nuyorican literature. Nevertheless class *is* the axis on which the entire argument around identity rests.

For the problem is that cultural hybridity and the cross-cultural experience which were the commonplace of working class and emigrant life have now become high fashion. In a pluralistic society, in the global village, everyone can claim to be bilingual and bicultural. We are all, in some way, marginalized. So what is particularly significant about Puerto Rico?

Flores's first strategic move is to map a politics of culture in which hybridity and heterogeneity are not simply constituted out of a general multicultural repertoire but are produced by lived relations between workers (Jamaicans and Puerto Rican farm laborers), between ethnic groups and between immigrant groups in New York. His second strategic move is to provide a new genealogy which links contemporary struggles over language to both the New York working class movements of the thirties, popular musical culture and the emergence of Nuyorican writers in the 1950s and 1960s.

It is this historical perspective which prepares the ground for the essays on language and on new social movements which complete the book. For Flores, identity is not fixed in some "authentic" place, nor is it tied to evolutionary history whether that of the working class movement or of popular culture. Contemporary language struggles do not grow like a sampling from the seeds of prior events, for the experience of immigration is essentially discontinous. This is why identity comes to be seen in terms of strategic responses to hegemonic rationality—for instance, the pressure to "assimilate" as the only way forward, or pressures to adopt the dominant language because it is a practical way of negotiating demands in U.S. society. Counter-hegemonic identities will be forged precisely in defiance of this rationalization. But doesn't this deny the very notion of identity? Not so, according to Flores. The language play of Tato Laviera, crossover genres of Rubén Blades, the cultural refashioning proposed by Gloria Anzaldúa are counter-hegemonic tactics in which "Latino" and Puerto Rican identity is there to be claimed and won, not as some pre-given category.

Flores' book is a powerful statement of the role of culture and language in counter-hegemonic struggles. The clear prose of these essays is in stark contrast to much contemporary academic writing. It is a clarity that encourages further debate and is directed to a broad community of those for whom forging alliances does not mean loss. In this light the fact that Puerto Rico is absent from the map of Latin America and appears only marginally on the map of the United States forces all of us to reconsider the meaning of identity.

Jean Franco
May, 1992

I

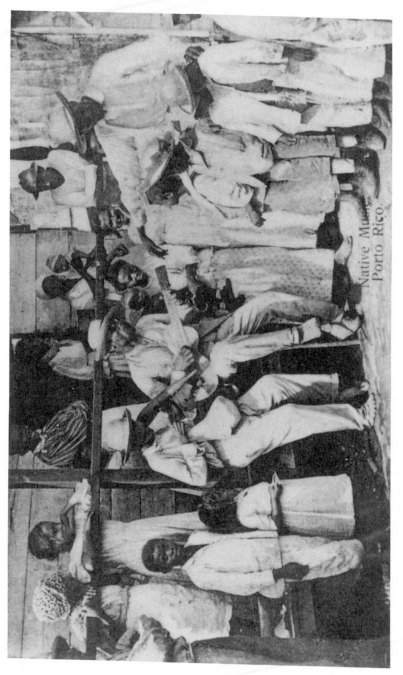

"Native Music. Porto (sic) Rico." Postcard, ca. 1900s. General Collection. Centro de Estudios Puertorriqueños, Hunter College, CUNY.

The Insular Vision: Pedreira
and the Puerto Rican Misère

New Contexts, New Readings

The wholesale exportation of working-class families from Puerto Rico to the United States carries a social and cultural impact of significant proportions. The massive presence of Puerto Ricans in New York and other urban centers and rural pockets, serving on ready reserve at all levels of the labor process, has introduced a new dimension to class and national contention both in the United States and in Puerto Rico. The cliché of Puerto Ricans as a "bridge between two cultures" was coined in a reactionary, assimilationist spirit, to suggest the convenient marriage of that age-old mythical pair, Anglo-Saxon materialism and Latin spirituality; or in its more pertinent, "commonwealth" version, the neighborly co-existence of the benevolent, self-sufficient colossus and that helpless speck of tropical subculture. Such "bridges," of course, are no more than colonialist wish-dreams, invidious constructs intended to conceal and legitimize the real relations between North American and Puerto Rican societies.

Yet in the deeper historical sense, Puerto Ricans in the United States do indeed generate new linkages. Cultural interactions and exchanges with Black people in the United States are clearly the most prominent, but only one in a growing array. Contact with peoples from other Caribbean and Latin American countries—in New York and San Francisco—and with Mexicans and Mexican-Americans—in Detroit, Chicago and Los Angeles—is becoming increasingly significant, as is the long-standing association with

First appeared as a Working Paper, Centro de Estudios Puertorriqueños, 1980. The Spanish translation, *Insularismo e ideología burguesa*, was published in Havana: Casa de las Américas, 1980, and Río Piedras: Ediciones Huracán, 1980.

working-class Americans of Italian, Irish and other European descent. The quality of these various cross-currents differs greatly, of course, depending most of all on the relative position historically of the interacting peoples and cultures within the expanding network of world imperialism and its projections within the United States. If the main design of the dominant culture is assimilation, the enforced melting-down of genuine cultural diversity, the most telling effect of the Puerto Rican cultural presence in the United States remains its emphasis on difference, and most notably on the distinction between cultures of colonial peoples and that of imperialist society. It is that core of resistance and self-affirmation that makes the Puerto Rican case so deeply revealing of the true content of newly furbished ideologies of pluralism for the colonized, whether at home or in the heart of the metropolis. In this sense, the Puerto Rican experience is indeed a link spanning outward toward the cultures of the entire hemisphere and the colonial world.

The Puerto Rican presence in the United States does inject a stream of anti-colonial, Latin American and Caribbean culture into the artery of North American life and, conversely, it has projected the development of Puerto Rican cultural history into a setting of intense multicultural interactions, both events unprecedented, in the senses described, within the history of either society. But as long as Puerto Rico remains in direct colonial bondage to the United States, Puerto Rican cultural expression in the United States evokes the relation, above all, between Puerto Rican people here and there, between the expressive life of the migrant population and the long-standing traditions of struggle and articulation of the Island culture. Whatever else is said about the cultural activity of Puerto Ricans in the United States, critical analysis will inevitably and ultimately hinge on the explanation given to the continuities and interruptions between cultural life in the new setting and its most relevant historical backdrop—Puerto Rican national culture.

Recognition of this national referent, however, does not by itself guarantee the accuracy and appropriateness of an interpretation of the cultural experience of Puerto Ricans in the United States. The most noteworthy and representative attempts to describe the culture in this setting, in fact, operate within just such a frame, steering clear of both overtly assimilationist and abstractly cosmopolitan positions and drawing many lines of comparison and contrast to the Island legacy. Yet despite their proper attention to identifiable national links, all of these approaches fall short, for different reasons, of a coherent and theoretically elaborated presentation of the problem. In all their diversity, the major commentators on Puerto Rican culture in its United States manifestations have recourse to a similarly static and fragmentary conception of cultural development. Considered individually and in conjunction, they project a confused and disorienting image of the cultural situation of Puerto Ricans in the United States.[1]

Now these theoretical deficiencies, and the major issues and concerns involved in the cultural identification of Puerto Ricans now in the United States, are rooted in the cumulated tradition of philosophical self-definition on the part of Island-based Puerto Rican thinkers. A critical review of some of the more widely recognized "classical" conceptions and misconceptions of Puerto Rican national identity, therefore, may identify the range of discourse concerning the cultural reality of Puerto Rican people living in the United States. To this day, despite intervening social changes and numerous subsequent attempts to delineate the national character and culture, Antonio S. Pedreira's *Insularismo: Ensayos de interpretación puertorriqueña* (Insularism: Essays on Puerto Rican Interpretation) stands, since its publication in 1934, as the watershed and germinal source of thinking about Puerto Rican culture. For this reason, and because the book has never received adequate intellectual scrutiny, detailed critical treatment of *Insularismo* is crucial to an assessment of the cultural life of Puerto Rican people, whether in Puerto Rico or in the United States.

At the same time, it is to be hoped that the vantage point provided by active interest and involvement in the current cultural production and political struggle of Puerto Ricans in New York City may help shed some fresh light on these deep-lying yet broadly contested assumptions. The process of intensive capitalist industrialization and the tidal-wave of migration, which cast up nearly half of the Puerto Rican working class in North American barrios, constitute the main historical developments separating Pedreira's time from the present. The cultural ferment to which that movement has led, the probing search for a critical, Puerto Rican perspective on their own production by cultural workers in this new setting, are the unforeseen events which confront Pedreira's vision. The disturbing, irreverent paintings of Jorge Soto, the varied poetic voices of Pedro Pietri, Sandra Esteves and Victor Hernández Cruz, the stark yet dramatic experiments of *Teatro 4*, the innovations in the music of Eddie Palmieri and popular ensembles of the last decade—compelling evidence of the manifold cultural experience of Puerto Rican people—escape interpretation within the cramped intellectual horizon of *Insularismo*.[2]

The Metaphor of National Identity: Isolation and Docility

In 1644, while Puerto Rico was languishing under entrenched Spanish rule, Damián López de Haro, who was the Bishop appointed to the colony, offered one of the very few available descriptions of conditions on the Island at the time. Among the realities which came to his attention, and which he recorded in rather sarcastic tones in a letter to Juan Díaz de la Calle "with a most curious account of his voyage and other matters," the Bishop made note of the dire poverty of Puerto Rico and the general state of terror caused by ceaseless acts of plunder on the part of Dutch pirates at large in the Caribbean. "Here we are so besieged by enemies," he wrote, "that they (the Puerto Ricans) dare not set out to fish in boats for fear that the Dutchman will get them" (161).³

This portrait of a people forced into confinement and isolation from even their most immediate surroundings and insulated, as it were, from the inimical world outside, hangs with symbolic import over the entire history of Puerto Rico. It is this commentary by Bishop López de Haro, in fact, which forms the metaphorical crux of the single most influential study of Puerto Rican culture: *Insularismo: Ensayos de interpretación puertorriqueña* (1934). Its author, Antonio S. Pedreira, had all the credentials necessary to undertake such a broad-reaching theoretical meditation on the "character" and cultural "personality" of the Puerto Rican people. Virtually every modern Puerto Rican writer and critic of any prominence—Tomás Blanco, Vicente Géigel Polanco, Emilio S. Belaval, Enrique Laguerre, Concha Meléndez, María Teresa Babín, Francisco Manrique Cabrera, José Antonio Dávila, Evaristo Ribera Chevremont, Washington Lloréns, Samuel R. Quiñones, Margot Arce de Vázquez, José A. Balseiro, Félix Franco Oppenheimer, to name a few—have paid explicit homage to Pedreira's paramount contribution. He was also praised highly by none other than Gabriela Mistral, who called him "a man of the stature of Hostos" ("gente hostosiana es ella"), and by Juan Ramón Jiménez in a letter to Margot Arce de Vázquez at the time of his death. In the only extended discussion of *Insularismo* to date, Manuel Maldonado-Denis singled out that book as "the classic work par excellence of Puerto Rican interpretation."⁴ With little hesitation, Pedreira is considered the father of modern Puerto Rican letters.

Born in the traumatic year of 1898, Pedreira emerged as a budding "postmodernist" poet and was active in university student affairs in the early 1920s. In addition to travels to Spain and the European countries, he did his graduate work under Federico de Onís at Columbia University, receiving his degree in 1927 for a thesis on Eugenio María de Hostos. On returning to the Island, he was named the first director of the newly founded Department of Hispanic Studies at the University of Puerto Rico. Aside from his teaching and directing activities, he was one of the co-founders, in 1929, of the journal *Indice*, which immediately became one of the most important forums of Puerto Rican intellectual debate. His critical and academic writings broke major ground in a wide range of areas of Puerto Rican cultural history. A mere listing of his works may suggest the scope of his contribution: *De los nombres de Puerto Rico* (About the Names of Puerto Rico, 1927), *Arista* (1930), *Hostos, ciudadano de América* (Hostos, Citizens of America, 1932), *La actualidad del jíbaro* (The Contemporary Jíbaro, 1935), *El año terrible del '87* (The Terrible Year of 1987, 1937), *Un hombre del pueblo: José Celso Barbosa* (A Man of the People: José Celso Barbosa, 1937), *El periodismo en Puerto Rico* (Journalism in Puerto Rico, 1941) and the compilation of his articles for *El Mundo, Aclaraciones y crítica* (A World of Clarifications). This legacy of pioneering studies, and especially his major work *Insularismo*, has marked the standard and prevalent philosophical tone for Puerto Rican cultural interpretation since his death in 1939.[5]

Pedreira sets the Puerto Ricans' fear of the Dutchman into the sweeping trajectory of colonial isolation and subjugation. The particular historical fate of the Island, having been passed from one imperial orbit to another and falling prey to whatever greedy and aggressive designs lurk in the Antilles, has served to accentuate the already restrictive effect of its diminutive, "insular" geography. Unending dread of invasion and political answerability to foreign metropolitan powers—total absence of national sovereignty—have forced Puerto Rican culture into a prostrate, submissive position, sealed off from all interchange and solidarity with other peoples. At the same time, Pedreira emphasizes the spirit of resistance and the struggle for self-identification which constitute the real quality of Puerto Rican history; his chapter "Afirmación puertorriqueña" is undoubtedly among the most moving, eloquent words of homage to the nineteenth-century autonomist movement in all Puerto Rican writing, and is in large measure responsible for the book's influence on subsequent progressive approaches to Puerto Rican history. Pedreira calls upon his compatriots to break out of their isolation and overcome their fear of the threatening pirate who, he observes, "has not always been a Dutchman." "For the world to get to know us and to impel us forward, we have to stop being Robinson Crusoe. Let us set out to fish, though we be caught by the Dutchman. The day may come when one of us will return with his nets full!" (163).

Yet the sense of affirmation pronounced by Pedreira runs deeper than evidence of political history; the real attraction of the book is that it poses the problem at a philosophical, ontological level. *Insularismo* was written to crown a debate among Puerto Rican intellectuals of those years, a debate consisting of responses solicited in 1929 by the editors of *Indice* to the agonizing question of national identity—"what are we and how are we?" ("¿qué somos y cómo somos?") The issue had been raised many years earlier, in the wake of North American occupation, in the famous words of Rosendo Matienzo Cintrón (1903): "Today, Puerto Rico is nothing but masses of people; but when these obtain a soul of their own, then Puerto Rico will become a homeland." The immediate spark for the contemporary debate, however, was the comment by the official Puerto Rican historian Mariano Abril in 1929: "But ... is there such a soul? And a distinctively Puerto Rican one? A surgeon would be hard put to find it with his scalpel; a physiologist would doubt its existence. The country is all out of joint ... it resembles the Knight of Death in Dürer's painting, whose coat of shining armor served only to conceal a vile skeleton" (167). While avoiding the crass and morbid imagery of Mariano Abril, most of the respondents to *Indice* tended to deny the existence of a Puerto Rican "soul" and to cast their national characterization in extremely negative, demeaning terms.

Pedreira allowed himself several years of reflection and study to formulate his contribution to this discussion, knowing that the clinical and pseudo-scientific terms in which the question was being framed could not possibly lead to an adequate answer. His conclusion, in *Insularismo*, is qualified, but can leave no doubt as to the existence of a Puerto Rican national spirit: "It is our honest belief that a Puerto Rican soul does exist, though it be disintegrated, disperse, latent, still in thousands of shiny pieces like a painfully difficult jigsaw puzzle which has never been successfully assembled" (168). The national psyche is in formation, he contends, and despite the many historical obstacles and contradictions, there is an incipient, or at least potential, Puerto Rican personality. It is this affirmation, however conditional, of national identity, and the evident circumspection and intellectual attention paid to its definition, which account for the germinal significance of Pedreira's book for subsequent cultural study. From this point onward it could no longer be said of Puerto Rico that it lacked the kind of self-interpretative essay enjoyed by most of the other Latin American countries. *Insularismo* put Puerto Rico on the intellectual map, and lent its claim to nationhood, however belated and mimetic, a measure of authority and, one might add, respectability.

Yet this spiritual recognition and patriotic homage is about all there is by way of national affirmation, and seems to have been purchased at the price of attributing to the Puerto Rican people, as inherent national traits, all the symptoms of colonial rule. In Pedreira's judgment, Puerto Ricans are characteristically a weak, complacent, ignorant and confused people, with a penchant for rhetorical excess, plagued by fits of lyrical melancholia, and cowardly and passive in the face of adversity. The isolation represented by the fear of Dutch pirates is generalized as a lack of solidarity with other peoples and of intellectual and cultural achievements matching up to international standards. The peaceful, non-violent nature of the people, presented as a singular Puerto Rican virtue, is then inverted at a more speculative level of thinking into weakness of will and a deficient sense of collective determination.

The catch-word, of course, is docility or, in its pungent, "native" expression, "aplatanamiento" (bananization?). As Pedreira defines this national condition, "*Aplatanarse* in our country is a kind of inhibition, mental lethargy and lack of assertiveness—following life's course complacently, routinely, never getting worked up about anything; nodding our heads at all aspirations and crouching in the face of whatever the future may bring" (39). Puerto Ricans are typically and collectively on their haunches, "*ñangotado*," according to Pedreira, who makes no note of the attribution of precisely the same identifying pose to other peoples, notably the Mexican peasantry. And in describing Puerto Rican society as sick and without motivation, Pedreira is only giving classical stature to similar observations made by earlier Puerto Rican intellectuals, such as Luis Muñoz Rivera in his poems and proclamations and Manuel Zeno Gandía in his four-part novel series entitled "Chronicle of a Sick World" ("Crónica de un mundo enfermo"). What is perhaps most important, however, is that Pedreira handed this tradition on to more recent portrayals of the Puerto Rican character, not only among North American anthropologists, but among some of the country's most prominent writers, notably René Marqués in what might be regarded as a sequel essay to *Insularismo*, the award winning *El puertorriqueño dócil* (The Docile Puerto Rican, 1962).[6]

The value of *Insularismo* in developing a critique of this generic attribution is its pivotal position within an extended controversy, but also derives from Pedreira's attempt to account for this collective trait by probing the roots of the national "essence" and tracing its development through the centuries. Getting out from under the Puerto Ricans' most burdensome, typological cliché involves most evidently in this case, therefore, a total recasting of historical vision, a radical reinterpretation of the meaning of ethnicity and an abandonment of outworn theories and methods of analysis.

Versions of Puerto Rican History

In Pedreira's view, Puerto Rico is in the third major stage of its historical development. "I perceive three outstanding moments in the development of our people: the first, the stage of passive formulation and accumulation beginning with the discovery and conquest and extending through the beginning of the nineteenth century; the second, one of awakening and initiation, which spans the nineteenth century through the Spanish-American War; and the third, which is the moment of indecision and transition in which we presently find ourselves" (15). Pedreira is confident about the accuracy of this periodization, and at times presents his vision in the poetic images of a seafaring voyage: "Three centuries of slow, tranquil navigation were not sufficient to discover the path leading to El Dorado. In the nineteenth century we began to trace the shores of our collective conscience in the mist, and then, just as we were preparing for the jubilant cry of 'Fatherland in view,' a warlike hand smashed our rudder to pieces, leaving our ship adrift at sea" (168). Puerto Rican history begins, then, with the Spanish conquest, and after three centuries of gestation and gradual differentiation from Spain, the process of national self-definition accelerates with the advance of the nineteenth century, only to be brought to an abrupt halt under the North American occupation since 1898. In the twentieth century, with Puerto Rican culture being saturated by foreign, "Anglo-Saxon" values, the society is considered to be in a state of confusion and "transition," and its movement toward national consciousness derailed.

This conventional panorama of national history, as helpful as it is in its indication of general contours, actually serves to obscure and distort the most salient features of national self-definition. Most obviously, the point of departure is taken to be the arrival of European conquerors, such that the cultures and struggles of pre-Columbian times are assumed to have no bearing on subsequent development. Because of its rapid extinction at the hands of the invaders, the indigenous population is dismissed summarily as a component of national identity; all that the Taínos contributed, after the Christian baptism of the Island, were some quaint folkloristic remnants like the typical hut (*el bohío*), the gourd hand instrument (*el güiro*) and the hammock. This deletion of the Indians from the historical record and diminution of their enduring cultural significance are earmarks of a colonialist frame of thinking. Though largely corrected by the subsequent anthropological work of Ricardo Alegría, Eugenio Fernández Méndez and Jalil Sued Badillo and, in a wider context, Francisco Moscoso and José Juan Arrom, this relegation of the indigenous heritage or, what is but the logical converse, its romanticized mystique, continues to blur any scientific account of Puerto Rican history.[7]

It is true, of course, that compared to countries like México, Perú, Bolivia and Guatemala, indigenous presence as a social force during the forging of modern Puerto Rican life is negligible; there are no living Indian languages or forms of social organization, no indigenist literature and therefore no indigenous participation in any of the formative struggles of modern history. For that reason, any claim to the effect that Puerto Ricans are "essentially" Taínos or endeavor to trace the national culture to some Indian "spirit," divorced from what can be determined to have been the mode of social organization of the indigenous peoples, lead inevitably to a mystified and reductionist escape. However, the extermination of the original population and relative extinction of their cultural remains in no way justify the exclusion of an indigenous, "primitive" perspective from the trajectory of Puerto Rican cultural history.

Even Pedreira, in fact, cannot totally ignore this dimension of the struggle for national self-definition. In the course of his enthusiastic homage to the nineteenth-century autonomist movement, he calls to mind the "first Puerto Rican to speak valiantly and clearly of separatism" (179), the poet Daniel de Rivera. In 1854, a Ponce newspaper published de Rivera's poem "Agüeybaná el Bravo" (Agüeybaná the Brave) in which the demand for independence—"let those born in Spain return to Spain" and "set this pearl free from the Iberians"—is uttered through the persona of the Taíno chieftain who led the earliest resistance against the conquistadores. This publication led to the immediate suppression of the periodical, confiscation of the press and persecution and exile of the poet. Pedreira goes on to document the powerful political impact of the poem in the famous manifesto of 1864, exhorting Puerto Rican soldiers enlisted in the Spanish colonial army to desert rather than fight their brothers in Santo Domingo. "The *jíbaros* of Puerto Rico," the proclamation reads, "sons of Agüeybaná the Brave, have not lost their sense of dignity and will show their oppressors, just as the valiant Dominicans are doing right now, that though they may be easy to govern as long as they believe they are being treated justly, in no way will they allow themselves to be abused with impunity." In what is the strongest note of internationalist solidarity in the pages of *Insularismo*, Pedreira summarizes the meaning of this "Indian" perspective: "The name of that Indian, then, the first to rise up against the conquerors, became a symbol of redemption. With an inspiring pride we proclaim ourselves in lofty tones the sons of Agüeybaná the Brave, and just as we declared war against the Spaniards, feelings of Antillean solidarity were loudly expressed" (179).

Yet such passages are rare in Pedreira's writing, and only feebly counteract his markedly Hispanic conception of Puerto Rican identity. At no point does he go beyond a symbolic and more or less rhetorical reference to the indigenous background, or show any interest in probing the deeper strains of continuity between Indian and later, national forms of resistance to colonial oppression. Puerto Rican history is, in his view, no more than a process of differentiation, almost regional in character, within the orbit of Spanish history, a movement from an initial state of "faithful prolongation" of Iberian culture and values to a growing conflict between Spaniards "from here" and Spaniards "from there." Needless to say, Pedreira's allegiance to Spain, like that of so many Latin American Hispanophiles, really betrays a selective loyalty, since it highlights only the patrimonial, feudal legacy of Spanish culture. (The progressive and revolutionary traditions of modern Spain, which were assuming visible expression in the very years of *Insularismo* and have such a strong potential bearing on the cultural struggle throughout Latin America, find no repercussions whatsoever in Pedreira's writing.[8])

This "criollo" vision, so common among Puerto Rican intellectuals when confronted with the reality of North American cultural imposition, leads Pedreira to a variety of Eurocentric distortions. He notes with remorse, for example, that Puerto Rican history lacks its Middle Ages and Renaissance, as though these periods inevitably befall all societies and are yet to "arrive" in Puerto Rico before it can attain to its full cultural realization. He summarily writes off the "first three centuries"—the sixteenth, seventeenth, and eighteenth—as "the Dead Sea," "blank centuries," and "a hopeless desert" (52–3), implying that all artistic expression must be measured against the Siglo de Oro and that there can have been no cultural life but that of the chronicles and memoirs of the Spanish missionaries.[9]

Even in his account of the heralded nineteenth century, the period of real national awakening, Pedreira points to the triumph of liberalism in Spain, rather than to the Latin American independence struggles, as the direct impetus of democratic movement. In a similar spirit, he considers the abolitionist literature of the Island and Spain and not the waves of slave rebellions to have been the backbone of social reform, and the repression of illustrious liberals like Ramón Baldorioty de Castro and the Spaniard Laureano Cepeda in the "year of terror 1887" of more transcendent historical importance than the "so-called Lares revolution." It is significant that in his hymnic praise of Puerto Rican national affirmation, the names Betances and Hostos are mentioned only in passing; and that while Alonso's *El Gíbaro* is enthroned as the *Poema del Cid* and *Martín Fierro* of Puerto Rican literature, and similar stress is placed on the romantic lyrics of José Gautier Benítez, there is little attention given to the critical, realistic novels of Manuel Zeno Gandía or to the revolutionary poetry of "Pachín" Marín. Pedreira did, of course, devote a full monograph to Hostos ("Citizen of America"); but here too his Hispanophile, anti-indigenous bias prevails. This distortion is most evident in his nearly total disregard for Hostos' diary novel *La peregrinación de Bayoán* (The Pilgrimage of Bayoán, 1863)—his only work of fiction—and the deep personal and political crisis it represented.

Small wonder, then, that Pedreira comes to characterize the twentieth century as an "intermezzo," a "transition" period in which the ship of Puerto Rican history is "adrift" ("la nave al garete"). Here all sense of historical actuality, dim as it is throughout *Insularismo*, gives way to the metaphysical dualism of contrasting "life-styles": "From a polarization with Europe we passed unwittingly to a polarization with North America" (96). Spain having been the sole center of gravity of Puerto Rican national formation, the engulfing occupation of the Island by the United States—extending, be it noted, to the imposition of English in the schools—is regarded by thinkers like Pedreira as an "interruption" of that process, the implication being that the colony will in the future somehow return to its true path of interaction with Spanish culture. Over against North American utilitarianism, progress and democracy, Pedreira calls upon Puerto Rico to uphold the legacy of Christian spirituality and elitist grace inherited from its patrimonial Spanish past.

This polarity, summarized in the familiar opposition between "culture" and "civilization," is of course not Pedreira's invention, but merely the Puerto Rican version of the central cliché of Latin American cultural nationalism and European cultural pessimism. It is best, therefore, to consider these more contemporary reflections of *Insularismo* in their relation to the theories of Enrique Rodó, José de Vasconcelos, José Ortega y Gasset and Oswald Spengler, these being the thinkers who stand as the evident sources of Pedreira's analytical method and broader philosophical orientation. These influential and wide-ranging intellectual currents bear most directly on Pedreira's response to conditions in the twentieth century, and are appropriately assessed in that context. Filling in the background to a rounded ideological placement, however, calls first for a critical review of his assumptions about some enduring issues central to an interpretation of Puerto Rican cultural history: the meaning of the Spanish conquest, the relation of print to oral culture, and the role of racial and environmental determinism in legitimizing colonial subordination.

The Culture of the Conquest: Enlightenment or Alienation?

There is a deep dimension to the discounting of indigenous origins and the Latinized conception of national identity which, while given a classical formulation in *Insularismo*, continues to find currency even in anthropologically grounded correctives to this frame of thinking. At this level, the very meaning of the concepts of culture, progress and civilization come into question, and any given interpretation of social developments calls for close ideological scrutiny. The question is not whether or not there existed a pre-Columbian world, nor the bearing of these cultures on the society after the conquest, since these realities have been and continue to be documented. In reference to Puerto Rico, in fact, by Pedreira's time much had already been recorded by early Puerto Rican historians such as Salvador

Brau and Cayetano Coll y Toste, and by the North American anthropologist Jesse Walter Fewkes as early as 1903. In recent years, Eugenio Fernández Méndez has contributed a valuable overview and economic periodization of indigenous society and European colonization in his *Historia cultural de Puerto Rico* (Cultural History of Puerto Rico, 1970). Unfortunately, his presentation remains eclectic and arbitrary, ranging from far-flung Kantian abstractions to rather tedious and pointless compendia. What is needed is a systematic historical study of social production before and after the conquest, and a dialectical interpretation of the resulting ideological and cultural transformations.

What, then, did Spain actually bring to the "New World" by way of a cultural superstructure understood in its broadest sense? The task is to define the nature of the "civilizing" European influence and the cultural content of the collision between the Spanish conquerors and the native societies in such a way as to account for the deeper continuity between European and North American colonialism. There can be perhaps no more suggestive a starting point for this manner of posing the issue than in the life and writing of José Martí. Evoking the radical spirit of Latin American independence from Spain, and with an eye of foreboding cast toward the North, Martí drew the deepest lesson from the "history of America, from the Incas to the present": "the foreign book has been conquered in America by the natural man. The natural men have vanquished the artificial, lettered men. The native born half-breed has vanquished the exotic creole. The struggle is not between barbarity and civilization, but between false erudition and nature."[10] Time and again in his famous, programatic essay "Our America" ("Nuestra América", 1891), Martí refers to the book and the printed word as crucial factors in the imposition of foreign culture on the "natural," native population. "The European or Yankee book," he writes, "could not provide the answer to the Hispanic-American enigma."[11]

To a mind like Pedreira's, Spain was above all the bearer of civilization and culture to the Americas. Despite the greed and arrogance which motivated them, and the violence and despotism of their colonial rule, the conquerors introduced into a primitive and inarticulate wilderness like Puerto Rico the values of Renaissance and Enlightenment humanism, and the means by which this tiny, isolated province could be drawn into the mainstream of modern world culture. The "culture" of the Island goes on record, therefore, in the surviving chronicles and reports of the soldiers and missionaries and, with the arrival of the first printing press in 1806, the gradual awakening of a native *criollo* expression. The arrival of an internal print culture is regarded, in fact, as marking the direct stimulus to the "birth" of genuine cultural life, and its lateness in reaching the Island—the first press came to México in

1539, to Lima in 1584, to Cuba in 1723 and to what is now the United States in 1638—as the central reason for the retardation of a specifically Puerto Rican culture. "Everything reached us late and on a small scale," Pedreira writes. "The press, the newspapers, the book trade, libraries, institutions of higher learning, the thirst for reading, belles-lettres, in short, literature with its many conditioning factors, was the exclusive creation of our nineteenth century" (54). Even more clearly and specifically than in *Insularismo*, Pedreira betrays his one-sided view of the role of the colonial press in his otherwise valuable study *Periodical Literature in Puerto Rico*.[12]

The unqualified tribute to the progressive, path-breaking influence of a literary print culture by no means began or ended with Pedreira; it characterizes, in one variety or another, the most authoritative recent histories of Puerto Rican literature, such as those of Francisco Manrique Cabrera (1971), Josefina Rivera de Alvarez (1970) and José Luis González (1976).[13] On a broader scale, the interpretation of the uniformly progressive influence of literate expression underlies even more contemporary histories of printing, such as Lucien Febvre's *L'Apparition du livre* (an English version entitled *The Coming of the Book* was published in 1976 by New Left Books). Febvre's description of the introduction of the press into the "New World" illustrates clearly how harmoniously this up-to-date cultural history can mesh with the most Eurocentric, colonialist understanding. For Febvre, the printing press complemented harmoniously the simultaneous process of European expansionism, two "great discoveries," in his words, which "rapidly enlarged the horizons of the world known to Western man. ... The epoch which begins with these discoveries has yet to come to an end, and throughout it Western civilization has acted to transform the rest of the world." "In the conquest of the Americas," he continues, "printing from the beginning had an important influence. We wonder what motive lay behind the assaults by the Conquistadors; was it greed for gold, a taste for adventure? These had their part to play. But their vision of the Indies had been fed by countless stories of chivalry printed on Spanish presses during the late fifteenth and early sixteenth centuries; in these, far-off lands were described populated by happy peoples blessed with fabulous riches."[14]

A very different conception of the meaning of these historical events is called to mind by José Martí. For Martí, the contradiction between the barbarous inhumanity of the conquest and slave trade and the humanistic claims which accompanied the arrival of print assumed a more basic, anthropological urgency. In a direct extension of Martí's thinking, and serving to dramatize clearly the contrast between his outlook and that of Pedreira, Febvre and so many other cultural historians, Jean Franco has set the role of European literate and print culture into the context of colonialist control and cultural imposition: "the dichotomy between civilization and barbarism was clearly expressed in the difference between enclave and rural cultures." While the enclave culture of the colonial powers "was highly controlled through censorship, the Inquisition, and the monopolization of the printing presses ... ," she observes, "the secret weapon of the Indian group was oral tradition in the native language. Indeed the most significant feature of colonial culture is this differentiation within the production process itself, between an oral culture dependent on a community and written culture, which was overwhelmingly associated with domination. In order to understand the colonial period at all, therefore, it is necessary to study oral narrative and poetry not simply as folklore (a nineteenth century invention) but as an integral part of the living culture which, as in medieval Europe, provided an outlet for the unofficial activities and responses of the indigenous peoples."[15]

This change in modes of cultural communication, rooted as it is in the production process of the society, has a direct bearing on the relative quality of artistic experience, and on the very definition of culture. Jean Franco's rejection of a unilinear conception of cultural "progress" is of key interest and, as she mentions, carries ample relevance to interpretations of contemporary cultural colonialism:

> It is this direct relationship between the oral performer and the community which makes the persistent survival of oral narrative and poetry a matter of more than antiquarian interest. For at the very time when in Europe this direct current was being replaced by published books, when poetry was gradually becoming something to be "overheard" rather than heard (to use John Stuart Mills' distinction), in Spanish America it was the slave barracks and the urban barrio as well as the Indian *comunidad* which produced exciting new variants of language and form. The presence which oral performance implies thus comes to seem, not a stage which writing happily superseded but a different and less individualistic form of art, and one which can teach us much at the present time when the privileged position so long accorded to print culture has been threatened by mass media. To recognize the co-existence and the dialectics of oral performance and print culture also helps us to detect the weakness of certain modern critics whose exclusive concern with print needs correction.[16]

What Martí meant by his poetic opposition between "nature" and erudition, between "natural men" and "artificial men of letters" ("los letrados artificiales"), is that Spain brought to the Americas not "civilization" in general, but a certain form of cultural experience which corresponded in many ways to its highly uncivilized and anti-humanist presence in colonial America from the outset. From this vantage point, the introduction by the Spaniards of print culture, that is, an artistic life which depends for its generation and promulgation on the existence of writing and printing, constituted a spearhead in the imposition of the cultural alienation of advancing European capitalism. The economic consequences of commodity production—the supercession of use-value by exchange, the separation of the producer from the object and activity of labor, and the general intensification of the divisions of labor—all of which were brought to the Americas by the Europeans, have as their cultural correlatives the breakdown in communal spontaneity, the relegation of oral transmission and the instrumentalization of social experience. The evidence of this "alienation" of artistic life within sixteenth-century Europe, as it stems from economic and political reality and projects into subsequent cultural developments down to the twentieth century, has been presented persuasively by Arnold Hauser, especially in *Mannerism: The Crisis of the Renaissance and the Origin of Modern Art*.[17] And yet it seems that the magnitude of this change, and its deeper anthropological implications, stand out in sharpest relief only when viewed in the light of the cultural collisions ensuing from the process of colonial expansion.

There are dangers, of course, in considering the arrival of print in Latin America as a strictly repressive tool, as though the printing were, in itself, an instrument of capitalist exploitation, and in imputing to the indigenous cultures an idyllic communist harmony. But in the sphere of intellectual and cultural production, the "circumstances" surrounding the introduction of the Spanish-owned and controlled press into Latin America were those of commodity production and the reproduction of early capitalist relations. With the same confidence as is evident in Pedreira's attribution of a germinal, formative impact of the printed word on the development of national consciousness in Puerto Rico, it may be argued that it was only in the deliberately subversive use of the press, and in the documented evasion and exposure of its official purpose in the colony, that the real differentiation of a national culture and politics came into being. This perspective on the meaning of the printing press is, in fact, particularly relevant in the case of Puerto Rico. According to the most reliable accounts, the first press was actually brought to the Island by an adventurer and refugee from the French, Spanish and United States governments. The governor at the time, Toribio Montes, fearful of its political potential, immediately purchased the press and put it to use for the publication of an official government gazette. For the first years, it seems, the only publication aside from this *Gaceta de Gobierno* was Ripalda's *Catechism*, which was used as required reading in the schools. As

Alejandro Tapia y Rivera noted in his memoirs (*Mis memorias*), "it seems that the only press on the whole Island was the not very noteworthy one of the Government, which according to the *Gaceta* was in the charge of Don Valeriano Samillán."[18] It is not the mere presence of print communication, therefore, but the response to its pervasively repressive influence and total official control, which served to generate an anti-colonial, patriotic spirit.

The remarks of Hostos in his important prologue to the second edition (1873) of *La peregrinación de Bayoán* provide telling evidence of this crucial cultural reality. Commenting on the tight censorship of his novel in Puerto Rico, Hostos observed, "Prohibiting it only made the persecuted book more sought-after and more widely read and better understood. It is in large part to that prohibition that I owe the authority my words still carry in my country . . . "[19] Even Manuel Alonso's *El Gíbaro* in fact, generally regarded as the birthstone of Puerto Rican national literature, provides an excellent example. The extent to which the book's original appearance in 1849 was conditioned by censorship and rigid monopoly of the press was persuasively narrated as early as Salvador Brau's prologue to the second edition of 1882, and has been faithfully reiterated in subsequent literary and cultural histories. Any account of the impact of these repressive conditions on the thematic concerns and particular formal and linguistic qualities of the work itself, however, is conspicuously absent from the critical literature to date. Lacking such a structural and sociological interpretation, which would seat the book in the circumstances of literary production of its time, *El Gíbaro* will remain no more than a treasure-chest of bygone "customs" and nostalgic curiosity, in Pedreira's words a portrait of "the childhood of our traditions, our sorrow, our beliefs, virtues and defects, and the age-old features of our character" (58). Beneath the harmless surface, Alonso was responding, slyly and sarcastically, and by use of intriguing artistic devices drawn from popular modes of expression, to the die-hard colonial conditions in mid-nineteenth century Puerto Rico. The dialectical relation of an astute colonial author to the tightly-guarded means of print communication was clearly paramount among these conditions, and played a key role in the forging of a distinctly national literary expression.

The Continuity of Popular Culture

As for the interpretation of indigenous peoples, the imputation to their cultures of a non-alienated, integral, communal character need not involve any romantic presumptions or stretches of fantasy, nor discount the potentially progressive importance of print and writing. The condition for such an assessment is that the historical position of the indigenous peoples be understood not only in moral, racial or cultural terms, but also in relation to the prevailing social, economic and political reality. It is in such terms that José Carlos Mariátegui posed the "problem of the Indian," and it is perhaps to a country like Perú, with its forceful traditions and unbroken presence of Indian resistance as a central component of the movement for national liberation, to which a reappraisal of Puerto Rican cultural perspectives needs to turn. With his thumb to the pulse of the Peruvian revolution, Mariátegui explained the organic relation between the indigenous movement in Spanish America and the ideals of socialism, making clear that it is not by virtue of "civilizing" European influences that this connection first suggests itself: "Faith in indigenous resurgence does not derive from any 'Westernizing' process, in a material sense, of Quechua lands. It is not civilization, it is not the white man's alphabet, which elevates the soul of the Indian. It is the myth and the idea of socialist revolution. Indigenous hope is totally revolutionary. The same myth, the same idea, are the decisive agents which have been awakening other peoples and races from ancient times, such as the Hindus and Chinese. World history tends today, as never before, to be oriented by the same dial. Why should the Inca people, who constructed the most advanced and most harmonious communist system, be the only ones insensitive to this world-wide emotion? The natural affinity between the indigenist movement and the currents of world revolution is too obvious to require documentation."[20]

Mariátegui does, indeed, document his claims, and provides an analysis of the economics of Spanish colonialism in the Americas which is readily applicable to Puerto Rico and the extermination of the Taíno peoples.[21] In fact, it is not even necessary to employ the methods of modern political economy to substantiate the sharp contrast between the economic assumptions of the indigenous societies and those of the European invaders. The early chronicles themselves, amidst their flurries of utopian fantasy and missionary zeal, contain ample observations about the strikingly different social and property relations among the native population. Columbus, for example, in his historic *Letter on the Discovery*, said of the native islanders of the Antilles that "they are so guileless and so generous with all that they possess, that no one would believe it who has not seen it. Anything they have, if it is to be asked of them, they never refuse; on the contrary, they offer it, and they show as much love as if they would give their hearts."[22] In his *Letter to Piero Sederini (The Four Voyages)*, Amerigo Vespucci made observations on the economic life of the Indians he encountered in Brazil: "They engage in no barter; they neither buy nor sell ... They are contented with what nature gives them. The wealth which we affect in this our Europe ... they hold of no value at all ... They are so liberal in giving that it is the exception when they deny." And the cultural, social significance of this unalienated economic reality is pronounced most emphatically, though in rather Arcadian tones, by the great humanist Peter Martyr in his *De Orbe Novo* from the early sixteenth century; of the Taínos, he had the following to say: "They go naked, they know neither weights nor measures, nor that source of all misfortunes, money; living in a golden age, without laws, without prevaricating judges, without books, satisfied with their life, and in no way anxious about the future ... It is proved that amongst them the land belongs to everybody just like the sun or the water. They know no difference between *meum* and *teum*, that source of evils. Little suffices to satisfy them ... It is indeed a golden age; neither ditches, nor hedges, nor walls enclose their domains; they live in gardens open to all, without laws and without judges; their conduct is naturally equitable, and whoever injures his neighbor is considered a criminal and an outlaw."

In the case of Puerto Rico, of course, the cultural counterpart to colonial economic transformation—the relegation of oral culture—must be understood in a broader sense than a historical account of Indian societies would suggest. Though the absence of Indians in modern Puerto Rican history and the seemingly diminished role of African slave backgrounds—compared, say, to Cuba or Brazil—in no way invalidate a strongly indigenist orientation, this perspective must extend to all groups among the population who practice oral popular culture. For, as Jean Franc points out, the "oral tradition in Spanish America is not confined to the Indian community or the black ghetto. Precisely because of the remoteness of many rural areas, Hispanic folk tradition which transmitted down to recent times something of the medieval folk tradition has also constituted a dynamic factor in the culture of the continent. Until recently, for instance, the improvisation of witty verses, often as a part of a contest between rival males was a feature of popular cultures in countries as diverse as Cuba, Brazil, Argentina, and Chile."[23]

Such a popular form, in Puerto Rican poetry, is the *décima*, to which a great deal of editorial and critical attention has been accorded in recent folklore study.[24] Along with the *copla* and other short narrative forms, the *décima* enjoyed a long oral tradition among the illiterate rural population in the colony prior to the arrival of printing, and in its local adaptations bears an emblematic significance as a representative mode of Puerto Rican poetic expression down to the present. A writer like Pedreira, though, can with a characteristic brush of the hand dismiss this entire legacy of peasant-based verse. In his futile groping after a distinctly "Puerto Rican" currency for the national poetry, Pedreira writes off "those pitifully crude and hideous peasant *décimas* made here, so lacking as they are in all consequence for those who perpetrate them. To cultivate our *criollo* spirit, one must be thrifty; and casting such doggerel into the world to the sound of a three-string guitar and the *bordonúa* is like passing a check with no money in your bank account" (71). It is hardly surprising that with such a disposition toward the popular poetic idiom Pedreira's quest for authentic literary inspiration ends in frustration; while giving his blessing to any and all technical innovation, he can still ask, "What mark of native criollo originality have we made in the normative European technique?" His sense of expressive sources is so rarefied that he makes no mention of the reliance of Luis Lloréns Torres on precisely the *décima* form, nor of Luis Palés Matos' important experiments with Afro-Antillean rhythmic possibilities. Rather, he is left with an abstract call for "encyclopedic" knowledge like that of Unamuno, and for "a criollo art superior to that of our Manuel Alonso." "Our literature," he concludes remorsefully, "has not yet captured in expressive form the interesting life of the indigenous population, nor the enlightened manner of the conquerors, nor the sap or our formation, nor the bitter root of our beginnings, nor even the disturbing restlessness of our own times" (175).

Another example of Pedreira's disdain for the popular, indigenous moorings of Puerto Rican culture is his view of music. In the chapter entitled "These Are Our Roots" ("He aquí las raíces"), Pedreira refers to the *danza*, "with its feminine, tender, romantic quality," as the exclusive pillar of the national music. Though denying it the sublime quality of "pure" world art, he considers the *danza* to be the "island's saving grace" and, as exemplified in the national anthem, "La Borinqueña," "a legitimate daughter of our culture" (198–199). In this case, a forceful and pointed corrective may be found even within Pedreira's immediate intellectual environment: the other major essayist of the 1930s, Tomás Blanco, responds directly to this alienated, patrimonial cultural ideal, juxtaposing to it the "natural," popular form of the *plena* with its strong strains of African origin. In his 1935 essay, "Elogio a 'La Plena' " ("In Praise of 'La Plena' "), Blanco declares, "some claim to prefer the cultured quality of the *danza*, dismissing the *plena* as vulgar. They forget, though, that culture is not solely the domain of polished, refined society, just as vulgarity is not an irrevocable element of whatever is popular."[25] Blanco points out that it is not the *plena* but the *danza* which faces extinction as a living art form, since it is basically a cultural transplant whose regional features are more external than intrinsic to the style: "all attention and care went to the foliage and the blossoms at the expense of the stem and the roots. They were too quick to cultivate and stylize the form, not allowing time for the genius of the people to temper the sap running through it."

It is true that the most glaring distortions of Pedreira's Hispanophile approach have been duly addressed in subsequent interpretation of Puerto

Rican cultural and social history. In fact it is in the artistic expression of his own time that the importance of Indian and African contributions to the national culture gained increasing recognition, as is most evident in Tomás Blanco and in the poetry of Luis Palés Matos and Juan Antonio Corretjer. Corretjer's long historical poem, "Alabanza a la Torre de Ciales," ("In Praise of the Tower of Ciales" 1950), pronounces a strong indigenist perspective on Puerto Rican cultural history. But Pedreira's anti-indigenous orientation is still present, as mentioned, in the standard histories of the literature and of the music, and even in the well-known anti-colonialist history, *Puerto Rico: Una interpretación histórico-social* (Puerto Rico: A Socio-Historical Interpretation, 1969) by Manuel Maldonado-Denis, which virtually omits any mention of pre-Columbian island conditions. But by now references to the Taíno and slave backgrounds and to the "popular" culture of the peasantry are more accepted commonplaces than original insights in the description of "authentic" cultural history.

The question is whether this vindication of the "primitive" and the "popular" has yet transcended the symbolic level and approached the radical vision of Martí, the full consequence of which can only be construed in broad socio-historical terms. For it is only when the conquest and the introduction of slavery are understood as the violent disruption of communal economic arrangements and their replacement by commodity production, the incorporation of pre-capitalist societies into the global process of early capital accumulation, that indigenous and popular cultural practices come to assume full analytic importance. Corresponding to this enforced economic upheaval, and the brutal political despotism aimed at assuring its unhampered development, came not only the imposition of a foreign culture, but the supercession of an entire universe of cultural assumptions by another. This "new" cultural domain, with all its claims to humanism and civilization and its evidence of technological progress in literacy and the printing press, had as its most telling effect the breaking apart of the spontaneous, organic relation between humans and nature, and between individual and community, which had characterized the primitive, oral cultures it replaced.

The real restitution of the "primitive" in Puerto Rican cultural history—whether it be the Taíno or the African legacy—can come not through the mystified distortions of romantic yearning, nor by detecting "symbols of resistance" in the recorded feats of Indian and slave rebellion. The inheritance of this legacy falls to modern "popular" culture, with its most direct lines of continuity to the cultural experience of the popular classes: the peasantry and the proletariat. For it is the working classes who stand in fullest opposition, not only to Spanish and North American cultures as imposed foreign cultures but, like the Indians and slaves, to the entire system of bourgeois cultural alienation. Thus, the tradition of indigenous, slave and working class cultural life, though rooted in the productive majority of the society, is not oriented toward a "class culture" in any narrow sense. Rather, this continuum, along with the many strains of internal resistance within the dominant colonial and *criollo* cultures, contains the anticipation of a radically alternative cultural field.[26]

From Hispanism to Racism

How far Pedreira is from scientific thinking about man and society is clear in the very structure of *Insularismo*. After some introductory reflections, the book opens with a section entitled "Biology, Geography, Soul" ("Biología, Geografía, Alma"). What comes first, not only sequentially but conceptually as well, are the biological—that is, racial—and geographical conditions of the people, which go to determine the state of their "soul" (*alma*). The "fusion" of different races accounts for their "confusion," their habitation on a tropical and small "insular" terrain for the sense of inferiority and isolation which characterize the national psyche: "The climate weakens our will-power and causes the rapid deterioration of our psychological make-up. The heat ripens us prematurely, and prematurely decomposes us as well" (38). This crude racial and geographical determinism, derived from such dated nineteenth-century European writers as Taine and Gobineau, has influenced widely the Latin American intellectual elite, most notably the Argentine Carlos Octavio Bunge in his *Nuestra América* (Our America, 1903) and Alcides Arguedas in the book about his native Bolivia *Pueblo enfermo* (A Sick People, 1908).[27] As has been shown, these early twentieth-century theories harken back, in turn, to that infamous tract by Domingo Faustino Sarmiento written late in his life, *Conflicto y armonías de las razas en América* (Conflict and Harmony Among the Races of America, 1883).[28] Pedreira, then, is not alone in his racial theorizing, as is most evident in a comparison of his ideas with those of José Enrique Rodo's influential essay *Ariel* (1900) and José Vasconcelos' *La raza cósmica* (The Cosmic Race, 1925).

Like most of these books, *Insularismo* has as its underlying premise not only the determining power of race, but the inherent inferiority of the indigenous and African "races" to the Europeans, the Spaniards in particular. Not only does he eliminate the Indians as a constitutive force in subsequent national formation, but Pedreira explicitly attributes their rapid extinction to biological weakness and deficiency. Even more shocking is his treatment of the African slaves—without a note of reservation, Pedreira speaks of the Blacks as an "inferior race," capable of hard work but lacking in "the intelligence of white people." While Pedreira considers the Spaniards as the founders and forgers of Puerto Rican character, it is the admixture of African "blood" which is held responsible for the most characteristic traits of the national personality:

> The fortitude and strong will of the European is coupled with the doubt and resentment of the African. So that at the crucial moment of the weightiest decisions they find themselves wavering in an endless hither and thither trying to accommodate them. Our rebellions are momentary, our docility permanent. In moments of great historical importance, the martial rhythms of European blood blossom forth in our every act; we are capable of the loftiest endeavors and the most valiant feats of heroism. But when our aspirations are drenched in waves of African blood we become indecisive, as though we were stupefied by a string of colored beads, or panic-struck before a cinematic vision of witches and fantasms. (29)

Nor was Pedreira the first Puerto Rican writer to conjure up these "secret biological stimuli" from the subsoil of a presumed national character, nor were his forebears, among the most enlightened and progressive thinkers of their time. Salvador Brau, for one, the historian and dramatist whose *Puerto Rico y su historia* (Puerto Rico and Her History, 1894), *Historia de Puerto Rico* (History of Puerto Rico, 1904) and *La colonización de Puerto Rico* (The Colonization of Puerto Rico, 1930) continue to furnish key sources of modern historical study, had the following to say in his description of the Puerto Rican peasantry, *Las clases jornaleras* (The Journeyman Classes, 1882):

> And there you have the primordial source of our character: From the Indian that remained was his indolence, taciturnity, disinterestedness and his sense of hospitality; from the African (came) resistance, vigorous sensuality, superstition and fatalism; while the Spaniard injected into our character its chivalrous sincerity, its characteristic pride, its festive taste, its austere devotion, constancy under adversity, and its love for the homeland and for independence.

Significantly, in his *Historia de la literatura puertorriqueña* (History of Puerto Rican Literature, 1971), Francisco Manrique Cabrera cites just this passage from Brau, commenting only that it has to do with "those traits which are proverbial to all Puerto Ricans."[29] This type of racial attribution also appears at points in the writings of the foremost Puerto Rican novelist and democratic journalist, Manuel Zeno Gandía. In his widely-read novel *La charca,* (1894), the influence of the naturalist theories of Zola and of Herbert Spencer's Social Darwinism leads Zeno Gandía to include among the ruminations of his main character, the landowner Juan del Salto, recurrent thoughts on the racial composition of his *campesinos:* "He was fully aware of the position that those classes occupied in the colony. He saw how they descended directly from racial admixtures as a result of which they were contaminated from birth by a morbid weakness, an invincible weakness, a weakness which has overwhelmed their entire species and left them without blood in their veins, nervous fluid in their brains, or strength in their arms, hurling them into the world like an organic mass incapable of being shaped by life, bent over in misery, demoralization and death."[30] In this case, of course, racialist thinking appears in a muted, conditional context, and can be attributed only indirectly to Zeno Gandía himself—the speaker is a fictional character, with an abruptly vacillating personality and only partially identifiable as a spokesman for the author. Further, his central role is counteracted by the figure of Silvina, the young peasant woman whose finely drawn personality contrasts sharply, and as a kind of subliminal correlate to the social struggle, with the disjointed clinical observations of the *hacendado*.

No such narrative perspective and fictional contextuality surround Pedreira's racial notions, however, nor are they uttered, like those of Salvador Brau, by way of more or less passing remarks within a larger historical panorama. Despite its metaphorical eloquence, *Insularismo* is a book of discursive argument, of which racial determinism figures as the conceptual pillar and structural pivot, and the accompanying geographical attribution as the leading, defining metaphor. Time and again throughout, conclusions about the Puerto Rican character are traced to "biological heredity" and to climatic, topographic or demographic milieu with a definitiveness and directness of attribution not present in those more circumspect interpretations of national identity.

An even more important difference between the racist thinking of such writers as Salvador Brau and Zeno Gandía and that of Pedreira is the historical periods in which they were postulated. By the time of *Insularismo*, theories of racial "values" and "qualities" like Pedreira's were already largely discredited by modern science—which is not to say, of course, that they have not reappeared, in more "sophisticated" form and with continuing appeals to scientific authority, down to the present day. Pedreira might have been warned, had he been alert to the ideological currents supporting Hitler's ascent to power during the very years in which he was writing, that racialist typologies had become the tools of the most reactionary thinkers of his time. What is perhaps even more ironic—and pertinent to the case of Puerto Rican history—is that it was this very ideology which was appealed to in justifying the United States occupation of Puerto Rico. In 1900, Senator A.J. Beveridge of Florida pronounced the following words to Congress in arguing for the expedient take-over of the Caribbean: "God has not been preparing the English-speaking and Teutonic peoples for a thousand years for nothing but vain and idle self-contemplation and self-admiration. No! He has made us the master organizers of the world to establish system where chaos reigns ... He has made us adept in government that we may administer government among savage and servile peoples."[31]

Now it would be wrong-headed and far-fetched to suggest any direct alignment between Pedreira's search for determining racial features of Puerto Rican culture and this imperialist rhetoric, based as it is in the decidedly anti-"Latin" Aryanism of H.S. Chamberlain and backed up as it is by the machinery of expansionist power. The political and economic conditions which gave rise to these versions of racial differentiation must be distinguished as must the intentions of their authors. But considered as ideology, as an explanation of human relations, Pedreira's account of Puerto Rican history as the gradual triumph of Spanish and European "blood" over the intrinsically retarding African and Indian influences no doubt bears closer resemblance to tracts like Chamberlain's *The Foundations of the Nineteenth Century* (1897) than to the kind of enlightened humanistic vision that guided José Martí. Writing in 1891, Martí proclaimed, "There can be no racial hate, because there are no races. The rachitic thinkers and theorists juggle and warm over the library-shelf races, which the open-minded traveler and well-disposed observer seek in vain in Nature's justice, where the universal identity of man leaps forth from triumphant love and the turbulent lust for life. The soul emanates, equal and eternal, from bodies distinct in shape and color. Whoever foments and propagates antagonism and hate between races, sins against humanity."[32]

This anti-racialist humanism of Martí prevailed, in fact, in Pedreira's own intellectual environment. While at Columbia University in the 1920s, he had no need to go far afield to come into contact with the enormous influence of Franz Boas in physical and cultural anthropology. And in Puerto Rico, Pedreira's closest contemporary and, according to the commonplaces of intellectual history, most kindred spirit, Tomás Blanco, held markedly different opinions about the issue of race. In his defense of the *plena*, Blanco presents a decidedly different account of the ethnic make-up of the Puerto Rican people, emphasizing that it is to be considered neither especially honorable nor dishonorable to be mestizo, white, black, yellow or red. His rejection of racial attribution goes even further than Martí's, and contains a reference to uneven economic and social development. "The notion of the essential inferiority of certain races," Blanco states, "is no more than an imperialist pretext, held only by ridiculous Nazis or picturesque retired colonels in the South of the United States, examples which we have no interest in emulating. The vindication of the values inherent in the diverse primitive cultures is a fact of tremendous importance to our times and a sign of the serious work being done in these fields. All that can be said today is that there are peoples in different stages of development: but one cannot attribute to the black race or the yellow or the red, any barbarism, savagery or inferiority."[33]

Somehow, these contemporary contributions to an understanding of human diversity escaped Pedreira's attention, and he was left with the typological speculations most characteristic of colonialist anthropology. Yet his closest intellectual company is no more Chamberlain and the forebears of National Socialism than it is Martí, Tomás Blanco or his revered Hostos, whose broad-minded article in defense of the indigenous basis of Peruvian national identity, "El Cholo" (1870), goes conspicuously without mention in Pedreira's monograph.[34] Rather, *Insularismo* is most accurately situated in relation to the writings to which Pedreira explicitly refers: Rodo's *Ariel*, Ortega y Gasset's *La rebelión de las masas* (The Revolt of the Masses) and Spengler's *Der Untergang des Abendlandes* (The Decline of the West). For despite the evident trappings of Eurocentric racialist thinking, and their central function in Pedreira's argument, the most pressing spiritual motivation of the book is directed not against the "backwardness" of non-European peoples, but against the political and social developments of modern Western civilization, meaning, most obviously, the United States. The ambiguities of this position as it appears in *Insularismo* can be unraveled only if account is taken of the direct and total domination of Puerto Rico by the United States and of the impact of this historical fact on all aspects of the colonial society. But precisely because of the inward, self-reflective, ahistorical and above all eclectic quality of Pedreira's speculations, the intellectual currents at work in the book assume a special importance and help greatly in explaining the shadings of his ideology.

Arielism and the Cosmic Race

More clearly perhaps than any other Puerto Rican writing, *Insularismo* belongs to the "Arielist" movement that swept through the Spanish-speaking intellectual world through the first three decades of the twentieth century. All of the ideological fashions inaugurated by José Enrique Rodó with the publication of his *Ariel* in 1900—elitism, individualism, rhetorical appeal to "youth" and national rejuvenation of the counterposing of Latin aristocratic grace to Anglo-Saxon utilitarianism and democracy—find their faithful echo in Pedreira's essay. The tone of the entire book is set by the spirit of *Ariel*, a debt which Pedreira acknowledges when, anticipating opposition to his pessimistic observations, he cites Rodó in the opening pages of *Insularismo*: "There is a kind of pessimism tantamount to a *paradoxical optimism*. Far from renouncing and condemning all of existence, they propagate, through discontent with the status quo, a need for change" (11–12). And the entire conclusion of *Insularismo*, entitled "La luz de la esperanza" ("The Light of Hope"),—especially the closing chapter, "Juventud divino tesoro" ("Youth, Divine Treasure," a title which derives from a poem by Rubén Darío)— seems to echo the words of Rodó's mouthpiece, Próspero: "Youth, which in the soul of all individuals and all generations stands for light, love and energy, exists and has the same meaning likewise in the evolutionary processes of society. Among peoples who feel life and view life as you do, the future always harbors fecundity and force."[35]

Such a defining influence of Arielist thinking on a writer like Pedreira is no surprise, since Rodó's style and orientation spread wildly among Spanish and Latin American intellectuals. Prominent Spanish philosophers like Rafael Altamira, Leopoldo Alas, Miguel de Unamuno and Juan Valera all received complimentary copies of *Ariel* in 1900, and responded with great admiration. Among Latin American intellectuals, from Cuba, Perú, México, Argentina and Chile, the reception was even more profound, and sparked an entire movement. As the Peruvian Luis Alberto Sánchez stated in his overview of nineteenth-century Latin American literature *Balance y liqui-dación del novecientos* (Balance Sheet of the Nineteenth Century), "the Arielists constitute the most important ideological movement in our America before 1930."[36]

The relevance of Rodó's manifesto to Pedreira's interpretation of Puerto Rican culture is located at the level of mythical polarity and its application to historical events. As has been pointed out, *Ariel* refers only indirectly to its original source, Shakespeare's *The Tempest*, the literary motif of Prospero, Ariel and Caliban having been transmitted to Rodó in the version of Ernest Renan's adaptation of 1878, *Caliban, suite de la Tempête* (Caliban, a Sequel to "The Tempest"). In this philosophical drama, the myth is given a decidedly reactionary cast, since Renan was responding with horror to the recent events of the Paris Commune: Caliban represents the vulgar masses, who conquer power from the aristocratic intellectual, Prospero, and send Ariel, the embodiment of spiritual value, into exile from human life. Rodó's indebtedness to Renan is acknowledged throughout his writings, and his ferociously anti-democratic ideas inform the elitist tenor of *Ariel*.[37]

Yet Renan's position is also overtly colonialist and racialist in its basic motivation, whereas Rodó was a colonial intellectual writing in opposition to modern imperialism. Between the time of Renan's influence on the Latin American "positivists" and the appearance of *Ariel* came the Spanish-American War and the ominous presence of North American expansionism. Rodó is known to have firmly supported the Cuban independence struggle, and his programmatic book must be understood, and appreciated, as a powerful voice of resistance to the United States. It has even been argued, with some justice, that "Rodó, in *Ariel*, ... is closer to Martí than Darío."[38] In any case, Rodó's immediate inspiration in taking up his leading theme was neither Shakespeare nor Renan, but the Argentine writer Paul Groussac, who in a Buenos Aires speech on May 2, 1898 made the statement: "since the Civil War and the brutal invasion of the West, the Yankee spirit had rid itself completely of its formless and Calibanesque body, and the Old World has observed with disquiet and terror a new civilization which intends to supplant our own, considered obsolete."[39]

It is this curious application of the Caliban symbol to the supposedly "advanced" modern civilization of the United States and the Anglo-Saxon "North," and the virtual inversion of the myth in its original conception, which characterizes Rodó's interpretation. For although he begins by speaking of Ariel as "the reign of reason and sentiment over the lowly stimuli of the irrational," and of Caliban as a "symbol of sensuality and vulgarity," the whole of Rodó's argument is directed against the very "rationalistic" and not very "sensual" values attached to North American life: "the utilitarian conception as the ideal of human destiny and the mediocre as the norm of society."[40] Caliban for Rodó is not the vulgar proletarian masses and inferior non-European races, as he was for Renan, but the spiritual void of materialism and leveling mediocrity represented by Yankee culture. The other pole of this typology, Ariel, stands for Christian spirituality, Platonic aristocracy and inspired creativity as characterized by the "Latin" south of the Americas.

It is this version of the Ariel-Caliban myth which underlies Pedreira's stance toward the influence of North American culture in Puerto Rico. Whenever he comes to speak of the United States, the familiar image of Rodó's Caliban makes its appearance. In fact, with its mournful phrases about "economic and utilitarian zeal," "the vulgarity of our times" and "plebeian intellectual impoverishment," the entire chapter on modern-day Puerto Rico reads like a paraphrase of *Ariel*. In general, the intellectual current introduced by Rodó and taken up by Pedreira may be regarded as the posing of the "Latin" idea as inherited from the former "mother country" against the contaminating influence of the real and present threat, Nordic, Anglo-Saxon culture. This recourse to Latinity, with its glorification of Ariel-like spirituality and revulsion toward the revised Caliban-image of Northern mediocrity, lies at the heart of intellectual and cultural opposition to United States imperialism for a significant sector of the Latin American elite.

As the case of Pedreira shows, Rodó's influence was riddled with ambiguities from the outset, and in many ways represents the equivocation and vacillation of the colonial intelligentsia in the face of modern imperialist domination. Thus there were Arielistas of all political stripes, from Julio Antonio Mella, who became one of the founders of the Cuban Communist Party in 1925, to Francisco García Calderón of Perú, who cited Rodó in calling, in French, for the increased immigration of Europeans to civilize the backward Indian masses. Similarly, a fellow countryman of Rodó, the Uruguayan Alberto Nin Frías, could make the claim, in 1907, that "of all the nations of America, the ones that have the greatest intrinsic value are Argentina and Uruguay: this is so because they have almost completely gotten rid of the autochthonous race."[41] The clearest example of this two-sided impact of "Arielism" in the work of a single Latin American intellectual is José Vasconcelos: while incorporating Indian and mestizo components into his vision of the Latin American "Cosmic Race" ("raza cósmica"), his pedagogical and ideological ideals as Mexican Secretary of Education were no less elitist, idealistic and, in fact, Hispanophile and European than those of other "Latinists."

In some important respects, José Vasconcelos may be viewed as the counterpart to Pedreira in Mexican intellectual life and, because of his international renown, in the Latin American "Arielist" movement generally. His heralding of the "fusion of races," including the Indians, as a new stage of humanity contrasts sharply, of course, with Pedreira's contention that racial fusion among Puerto Ricans is responsible for their "confusion" as a people. But despite this difference, and Vasconcelos's public role in Mexican politics, both thinkers are considered in a similar way to be the fathers of modern national self-definition, and have exercised a defining impact on institutionalized cultural interpretation in their respective countries. Further, both Pedreira and Vasconcelos attempted to apply the tenets of Rodó's Ariel-Caliban mythology in the years of entrenched imperialist presence in Latin America, and both served to frame the resistance to North America in primarily cultural, spiritual terms. How closely their conceptual and methodological approaches converge can be seen in comparing *Insularismo* with Vasconcelos's *Indología* (Indianology, 1927), a work which begins, significantly, with a lengthy account of his visit to Puerto Rico hosted by Pedreira's main academic patron, the University Chancellor Thomas E. Brenner. It seems more than possible that the very topics and structure of *Insularismo* were suggested by the contents of Vasconcelos' book, which begins with chapters entitled "the matter at hand" ("el asunto"), "the land" and "man" and leads up to "the conflict" and "the ideal." Whatever may be said of these more direct influences, the spiritual kinship and intellectual parallels are undeniable. The same social and cultural perspective inherited by both thinkers from Rodó's *Ariel*—and the same political ambivalence—characterize their interpretation of Latin American reality, such that the guiding words of *La raza cósmica* (1925) could well serve as a motto to *Insularismo*: "Only the Iberian part of the continent," Vasconcelos wrote, "possesses the spiritual qualities, race and territory that are called for to undertake the huge endeavor of initiating the universal era of mankind."[42]

The corrective to this "Arielist" conception involves nothing less than a return to the original framing of the myth, and an insistence that "Our symbol then is not Ariel, as Rodó thought, but rather Caliban." Roberto Fernández Retamar has taken up this intellectual and political challenge, reverting the figure of Caliban to its original etymological identification with "Canibal" and "caribe" and proclaiming, in unison with Simón Bolívar and José Martí, "what is our history, what is our culture, if not the history and culture of Caliban?"[43] Caliban is no longer the symbol of northern, Anglo-Saxon utilitarianism and materialism, but stands for the most severe victims and absolute antagonists of United States imperialist "rationality," the masses of oppressed Latin American Indians, slaves and peasants. And as for the "Ariels," Fernández Retamar attributes to them the role of the "traditional" intellectual, in Antonio Gramsci's sense, who stand in a tenuous, vacillating position between defense of the "old" society, that is, service to "Prospero," and alliance with the movement of Caliban for liberation. It is a thinker like Pedreira, who holds up his Latinized ideal to the reality of imperialist saturation and with all his "cultural resistance" could allow for the adoption of English as the official language of Puerto Rico, who is most aptly represented by "Ariel."

"Had Ortega y Gasset been a Puerto Rican ... "

The intellectual resonance of Rodó and Arielism probably came to Pedreira, and to Puerto Rico, by way of Spain, and in close association with the ideas of Ortega y Gasset. In any event, the prevailing trends of Latin American cultural theory form one part—and in fact the most progressive aspect—of the larger ideological current which informs *Insularismo*. By the time of Pedreira's own educational development in the 1920s, in fact, it was more Ortega y Gasset and Spengler than Rodó who set the tenor of contemporary intellectual fashion. The bearing of their writings on Pedreira—and he quotes them repeatedly—helps define even more precisely than the legacy of Arielism the political position assumed in *Insularismo*.

The enormous influence of Ortega y Gasset in Latin America, particularly in Argentina which he visited in 1916 and 1929, and among the Mexican philosophers Samuel Ramos and Leopoldo Zea, has been well documented.[44] His appraisal of the condition of modern Spain, in fact, served as a model for many of the essayists, including Pedreira, in developing critical interpretations of their native societies. Ortega y Gasset's international stature and weighty philosophical concerns extended the horizons of their analysis and allowed them, as Zea said, to "feel justified as participants in culture in a more general sense."[45] Not only did he help in the founding of the influential Argentine magazine *Sur*, but his *opus* includes two important essays about Latin America, "Hegel y América" ("Hegel and America," 1928) and "La pampa ... promesas" ("The Pampa ... Promises," 1929). As late as 1956 Leopoldo Zea entitled an article "Ortega el americano" ("Ortega, the American"). However, *Insularismo* does not take into account Ortega y Gasset's existentialist, philosophical system, nor even his relevant reflections on the national theme of "España invertebrada" ("Invertebrate Spain"). For Pedreira, Ortega y Gasset in *La rebelión de las masas* (The Revolt of the Masses, 1930) contributed above all a disdain for mass democracy and the social impact of modern scientific progress. In the beginning of *Insularismo*, Pedreira utilizes Ortega y Gasset to separate his search for the "essence" of cultural identity from any sense of historical progress. "Frivolous people," in the Spanish philosopher's words quoted by Pedreira, "think that human progress consists of a quantitative increase of things and ideas. No, not at all: real progress is the growing intensity with which we perceive those half-dozen cardinal mysteries throbbing in the shadows of history like perennial heartbeats" (13). And the definition of culture throughout *Insularismo* as "vital intensity" ("intensidad vital") is little more than a replica of the highly intellectualized vitalism which Ortega y Gasset posed as the only existential salvation from the overly rationalized, scientific society of modern times.

The real indication of the importance of Ortega y Gasset's social philosophy emerges when Pedreira comes to consider the situation of Puerto Rico in the twentieth century. In fact, Pedreira goes so far as to identify the thesis of *The Revolt of the Masses* with the entire history of Puerto Rico since the turn of the century. He asserts: "Had Ortega y Gasset been a Puerto Rican, he would have written *The Revolt of the Masses* twenty-five years ago" (104). For the main result of the transfer from Spanish to North American rule over the island is for Pedreira not the difference between traditional colonialism and modern imperialism, but the collective degeneration from a "cultured" to a "civilized" society. The most essential feature of this transformation is the replacement of aristocratic values and the primacy of spiritual quality over mass democracy and the "fallacy" of egalitarianism. "With the change of sovereignty," he wrote, "we stumbled upon democracy and in so doing were doomed to accelerate mediocracy." Pedreira goes on to pronounce this elitist position in terms derived directly from Ortega y Gasset: "the reign of numbers and of the just mean accidentally excludes the extraordinary collaboration of the select few. With equal opportunity for all, the mob has been quite content to see the ascendancy of its values at the cost of the decline of the cultured. In our day, cunning, trickery and boldness are more effective attributes than merit, dignity and principles. It is a painful sight to see in our people the withdrawal of superior men, who isolate themselves in the emptiness of their homes so as to defend their aristocratic spirits against the shameless dominance of the mediocre" (102–3).

It is true that Pedreira, like Ortega y Gasset, arrives at these anti-democratic conclusions by way of a response to the reification and quantification which accompany the development of modern capitalist society, a process which enveloped Puerto Rico with particular intensity upon the passage of the colony from Spanish to North American hands. Neither thinker, however, anchors this increasing alienation and disengagement of cultural values from technological advance in the economic structure of society; each attributes it to the impetuous ascent of the "vulgar" masses and the subordination of the chosen few who are by destiny called upon to direct society. Now in the case of Ortega it may be argued that his attack on "mediocrity" was directed, in a tactical sense, against the irresponsibility and corruption of the monarchy—*The Revolt of the Masses,* be it remembered, was written at the time when Ortega y Gasset resigned from his prestigious professorship in protest against the closing down of the University of Madrid in 1929. Pedreira, on the other hand, places the "blame" for the democratization of society squarely on the North American "liberals" and, by indirection, on the Puerto Rican "people" themselves. The "superior minority" has been forced out of public life into the ivory tower by the advent and political enfranchisement of the incompetent many. As if the "problem" introduced into Puerto Rico by the United States imperialists were democracy!

Both Pedreira and Ortega y Gasset ground their distinction between the elite and "mass man" in class differences, and no interpretation to the contrary stands the test of critical analysis.[46] As much as they may try, in all good faith, to couch their appeals to nobility in terms of abstract qualities, moral values and psychological types, it remains anything but coincidental that one writer on the Spanish philosopher concluded that the "higher classes generally have a larger share of excellent men than the lower."[47] Any tribute Ortega y Gasset may have paid to the working class—as when he proclaimed in 1931 that "for sixty years, the most energetic force in universal history has been the magnificent upward movement of the working classes"—appears as a rather idle gesture in the light of his naive idealistic notions about capitalist relations of production. The "idea of work," he contended, "should make the abyss that exists between workers and those who are not workers disappear, for as the former work with the hoe on the divine earth, the latter will work by means of their capital."[48] Similarly with Pedreira: while he pays passing respects to the "exquisite anonymous masses" (36) for their historical role, and even voices sympathy for the Puerto Rican worker who "has always . . . eaten poorly, lived badly, worked hard and earned little," he goes on to thank the select minority for having paved the nation's path to immortality, and to incorporate this enduring economic misery into the more encompassing framework of his atmospheric determinism: "Hurricanes, earthquakes and epidemics only aggravate from time to time the permanent economic imbalance, and under the rhetorical exuberance of an adjective we crawl through our bitter life with a vegetative languor" (143). It is this polarization of class "moralities," with the leading and defining role attributed to the "superior" minority, which guides Ortega y Gasset, and Pedreira, in their conception of national history and culture. A nation is, for Ortega y Gasset, "organized by a minority of select individuals"; regardless of its particular political or legal structure, "its living and extra-legal institution will always consist of the dynamic influence of a minority acting on a mass" (51). This process of social selection, which Ortega y Gasset elevates to the status of a natural law, provides the fundamental premise of all historical study.

The elitist orientation of Ortega y Gasset and Pedreira has its point of origin in modern cultural theory in Nietzsche's vehement ideological reaction to the European class struggle and, as with Renan, to the implications of the Paris Commune in particular. Ortega y Gasset's application of this Nietzschean anti-democratic thinking to twentieth-century conditions helps illuminate further the inversion of the Caliban myth as in Rodó and the Arielist movement, that is, the identification of modern democracy as "vulgar" and "primitive."

In Ortega y Gasset's view, "the type of man dominant today is a primitive one, a *Naturmensch* rising in the midst of a civilized world."[49] "If that human type continues to be master in Europe," he states in another passage, "thirty years will suffice to send our continent back to barbarism."[50] The ominous "revolt of the masses" is, in an allusion to a phrase of the German politician and industrialist Walter Rathenau, the "vertical invasion of the barbarians." "The actual mass-man is," he continues, "a primitive who has slipped through the wings on to the age-old stage of civilization."[51] Pedreira adopts this scorn for the "primitive" masses in his comments on the imposition of a supposedly democratic process in Puerto Rico. This equation of the barbarian morality of resentment and modern democracy underlies even his pejorative racial theories, as when he remarks, "the half-breed ("grifo"), having little white-man's blood, certifies his rights by aspiring ambitiously, and his resentment finds its escape-valve in democracy" (27).

Spengler a la mode

Ortega y Gasset's influence had the important and in some ways salutary effect of transmitting the concerns of modern Spanish philosophy to contemporary thinkers of Latin America, including colonially occupied Puerto Rico. His most significant contribution as an intellectual bridge, however, was his introduction of current philosophical issues and vocabulary from the rest of Europe, particularly Germany, into the Spanish-speaking world, both Iberian and American. In his own writings, and above all in his capacity as editor of the *Revista de Occidente*, he was the first to make the theories of Wilheim Rickert, Georg Simmel, Hermann Cohen, Martin Heidegger and many other German philosophers accessible to Hispanic intellectuals. In the founding year of its publication, 1923, the *Revista de Occidente* featured translations from that weighty German book which was attracting intellectual attention throughout the Western world, but was as yet relatively unknown among Spanish readers: Oswald Spengler's *Der Untergang des Abendlandes* (The Decline of the West).

To a large degree, the impact of Ortega y Gasset on a writer like Pedreira was really the impact of Spengler. Not that Ortega y Gasset's works may be considered a simple restatement of Spengler, nor that his theories lacked distinctiveness and authenticity, and a relation to far more sophisticated philosophical minds than that of Spengler. But the most "popular" ideas of Ortega y Gasset, those which struck a topical chord and found general intellectual currency, stand in closest running discourse with Spengler's and appear in many ways as a commentary to and cultural translation of *The Decline of the West*. Thus, whatever conclusions may be reached about Pedreira's reading and application of Ortega y Gasset are best drawn in the context of his adoption of the more presumptuous ideological framework represented by Spengler. The philosophy of history, concept of culture and political and class attachment of *Insularismo* all seem inspired by the fashionable dualities of the Spenglerian world-view. Here again, Pedreira was by no means alone among Latin American intellectuals of his time; Spengler was "in the air" in the early 1930s, as is evident even in thinkers far more "modern" and original than Pedreira, such as the Argentine writer Ezequiel Martínez Estrada and the Mexican philosopher Samuel Ramos.

Martínez Estrada's *Radiografía de la pampa* (X-Ray of the Pampa) and Ramos's *El perfil del hombre y de la cultura en México* (Profile of Man and Culture in Mexico), both bearing strong influences of Spengler in association with existentialist and psychoanalytical theories, appeared in 1933 and 1934 respectively.

Pedreira not only situates Puerto Rican culture as "an American variation of the culture of Spain" but, utilizing the universalist terms of Spengler, he says of Spain that it is no more than "a phase in the school of Western culture." By "Western culture" Pedreira is actually referring to a "stage" in the development of the Greco-Latin tradition, the features of which were drawn by Spengler: "In his widely discussed *The Decline of the West*," Pedreira writes, "Oswald Spengler divides the former (world culture) into two major stages: ancient culture which is Apollonian in spirit, and Occidental, Faustian culture. The serenity of one and the restlessness of the other make up the difference between them" (14–15). The culture of Puerto Rico, according to this scheme, constitutes a minor offshoot of the "Faustian" culture of passionate striving which, in Spengler's words, "blossomed forth with the birth of the Romanesque style in the tenth century on the Northern plain between the Elbe and the Tagus."[52] The Teutonic cradle and content of this cultural "stage" is strongly emphasized. Indeed, the very dichotomy between classical serenity and modern romantic yearning is a recurrent theme in German cultural theory, as in Schiller's distinction between "naive" and "sentimental" poetry. The category of "Apollonian" poise attached to Hellenic culture stems most directly from Nietzsche's *Birth of Tragedy* (1869), though Spengler significantly misrepresents his source by failing to mention that Nietzsche considered the real origins of Greek culture to be not "Apollonian rationalism" but the "Dionysian" stage of ecstatic rapture with its roots in the ancient Orient.

In any case, Pedreira's receptive reference to Spengler's "macrocosmic" polarities indicates that he traced the lineage of Puerto Rican culture not only to Catholic Spain but, on a universal plane, to the medieval and modern "Germanic" stages of the Greco-Latin tradition. This identification with the "Faustian Soul" in 1934, the founding years of the Third Reich, swarms with political and ideological implications. The same Occidentalist vision was expressed in Puerto Rico before *Insularismo*, and in even more memorable language, in the poetry of Luis Lloréns Torres. In his poem to Ponce de León, in fact, the conquistador is mythicized not only as Don Juan and Don Quixote, but as the "Faust" of Latin American history.[53] In Pedreira's own time, even the most forthright and articulate demands for Puerto Rican national sovereignty were characteristically framed by an extended, Western universalist version of the Hispanophile ideal. Vicente Géigel Polanco, for example, established in just such terms the fully developed nationhood of Puerto Rico at the inception of North American political control over the Island. "By 1898," he wrote in 1936, "our people ... already disposed of a homogeneous population of over a million souls; a definite historical personality; ... a common language; a spiritual formation based on the ethical teachings of Catholic Christianity; a clear concept of justice and the law derived from Roman sources: and a solid culture firmly implanted in the noblest Greco-Latin traditions."[54]

But the most compelling attraction of Spengler's "morphology" of world history was his contrast between "culture" and "civilization." This conceptual polarity also informs the cultural speculations of Ortega y Gasset—despite his insistent claim to the contrary—and is likewise but a schematized popularization of a long-standing current in German philosophy going back to Kant and Hegel. In Spengler, though, the dualism is expounded in its sharpest relief, forms the crux of an organicist theory of history and gives voice to the widespread cultural despair among European intellectuals in response to World War I and the Bolshevik Revolution. Pedreira, therefore, picks up not only a set of philosophical categories, but an entire theoretical and historical context when he applies Spengler to his explanation of Puerto Rican cultural history.

"Culture" is identified as the vibrant, living expression of the "soul" of a people or an epoch. "Every culture," according to Spengler, "passes through the age-phases of the individual man. Each has its childhood, youth, manhood and old age."[55] This crass dogma of cultural life-cycles rests on a decidedly mystical concept of culture which, in Spengler's words, "is born in the moment when a great soul awakens out of the proto-spirituality of ever childish humanity, and detaches itself, a form from the formless, a bounded and mortal thing from the boundless and enduring. It blooms on the soil of an exactly definable landscape, to which plant-wise it remains bound. It dies when this soul has actualized the full sum of its possibilities in the shape of peoples, languages, dogmas, arts, sciences, and reverts into the proto-soul."[56] "Civilization," on the other hand, is identified with the death of culture, "the inevitable *destiny* of the Culture." "Civilizations are the most external and artificial states of which a species of developed humanity is capable." Speaking of the transition from Greece to Rome, Spengler juxtaposes "soul" and "intellect," "and this antithesis is the differentia between culture and civilization." "Again and again," Spengler continues, in a description which Pedreira would certainly have identified with the North American cultural invaders, "there appears this type of strong-minded, completely non-metaphysical man, and in the hands of this type lies the intellectual and material destiny of every 'late' period. *Pure* civilization, as a historical process, consists in a progressive exhaustion of forms that have become inorganic or dead."[57]

In defining the difference between nineteenth and twentieth-century Puerto Rico, Pedreira speaks of a collective passage "from the cultured to the civilized" ("de lo culto a lo civilizado," 97); "today we are more civilized, but yesterday we were more cultured" (99). The most telling effect of imperialist occupation was, for Pedreira, the rude interruption of the life-span of Puerto Rican culture and its replacement with cosmopolitan progress and civilization. Pedreira draws this perspective directly from Spengler, who in another rhetorical formulation of his main theme portrays the process of decline in just those terms with which *Insularismo* is charged: "In place of a type-true people, born of and grown on the soil, there is a new sort of nomad, cohering unstably in fluid masses, the parasitical city-dweller, traditionless, utterly matter-of-fact, religionless, clever, unfruitful, deeply contemptuous of the countryman and especially that highest form of countryman, the country gentleman." This urbanized "mob" shows an "uncomprehending hostility to all the traditions representative of the culture (nobility, church, privileges, dynasties, convention in art and limits of knowledge in science)," a "keen and cold intelligence" and habits which go "back far to quite primitive instincts and conditions" such as "wage-disputes and sports stadia."[58]

At the core of the distinction between "culture" and "civilization"—as it is adopted by Ortega y Gasset and Pedreira from Spengler, and anticipated in a Latin American context by Rodó—is the categorical separation of "soul" and "mind." The central question motivating *Insularismo*, be it recalled, was: "Is there a soul? And a Puerto Rican one?" And the whole import of the book is to affirm the existence of a Puerto Rican soul. And, as in Spengler, "soul" means for Pedreira precisely what is not mind, what is "forever inaccessible," in Spengler's words, "to the lucid mind, to the understanding or to empirical, factual research ... One could sooner dissect with a knife a theme by Beethoven or dissolve it with an acid than analyze the soul by means of abstract thought."[59] "Soul," in fact, is divorced not only from scientific reason and intelligence, but from the external, material world itself. It is lodged and sheltered in the "inner existence" of man, separated, as Spengler says, "from all that is real or has evolved, a very definite feeling of the most secret and genuine potentialities of his life, his destiny, his history. In the early stages of the languages of all cultures, the word soul is a sign that encompasses all that is not world."[60]

In the circumstances of a colonial society, of course, the attribution of a "soul" to the conquered people constitutes a form of resistance and defiance, since the message of the colonial missionaries was precisely the denial of "soul" among the native population. It is significant, therefore, that Pedreira's assertion of a Puerto Rican *soul* occurs at the outset of the chapter "Puerto Rican Affirmation." The content of "soul" and "culture" in Pedreira's writings, however, and the ideological function of these concepts in *Insularismo* pertain less to an anti-colonialist intellectual tradition than to the trappings of apologetic bourgeois aesthetics. A penetrating analysis of this metaphysical polarity occurs in the early essay of Herbert Marcuse, "The Affirmative Character of Culture" (1934), which was directed largely against Spengler and applies cogently to Pedreira's most heart-felt cultural assumptions:

> There is . . . (a) fairly widespread conception of culture, in which the spiritual world is lifted out of its social context, making culture a (false) collective noun and attributing (false) universality to it. This . . . concept of culture (clearly seen in such expressions as "national culture," "Germanic culture," or "Roman culture,") plays off the spiritual world against the material world by holding up culture as the realm of authentic values and self-contained ends in opposition to the world of social utility and means. Through the use of this concept, culture is distinguished from civilization and sociologically and valuationally removed from the social process. This concept itself has developed on the basis of a specific historical form of culture, which is termed "affirmative culture" in what follows. By affirmative culture is meant that culture of the bourgeois epoch which led in the course of its own development to the segregation from civilization of the mental and spiritual world as an independent realm of value that is also considered superior to civilization. Its decisive characteristic is the assertion of a universally obligatory, eternally better and more valuable world that must be unconditionally affirmed: a world essentially different from the factual world of the daily struggle for existence, yet realizable by every individual for himself "from within," without any transformation of the state of fact. It is only in this culture that cultural activities and objects gain that value which elevates them above the everyday sphere. Their reception becomes an act of celebration and exaltation.[61]

What for Spengler, and Pedreira, would be a dynamic concept of culture is in fact a static one, isolated from the real movement of social history; what is intended as a spiritual protest against reification is a surrender to it, and the "soul" a seat of unfulfilled promises. Thus, the core chapter of *Insularismo*, "Afirmación puertorriqueña," turns out to be aptly titled in an ironic, unintended sense, since rather than an anti-imperialist claim to distinct cultural identity the book rests on an "affirmative" rationalization of the cultural status quo.[62]

Pedreira may not have been aware of the deeply reactionary implications of Spengler's theories which made him—despite his muddled objection—one of the undeniable spiritual fathers of German fascism.[63] He may not have recognized *The Decline of the West* for the sham that it was, culminating in a call for a very Western and decidedly Germanic "Caesar" to launch the new "stage" of world culture, and motivated by the kind of imperialist desperation that led its author to declare, in 1936, "Should the white peoples ever become so tired of war that their governments can no longer incite them to wage it, the earth will inevitably fall a victim to the colored man ... If the white races are resolved never to wage war again, the colored will act differently and be rulers of the world."[64] This fanatical propaganda, though it derives logically from Spengler's meta-cultural morphology adopted by Pedreira, plays no part in *Insularismo*. Rather, the "solutions" offered by Pedreira have the ring of a more conventional cultural idealism, very reminiscent, at times, of Schiller: the path to political freedom leads through the aesthetic, through the cultivation of Beauty and inner spiritual values.

But there is another feature of *Insularismo* which bears the mark, at least indirectly, of Pedreira's reading of Spengler. As Georg Lukács has pointed out, Spengler's basic degradation of science and scientific analysis led him to the explicit and methodical rejection of any sense of historical causality.[65] Instead, he chose to expound his ideas in the form of analogies and metaphorical generalities. Pedreira, too, is careful to preface his reflections by saying, "they are not the result of scientific analysis" and "we do not aim to make history, nor science, nor expect research based on statistics" (9). These introductory words of caution open the door, then, to the entire barrage of analogies and speculative metaphors, all of them exempt, as it were, from the test of scientific scrutiny and responding only to "a personal malaise, rooted in the discontent of our times." They are no more than "provisional reflections," "disperse elements," "seeds recently sown in the hope that the reader will make them sprout" (17). As with Spengler, Pedreira raises the negation of method to the rank of a guiding methodological stance.

Insularismo: Interpretation of What?

Lukács's polemical analysis of Spengler and German irrationalism—represented by Ortega y Gasset among Spanish philosophers—has a more substantial relevance to a critique of Pedreira. While appearing to attack the manifestations of capitalist culture and the "mediocrity" of bourgeois democratic society, thinkers like Nietzsche, Spengler and Karl Jaspers have as their real target socialism and the working class movement. The "hidden agenda" of the cultural pessimism of Ortega y Gasset and Spengler—and at times it is far from secret—is dictated by their panic fear of Bolshevism and the "threat" of proletarian revolution. The ominous "mass man" and modern Caliban, when stripped of his cultural and psychological mask, is none other than the modern working class.

The same class motivation underlies Pedreira's "Puerto Rican interpretation." It is more than coincidence that *Insularismo* was published in the same year as the founding of the Puerto Rican Communist Party. 1934 was also the year of the historic strike of the sugar-cane workers; the entire period, in fact, that Pedreira bemoans as an "intermezzo" in Puerto Rican life and a detour from the course of Puerto Rican cultural destiny, witnessed the growth of a militant, indigenous labor movement.[66] It also coincided with the ascendancy and expanding influence of the Nationalist Party. The specter of "mass democracy" and materialist civilization which caused Pedreira such alarm was really the historical reaction to intense imperialist oppression and the externally controlled capitalist consolidation, and rapid proletarianization, of Puerto Rican society.

Pedreira did not voice any explicit contempt for, or fear of, the Puerto Rican or North American working class, any more than he saved any kind words for the imperialist bourgeoisie or its frail colonial counterpart. Rather, he assumed a stance "above" the economic and social fray, cursing both houses in the name of aristocratic nobility. The butt of his scorn and cultural premonition was the rise of "economic man," who would appear to embody corporate businessman and plebeian consumer alike. He was not for or against capitalism or any other economic or political arrangement as such; what he opposed was the politicization of social life and the economic, utilitarian measurement of all values. "We have lost all creative leisure," he complains, "because someone told us that time is money" (105).

And yet, with all due reservations and qualifications, Pedreira's *Insularismo* remains a textbook example of bourgeois ideology. His sublimated, "affirmative" concept of culture, counterpoised as it is to "civilization" and the contradictions of social production to which it responds, is true to the letter of metaphysical aesthetic theory. By the same token, his unilateral identification of European "civilization," in the form of writing, print and formalized aesthetic norms, as the impetus to genuine cultural life constitutes but another variant of the dominant unilinear understanding of human progress. The complementarity of these seemingly diverse positions, and Pedreira's confusion about the entire relation between culture and progress, is evident when he traces his own intellectual lineage from Ortega y Gasset back to Rousseau (98). Yet what Rousseau opposed to the reified "civilization" of modern society was not idealized, effete cultural tradition, but the spontaneity and organic unity with nature, characteristic of communal life. Now Rousseau's vision of the "nobility" of pre-civilized man is of course romantic and mythical in quality.[67] Nevertheless, a clear distinction must be drawn between Rousseau's radical insights, centering as they do around a critique of private property, and the heritage of existentialism, nihilism and cultural pessimism with which they are often associated. More than Spengler, Ortega y Gasset and Pedreira, it is Martí and Mariátegui who stand closest to the perspective of Rousseau's criticism of modern civilization and culture.[68]

This separation of "culture" from economic and political reality has its bearing on Pedreira's understanding of Puerto Rico as a colonial nation. For, again in classical bourgeois fashion, he strives to isolate the "national culture" as the defining "essence" of Puerto Ricans, "in their totality" ("globalmente considerados" 10). Whatever seems to involve the participation of "all" Puerto Ricans—black or white, rich or poor, urban or rural—stands to define the cultural personality of the nation, and serves as its main instrument of collective resistance. Thus, in his enthusiastic description of clandestine economic opposition to Spain in the 1880s, Pedreira emphasizes this total participation: "All of Puerto Rico was stirred by the same aspiration: black and white, rich and poor, peasants and city-dwellers, workers and professionals" (184). The regressive quality of Pedreira's position is most glaring when he elevates this relatively cohesive perspective of the nineteenth-century movement for autonomy into an ideal for Puerto Rico well into the twentieth century.

Pedreira equivocates on the issue of Puerto Rico's political status, contending only that is impossible to gain any definite orientation because the juridical questions are so confusing (100). Nevertheless, despite this political evasion, Pedreira does indeed advocate a position, for which *Insularismo* provides, in many ways, an eloquent program: the position of cultural autonomy. He argues, and the kernel of his messages comes out in his concluding hymn to Puerto Rican youth, that the intellectual, educational and cultural formation of the nation should be allowed to flourish and develop "freely," regardless of whether or not this process takes place under the political and economic tutelage of the United States. The consequences of such a position in subsequent Puerto Rican history, with the institution of "commonwealth" status and "free associated statehood," are too familiar to require elaboration.

If Pedreira's spokesmanship for the Puerto Rican nation against imperialism was equivocal, and oriented toward cultural preservation rather than political sovereignty, his class partisanship was decidedly less so. His ideal of the "national culture" clearly and unflinchingly identified the criollo bourgeoisie as the defining force, often against the contaminating influence of the "vulgar" popular culture of the masses. Even economically, though, his emphasis is on the interests and mobility of the owning class, as in his admiration for the collective national involvement in the nineteenth-century boycott movement: "All of Puerto Rico," his thought continues, " ... united closely in the spirit of this new Free Masonry, whose influence was soon felt in the rapid flourishing of trade, industry and business on the part of the native population" (184). And it is significant that in his overly indulgent, sympathetic "revision" of *Insularismo*—as mentioned, the only extended discussion of the book to date—Maldonado-Denis interpreted Pedreira's warning words about North American "civilization" distinctly from the vantage-point of the colonial bourgeoisie and petty-bourgeoisie; "what is indisputable," he wrote in 1962, "are all those things which we can see with our own eyes: the large percentage of factories set up in Puerto Rico which belong to U.S. companies; the proliferation of supermarket chains which threaten the very survival of the small businessman; the installation of large department stores that endanger the future of the local retailer (not only of foodstuffs, but of clothes, shoes, etc.); the preponderant role played by North American finance capital in our industrialization program."[69] According to this more faithful than critical updating of Pedreira, the main threat involved in the economic saturation of the society is not to the working class, but to the native owners and individual producers, whose "freedom" and right to "self-determination" are becoming increasingly restricted.

Pedreira was, of course, not speaking on behalf of the small shopkeepers or artisans in any direct sense, any more than he was siding with the local capitalists. He was a university professor and eminent intellectual, who considered his deepest concerns to lie outside of the public arena. His class representation is betrayed not in any open political advocacy, but in the quality of his vision itself: the economic and political restrictions suffered by the colonial bourgeoisie and petty-bourgeoisie are paralleled in the intellectual restrictedness of Pedreira's cultural interpretation. *Insularismo*, according to its author, consists of no more than "personal" observations, stemming from his own "private" concerns; yet his projections, his prescriptions of educational autonomy and cultural dignity, are intended to apply to all mankind, and to all of Puerto Rican society in particular. This endeavor to generalize a personally perceived predicament and sense of emancipation within bounds set by the very structure of society is just what characterizes the intellectual representative of the petty bourgeoisie. Marx's portrayal of this relationship in *The Eighteenth Brumaire* (1852) remains resoundingly apt to an explanation of the class content of a position like that of Pedreira:

> Just as little must one imagine that the democratic representa-
> tives are indeed all shopkeepers or enthusiastic champions of
> shopkeepers. According to their education and their individual
> position they may be as far apart as heaven from earth. What
> makes them representatives of the petty bourgeoisie is the fact
> that in their minds they do not go beyond the limits which the lat-
> ter do not get beyond in life, that they are consequently driven,
> theoretically, to the same problems and solutions to which mate-
> rial interest and social position drive the latter practically. This
> is, in general, the relationship between the political and literary
> representatives of a class and the class they represent.[70]

"The Dutchman will get us!"—the perennial fear of Dutch pirates is Pedreira's standing symbol of Puerto Rican identity, the historical epitome of collective "insularism." Paralyzed by an inclement climate, diminutive geography and a disjointed racial fusion, Puerto Ricans are condemned to isolation from the world around them, economically, politically, intellectu- ally and culturally. On their haunches in the face of Destiny, and wills weak- ened by the tropical heat, they have recourse only to optimistic metaphors and overblown rhetoric with which to "sweeten the pill" of their historical misery. And yet, is it not Pedreira himself who resorts to these devices and assumes this posture? "Without the slightest reserve," he says of his coun- trymen, "we invent geological and atmospheric theories" (146), in a book which is steeped in the long-outmoded milieu theories of Taine, and which rests on intellectual improvisations like, "Our national temperature has been conditioned by historical climates which are not tropical" (160).

As it turns out, the metaphorical catch-phrase "insularismo" appears more a projection of Pedreira's own intellectual limitations than an appropri- ate characterization of Puerto Rican reality. The solitary, insulated condition of the colony is manifest in the confining horizons of its revered intellectual spokesman. "And that solitude," Pedreira reflects, "which is a restraining muzzle that cuts us off from the fraternal intellectual circles and deflects us from those new ideological currents which are stimulating the thinking world, does constitute still today one of the most repressive aspects of our culture and is indeed a contributing factor to our petrified personality" (160).

What better explanation of a writer like Pedreira himself, who in the year 1934—between the advent of fascism and the Spanish Civil War—could treat the European cultural pessimists Spengler and Ortega y Gasset as "fraternal intellectual circles" and continue citing Arielism among "those new currents of thought which are stimulating the thinking world?" What more apt description of Pedreira's own position than when he speaks of the chronic break-up of Puerto Rican national cohesion and solidarity: "whenever we could have formed the brotherhood of all Puerto Ricans our atomizing individualism has always blocked that cohesion, breaking us up into small, powerless and spineless groups?" (187).

Concluding Remarks: New Readings, New Tasks

It would be mistaken, and damaging to the cause of Puerto Rican liberation, simply to dismiss *Insularismo* as passé, as the pathetic relic of an outmoded mental disposition. More than a curiosity-item, *Insularismo* stands as the classic, and in many ways pioneering, statement on Puerto Rican national identity, in which the issue was first presented as the serious philosophical challenge that it is. Here credit is due, as Pedreira himself must be recognized as one of the first established intellectuals to study and document Puerto Rican culture as a national culture. It is because of its steadfast ideological pertinence and the prevalence of its guiding postulates that the book calls for more than polemical fanfare, or the facile presumption that Pedreira's negative vision may be overcome by pronouncing a bold new "positive" image in its stead.[71] What is needed, rather, is critical re-assessment, a new reading guided by and contributing to a dialectical understanding of our social and cultural history.

To begin with, the most nightmarish of Pedreira's premonitions of a commercialized and vulgarized national culture have been more than confirmed. By our time, a full-scale "Latin" culture industry flourishes by debasing Puerto Rican culture and by flaunting its supposed uniqueness, all the while adulterating it and effectively assimilating it into the venomous current of North American cultural propaganda. This process has come to saturate nearly all aspects of society in Puerto Rico, an example of cultural imperialism of the most thorough and "advanced" variety. But that uneven clash of cultures can only be understood in its full magnitude when account is taken of the political and cultural life of Puerto Ricans in the metropolitan United States.

Such a reading of *Insularismo*, therefore, immediately evokes the practical social context in which the Puerto Rican people have lived, with growing frequency, since 1934 and the death of its author in 1939. The process of capitalist industrialization has involved the radically changing social experience of a growing emigrant population. Mass emigration to the United States has confronted Puerto Ricans dramatically with the demands and opportunities of a multinational working-class reality, and thus thrown into jarring conflict many of the most cherished and assertedly essential marks of national identity. For the first time a setting is before us within which to unravel the mysteries and to confront the continued legacy of Pedreira's influential thinking.

A new evaluation of the national culture thus involves the retracing of cultural history and the development of social production, and specification of the particular class dynamics that impel and condition cultural and political life. In that way it is possible to situate instances and currents of cultural expression in their appropriate historical and ideological frame. This economic and sociological grounding of culture theory is crucial, but represents only a first step in transcending the most telling weaknesses of conventional interpretations of Puerto Rican culture. For neither a materialist sociology of art, nor folklore study aimed at unearthing and preserving the buried culture of the masses, harbors any final assurance that the sacred reign of the "isms" may be broken and arbitrary periodization by decades or biographical generations laid to rest. Focused attention must go to the stylistic and thematic texture of cultural practices, including that of the popular and "marginal" majority. The very notion of "popular culture" demands critical dissection according to the degree to which it represents an intentional alternative and opposition to the official mode of the national culture.

The consequences of this analytical distinction are obvious: not only does it underlie any critical assessment of the vast and growing folklore literature concerned with Puerto Rican culture; it also poses the turn-of-the-century period (1890–1920), which saw the incipient organization and artistic expression of the Puerto Rican proletariat, as an axis of Puerto Rican cultural development for very different reasons from those offered in standard historical accounts.[72] The abundant and diversified working-class and popular literature produced in Puerto Rico during the early decades of this century has only begun to be gathered and has still to be incorporated into critical debate. Writings such as those of Ramón Romero Rosa, Luisa Capetillo, Juan Vilar, Eduardo Conde and many others comprise a formidable cultural legacy replete with engaging historical experiences and aesthetic innovations. This wealth of evidence clashes with the pat cliché of the vacuum of silence and the spiritual trauma that is supposed to have engulfed Puerto Rican literary life in those very years. What a different sense emerges of the history of Puerto Rican culture than if one's view is restricted to the familiar luminaries of the national elite.

Along the same lines, it is of utmost importance to examine the cultural expression of Puerto Ricans in the United States as it captures the turbulent and life-rending exodus of working-class contingents from the Island. Voluminous and still largely unsorted materials illuminating the tribulations of the emigrant community are among the holdings of archives and libraries of New York City and elsewhere in the United States. Here is to be found the immediate historical background to contemporary Puerto Rican expression in the North American setting, indispensable testimony to the continuum of imperialist domination and the resistance it has unleashed. This background is indeed a crucial link in the reconstruction of Puerto Rican cultural history.

II

Rafael Cortijo, ca. 1960. (Album cover) Photographer unknown. Courtesy of Blanco Vázquez.

The Puerto Rico that José Luis González Built

A new vision of Puerto Rico is emerging in recent intellectual and cultural work, a revised understanding of its history and changing identity. Long viewed monolithically as an outpost of colonial Spain and, in the twentieth century, of the American empire, Puerto Rican cultural history is now being interpreted in more dynamic, differentiated terms. Growing attention is turning to the society's racial and ethnic composition, sexual divisions, and class hierarchy, as well as to alterations and gradations in the forms of colonial dependency. The result is a substantially modified account of the national history, with ideological and political implications of strategic consequence.

The recent essay "El país de cuatro pisos" by the well-known author José Luis González (1980a) is fast becoming a landmark in this unfolding critical project. Its appearance has occasioned a wide-ranging and lively debate among historians, sociologists, and political activists, such that it has become difficult to ponder and discuss Puerto Rican issues without making reference to that work. "El país de cuatro pisos" is to the 1980s what *Insularismo*, that classic essay of Puerto Rican self-reflection by Antonio S. Pedreira (1934), was to the 1930s: an engagingly written, metaphorically abundant watershed and germinal source for thinking about the issue of nationalism in a broad historical perspective. In fact, it is perhaps in its contrastive relation to *Insularismo*, and to "El puertorriqueño dócil," the other prominent example of the genre by René Marqués (1962), that the theoretical advances of José Luis González's reconstruction stand out in sharpest relief.

For unlike his predecessors, González delineates the stages of Puerto Rican cultural and national formation as a reflex of ongoing power relations within the colonial society and under the impact of persistent foreign domination. Rather than some gathering sense of spiritual affinity or chronic psychological idiosyncrasy, the national culture unfolds in direct correlation

First published in *Latin American Perspectives* 4/3 (Summer, 1984): 173–84.

to the exercise of political and economic authority. What seems manifest as the general culture of the Puerto Rican people in fact only goes to express, and thereby legitimate, the historical supremacy of some Puerto Ricans over others and, more or less directly, of European and North American interests over those of Puerto Rico. As such, to describe and interpret colonial culture means first of all to disassemble it, to probe beneath the official surface and seek out those latent cultural traditions that have been systematically smothered by the reality of colonial imposition, political despotism and slavery.

*   *   *

Puerto Rico, for José Luis González, is a four-story building. The first floor, constructed during four centuries of Spanish colonial rule and slavery, is the Afro-Caribbean popular base of the national culture. The second story, composed of the immigrants from South America and Europe, was added over the course of the nineteenth century. Construction of the third floor began with the North American occupation of the island in 1898. The fourth and top level, which we are still inhabiting in the present day, dates from the industrialization plan initiated in the 1940s.

Such is the scaffolding of González's newly reconstructed edifice. Its emphasis on socio-economic and political forces constitutes an evident advance beyond the idealist and subjective framework of earlier interpretations. González is most innovative when he puts cherished assumptions about national culture and ideology to the test of sociological and historical reality, and thus draws out some of the iconoclastic implications inherent in the work of contemporary Puerto Rican scholars like Angel Quintero Rivera (1972, 1976a, 1976b), Arcadio Díaz Quiñones (1982), and Fernando Picó (1981, 1984). Among the notable examples of these new lines of analysis are the importance given to nineteenth-century immigrants in the formation of a native elite and the critique of conservative ideological strains in twentieth century nationalism.

But the major contribution of "El país de cuatro pisos" to the tradition of Puerto Rican interpretation is the search for the popular grounding of the national culture. Here and in much of his earlier fictional and theoretical writing, González has sought to subvert the elitist and derivative dominant patrimony and arrive at the cultural life of the Puerto Rican masses—what he views as the repressed core of the nation throughout its development. He sees the need to undermine the traditional version of the national history that attributes the first stirrings and origin of Puerto Rican consciousness to the patriotic aspirations of the professional elite. What González concludes from this insistent quest is indicated in the title of one of his earliest and most successful short stories—"En el fondo del caño hay un negrito" ("There's a Little Black Boy at the Bottom of the Ditch"). Puerto Rican popular culture, and thus Puerto Rican national culture per se, is essentially and fundamentally African culture in its Caribbean transmutation. Beneath the layers of imposed European traditions and subsequent historical developments reside the creative and existential expression of slavery and its legacy, the productive foundations of Puerto Rican nationality. As González states in pointed dramatic terms, "the first Puerto Ricans were black Puerto Ricans."

The restitution of the Afro-Antillean dimension is, as mentioned, not new to González in this essay, nor is it new to Puerto Rican culture and theory. Rather, the twentieth century has seen the ascendancy of the African basis in the national culture, as in the growing prominence of the "plena" in the popular music, and in the veritable revolution brought to Puerto Rican poetic language by Luis Palés Matos and his introduction of African rhythms. Both of these influential tendencies were recognized in theoretical commentary by González's forebearer in the Puerto Rican interpretive essay, Tomás Blanco (1935, 1950). González has paid frequent tribute to Blanco, whose writings on Palés Matos and on "la plena" first appeared in the 1930s. A still earlier predecessor, not identified by González but certainly writing in the same spirit, was the working class leader Ramón Romero Rosa. In "A los puertorriqueños negros" ("To the Black Puerto Ricans"), a pamphlet circulated in 1899 and published in 1901, Romero Rosa states that "the children of Africa, ... those unfortunate beings brought over to settle this untamed region, constituted our first working people after the conquest" (1982, 31).

But it is in "El país de cuatro pisos" that this recovery of the buried African root is given full analytical articulation, and where the facile equation of Puerto Rican cultural identity with the syncretic fusion of Spanish-plus-Taíno-plus-African components is finally exploded. For here the African dimension appears not as just one other ingredient in the cultural stew but as the stock, or to retain the original metaphor, as the ground floor, the entryway into the national culture as a whole. And it is so not for any folkloristic, spiritual or racial reasons, but because of the situation of the bearers of African culture at the base of the social and economic hierarchy. They were the "first" Puerto Ricans, and their culture the origin and ground of the national culture, because they were the first to be tied inextricably to the country's productive system, the first with no other geographical or social recourse but to be Puerto Rican.

The strength of González's assertions is that they imply a theory of culture and work: the human source of a society's material wealth is also the cornerstone of its most distinctive cultural wealth. In countries whose process of national formation coincides with and relies upon the institution of the African slave trade and slave labor, this origin of national wealth—both material and cultural—corresponds to the slave population itself. The cultural redefinition of the Caribbean countries and even, ever so reluctantly, of the United States, has come to involve a recognition of this telling correspondence: it is the culture of black slaves and their descendants that eventually surfaces as the mainstay of the general culture of the society, especially at the popular level.

Thus the grounding of Puerto Rican cultural history on an Afro-Caribbean base has strategic implications not only for the sake of national unity and liberation; it is also a key step in the direction of regional and hemispheric solidarity. José Luis González signals that broader horizon throughout his essay, pointing out that the pattern and structure of cultural history common to the Caribbean area ultimately serves to counteract the political and linguistic divisions maintained and exacerbated by continuing imperialist design. When pronounced from the vantage of parallel cultural experiences, somehow the vision of a single, unified Caribbean community seems less utopian, even in a time of fractious contrasts like our own.

This first floor of González's edifice is certainly its sturdiest part, and constitutes the most striking architectural innovation. The emphasis on the nineteenth-century immigrants making up the second story, and the levels spanning the twentieth century (1898 and 1940), are decidedly less original for purposes of historical periodization and less carefully constructed as interpretive arguments. Yet even at ground level, at the Afro-Puerto Rican foundation, there are theoretical inconsistencies that necessarily affect the quality of the entire building. For in his welcome and justified endeavor to counteract the white-washing of Puerto Rican cultural history in its official version, González effectively substitutes a racial and ethnic category for the concept of class. This is evidently not his intention, which is avowedly Marxist and seeks to pose the contrast between black and white, African and European, in terms of the economic and social stratification system. But the argument (with which González begins his essay) that each national culture is actually two cultures refers explicitly and unequivocally to divisions of class. The dominant culture of the oppressors and the subordinate culture of the oppressed differ and interact as expressions of differential relations to social production, that is the premise that González claims forms the mortar of his whole construction. Curiously, he attributes the idea to "many sociologists" rather than to its real source in social theory—Lenin.

Of course, class contradictions never appear in "pure" form; and in the history of Puerto Rico and of other societies with slave pasts, the struggle between black and white is a primary manifestation of the class struggle. But as his accentuation of racial and ethnic contrasts proceeds, the class dimension of his argument fades from view, such that by the time the first floor nears completion we are left not with a dynamic socio-economic interaction but with an image of ethnic layering and typology. At one crucial point González even proposes two basic hypothetical "types" of Puerto Rican— one a white poet from Lares, the other a black dockworker from Puerta de Tierra—and attributes the primordial difference between them to the racial aspect. What is missing is not the reinstatement of class against the racial and ethnic reality, but a sense of the interaction between the two: How and in what ways do the black and the working class cultures correspond and diverge, and to what extent is white, European culture the manifest expression of the owning and politically dominant class?

This replacing of class analysis with a framework of ethnic relations may contribute to another serious drawback of González's structure: the denial that Puerto Rico was a nation in 1898 as it passed from Spanish to North American colonial rule. For if the process of national formation is seen primarily in terms of ethnic cohesions and contradictions, Puerto Rico by the end of the nineteenth century would indeed appear to have been too polarized between black-African and white-European to form an adequately coherent national entity. From that vantage point, Puerto Rico was still a nation "in formation," not yet a people ready for independent national life. It might be mentioned that Pedreira (1934) made the very same argument much earlier, although from a different ideological perspective. The question is, if Puerto Rico was not yet a nation in 1898, at what point and as a result of what subsequent changes did Puerto Rico become a nation? González does not address this question.

If, on the other hand, we maintain the class concept and think of the African-based cultural traditions as the major historical prefiguration of working-class culture, the stage of national formation reached by 1898 looks dramatically different. At that historical juncture, before and after the North American invasion, the class composition of Puerto Rican society was becoming openly pronounced at every level—economic, political, cultural and ideological. Of course there were marked ethnic and regional differences within the working class, just as there were varied and sometimes conflicting backgrounds and political orientations among the owning elite. But if the presence of modern, self-conscious social classes is any measure of the relative "maturity" of a nation (and in Marxist theory it is the most significant measure), then Puerto Rico by 1898 was assuredly a nation, as "developed" and eligible for national sovereignty as any nation that has gained independence in the twentieth century. Interestingly, the non-Marxist writer Manuel Méndez Ballester argued this point well in his response to González's essay (1980), although his critique is best read along with the rejoinder by Quintero

Rivera (1980).

González equivocates on the main condition or criterion of national formation, referring variously to the level of technological, ideological, political or cultural development as the key index. Thus the mid-section of his building sags noticeably, as his bold new account of the turning point in the national history remains unconvincing. Actually, it is not so new, since the idea that Puerto Rico was, and is, not yet ready to be free has long been the view upheld by the formidable line of accommodationists and apologists, a tradition to which González definitely does not belong but against whom his arguments fail to stand firm.

But aside from the faulty middle section, there are other lapses in construction, especially at the bottom and again at the top. González slights two essential stages in the history of Puerto Rican culture: the pre-Columbian, Taíno heritage and the cultural experience of Puerto Ricans in the United States. These two extremities, if they do not each constitute floors of their own, at least warrant consideration as the basement and the attic of González's building.

The enduring cultural relevance of Puerto Rico's indigenous people is familiarly dismissed, or diminished, by reference to their rapid physical extinction during the Spanish conquest and colonization process. Within two decades, González reminds us, genocide had taken its toll on the entire Taíno population, and he goes on to suggest that its subsequent contribution to the history of the Puerto Rican people is carried forward in the evolution of the Spanish and especially the African strains of the culture. The problem with this conception is that it reduces the idea of cultural tradition to the visible presence of its bearers and folkloric remnants. But the case of the Taíno legacy in Puerto Rico shows that culture is also alive as the constantly recurring image of an alternative, as a decimated but never fully extinguished origin of the people's history.

For generation after generation of Puerto Ricans, on the island and in the United States, the Taínos represent the culture of the island in its state of nature, so to speak, prior to and over against the arrival and imposition of European, capitalist values and ways of life. The evidence is abundant in the literary, musical and pictorial arts of the nineteenth and twentieth centuries, in the naming of children, places and events, and in the growing body of critical scholarship on Puerto Rican indigenous culture (see Moscoso, 1981, and Sued Badillo, 1978, 1979). The fact that this popular meaning of the pre-Columbian world often involves romantic idealizations and distortions, and that it has also been invoked for opportunistic or escapist motives, in no way negates its persistent symbolical force as a component of a culture of national resistance and affirmation. Rather than "archaic," Taíno culture harbors an enduring "residual" significance in the national history. In this sense, the indigenous culture may be considered the footing or foundation of the whole cultural construct.

At the top of the building, at the level of its attic or roof, is the cultural impact of mass migration and the resettlement of Puerto Ricans in the United States. In some ways, of course, this process may be seen as an addition to the fourth floor, since the migration of the 1940s and 1950s formed an integral part of the plan to industrialize and otherwise "modernize" Puerto Rican society. Accordingly, the cultural expression of the migration is further testimony to that development plan (Operation Bootstrap), the revised colonial relationship (Free Associated State) under which it was implemented, and its increasingly disastrous outcome in recent times. But Puerto Rican culture in the United States is also more than that, representing a qualitatively new turn in that it involves the extension and transformation of the national culture in a radically different, foreign setting. It also is inaccurate to omit this cultural reality from the national edifice by regarding it as North American culture with a Puerto Rican flavor or background, thereby equating the Puerto Rican case with that of other immigrant or ethnic groups in the United States. The sheer magnitude of the migration and above all the direct colonial relationship between the two countries go to invalidate such a facile analogy.

It is especially surprising that González disregards the emigrant and Nuyorican experience as a distinctive level of Puerto Rican cultural history since he was one of the first writers to introduce that reality as a theme in the national literature. Beginning in the late 1940s, when he himself came to spend some years in New York, González has written a range of fictional works and critical commentary treating the life of the Puerto Rican migrant (1973a, 1973b). One of his most memorable stories, in fact, entitled "La noche que volvimos a ser gente" ("The night we became people again"), builds to a final rooftop scene in El Barrio in which New York Puerto Ricans come to recognize their heightened spiritual affinity with the Island. It is unfortunate that the author did not elaborate this vision of cultural continuity and change in theoretical terms while completing the construction of his cultural building.

Thus, González's provocative new version of Puerto Rican cultural history suffers from some questionable sociological premises about the relation between race, class and nationality, and from consequential omissions of crucial historical stages. Beyond that, the structure is shaky because of inconsistencies in the type of building materials used at different levels. The various stages of periodization are marked off, alternately, by demographic, ethnic, institutional, political and economic variables, with no clear indication as to why one or the other of these factors is given greater weight at any given stage. González anticipates this objection to the essay's incompleteness and inconsistencies by subtitling his work "Notes . . . " and by explaining in the opening paragraph that it is intended as no more than the nucleus of a longer and more rigorous analysis. Indeed, the picture becomes significantly clearer and richer when a reading of the essay is complemented by his many other works of cultural historical import, such as his recent "chronicle" of the North American invasion, *La llegada* (1980b), and his influential theoretical writing contained in *Conversación con José Luis González* (1976a), the introduction to *Memorias de Bernardo Vega* (1977), "Literatura e identidad nacional en Puerto Rico" (1979), *Literatura y sociedad en Puerto Rico* (1976b) and others. Other commentators, such as José Luis Méndez (1982) and Manuel Maldonado Denis (1982), have attempted to provide a more inclusive critical account of González's contribution.

Nevertheless, "El país de cuatro pisos" is liable to remain the best known of the author's theoretical pronouncements and for many readers perhaps the only one with which they are familiar, and it therefore needs to be reckoned with on its own terms. As such, it begs the still larger question of interpretive method: Does the architectonic principle make for an appropriate, or even useful, metaphor for concretizing the course of cultural history? Does the process, not to say progress, of a people's culture really resemble the layer-upon-layer erection of a multistoried building? No more so, I would contend, than it resembles the roots, trunk and branches of a tree, or the seasons of the year. The mechanical metaphor, of which the architectural construct of José Luis González is an example, is no more adequate than the more familiar organic or cyclical metaphors in accounting for the dynamic development of cultural history. Metaphorical imagery is of course valid and helpful to bring aspects of historical experience closer to a contemporary understanding, but not when it is taken as the guiding principle of historical conceptualization.

* * *

In no direct way are these objections, however severe they may seem, intended to detract from the value of "El país de cuatro pisos" as a contribution to new thinking about Puerto Rico. The essay is full of striking critical insights, and the attempt to present the political and cultural process in lively graphic terms is more than welcome. It will be necessary to extend González's salutary emphasis on the Afro-Caribbean base of Puerto Rican popular culture and to fill in his reinterpretation of the national culture under North American domination. In broader terms, he offers a provocative reference point for approaching the culture in its relation to social history and political ideology. Such a structural conception is needed in order to challenge the elitist and ethnocentric assumptions still prevalent. A striking counterpart to González's essay in contemporary Puerto Rican writing is the provocative testimonial narrative by Edgardo Rodríguez Juliá, *El entierro de Cortijo* (1983), which also reflects on the African base of Puerto Rican culture.

But building on this theoretical project of "El país de cuatro pisos" involves, first of all, replacing the architectural metaphor with an account of cultural process based on the history of social formations. Rather than the floor-upon-floor blueprint suggesting successive layers, a concept of cultural history as the constantly interpenetrating dynamic of traditions and social practices makes for a more satisfactory guiding principle of interpretive analysis. For example, rather than merely locating Afro-Caribbean culture at the origins of Puerto Rican nationality, it is necessary to study how this basic strain of the popular culture is reconstituted, taking on new meanings and socio-cultural functions, in the varying contexts of national history—before and after the abolition of slavery; in its differentiated contact with indigenous, European and North American cultures; in relation to an emerging working class cultural life on the island; and in the radically new setting of the urban United States. The mechanical analogy of architectural construction tends to lock any given aspect of the national culture into the confines of its initial manifestation.

The understanding of cultural change as correlative to, and expressive of, interacting social formations also relates cultural practice more integrally with production and the organization of production. José Luis González's notion of culture identifies it strongly with ideology and artistic expression, especially literature; aside from some cursory remarks on Caribbean food, culture in his view remains rather rigidly superstructural. In this sense "El país de cuatro pisos" remains more conventional than innovative; the emphasis in the best of contemporary cultural theory has been on culture as a form of material practice in its relation to technology. It is precisely along these lines, by applying and expanding upon the work of Pierre Bourdieu (1977), Nestor García Candini (1977, 1979, 1982), Raymond Williams (1982) and others, that striking new insights into Puerto Rican cultural history might be developed. The dichotomies and interpenetrations between elite and popular cultures, on which González focuses his interpretation, are only partially understandable as contrasting ideological orientations and literary currents. The formation of Puerto Rican culture is grounded in other processes as well: the changing quality of labor from agricultural to artisan to industrial production; the collisions and interfaces of oral, literate and media traditions; the shift from rural to urban to metropolitan cultural environments; and the difference between walking, horses, trains, automobiles, ships and airplanes as the primary means of transportation. Another key dimension of the historical dynamic, unmentioned by González but emerging in recent socio-cultural analysis, is the specific cultural experience of Puerto Rican women (see Acosta-Belén, 1979, 1980).

Such are some considerations germane to a renewed vision of Puerto Rican culture. "El país de cuatro pisos" and the ensuing debate provide the needed contemporary impetus, and the point is neither simply to furnish the building nor to demolish it. The goal is to reconstruct the national history according to its own particular contours, not some extraneous metaphorical design. The guiding theoretical premises derive from an analysis of the structured relations of social power understood in their national and international dimensions. The substance of the national culture has to do with practical social experience—how Puerto Ricans live, work, interact, celebrate and struggle—and the articulation of that experience in symbolic and intellectual meanings. For Puerto Ricans, as for other colonial peoples, the purpose of reconstructing cultural history is to recapture it, to seize it from those who have denied and distorted it.

Refiguring *La charca*

Juan del Salto and Silvina never meet, yet *La charca* is essentially the story of their interlocking worlds. The two ends of the social spectrum—the rich *hacendado* and the poor peasant girl—are set in narrative counterpoint, the protagonists at no point actually coming into direct contact but always implying each other as the associations and analogies mount. Intermediate characters like Marcelo and Ciro, Galante and Gaspar, Dr. Pintado and Old Marta, and the suggestive coincidence of events, bring their disparate lives gradually to converge through the distance. Toward the end we even hear Juan del Salto speak sympathetically of Silvina—whose sad story he knows, at least "in part"—and it is significant that the last chapter begins by locating them at close range: "Two years later, Silvina was living in a hut situated in the heights of Juan del Salto's farm."

But, as the epileptic Silvina finally collapses and crashes to her death, Juan del Salto is off in Europe to attend the university graduation of his idolized son. *La charca*, in fact, seems to build toward their rapprochement, only to accentuate the unbridgeable gulf between them, the mutual irrelevance and exclusion of their lives and concerns. Silvina, the defenseless victim, may get a warm, comforting feeling when she gazes off in the direction of his hacienda and vast coffee plantation; and Juan del Salto, the powerful *caballero*, is typically wracked with pity and liberal outrage when he is made to think of the likes of suffering Silvina. But the story shows that their relation is ultimately one of contrast and conflict, not harmony, since they inhabit opposing extremes in an antagonistic class system.

This dynamic polarity between the two main characters forms the basic compositional principle of *La charca*, and is a feature of the book to which scant attention has been paid in previous critical writings. Even recent interpretations and relevant historical studies, while contributing valuable new

First published as "Introduction" to *La Charca*, trans. Kal Wagenheim (Maplewood, NJ: Waterfront Press, 1984).

71

insights on social and stylistic aspects, still largely overlook the specific elements of plot structure and characterization. (A selective bibliography of writings about, and relevant to, *La charca* is included.) The present comments will take the structured action and character relations of the novel as a springboard for reassessing some of its socio-historical and ideological dimensions, and then turn to the issue of its literary placement. Only occasional reference will be possible to the rich symbolical and stylistic qualities of *La charca*, a fascinating topic entered into by some earlier critics, but still awaiting more coherent analysis.

In addition to the central contrast between landowners and peasants, and mediating between them, there is a third social force at work in the novel. It is the world of *"el negocio,"* a single term referring to all the various deals and schemes—from business transactions, usury and hoarding to outright larceny and murder—which serve to propel the action. The characters here—Andújar, Galante, Gaspar and Deblás—are treated with unqualified disdain, often cast in pejorative racial tones. As befits their lack of spiritual and human depth, they tend to be flat and allegorical, varied incarnations of evil driven by a singular emotion, greed. It is only in the sequel to *La charca*, in the novel entitled *El negocio*, that these characters take on any psychological complexity and come to occupy the center of fictional interest.

In *La charca*, this business sector appears in its earlier, embryonic stage. Their names suggest that they are immigrants, signaling the preponderance of entrepreneurs from Spain and southern Europe in the unfolding of Puerto Rican commerce during the late nineteenth century. Indeed, they typically appear on the scene as foreigners intruding ominously and violently upon the native setting. But they are not outsiders to the plot. Rather, they are the collective catalyst of events, their abiding influence impinging on both Silvina and Juan del Salto and binding their disparate worlds into one indissoluble dramatic web.

These three class constellations—landowning elite, rural laborers and petty entrepreneurs—comprise the social ensemble of the novel; together, they are the human components of "la charca." Along with Juan del Salto, the *hacendados* are represented by his companions, Dr. Pintado and Father Esteban and, as extensions of his "ideal" and "practical" selves, his son Jacobo and his foreman Montesa, respectively. Silvina's world of the peasants and day laborers includes her mother Leandra, her beloved Ciro and his brother Marcelo, as well as Inés Marcante and a mass of other, nameless characters. The stagnation and pollution of the title indicates that the whole society is seen as a "sick world," though its moral affliction is overtly attributable to the contaminating role of *"el negocio."* The pollutant is the force of commercial greed, and the schemers and usurers who introduce and represent that motive. But the landed aristocracy and the "helpless" peasantry are equally caught up in the general social miasma. Their social interaction, in fact, makes for the very stagnation needed to allow the sickness to fester. And it is this relation that is of foremost interest in the novel. The stature and dimension accorded Juan del Salto and Silvina and the narrative structure by which their fates are systematically interwoven, make it clear that the story is really about them.

It is especially important to call attention to Silvina because she is so overshadowed by the commanding presence of the *hacendado*. She lurks, frail and almost indiscernible, at the edge of the forest (her name associates her with *la selva*), while he confidently oversees his vast plantation and ponders lofty philosophical truths. Juan del Salto bears so much of the intellectual weight of *La charca*, and so strongly suggests its author, that most interpretations have focused primarily on him. His words and thoughts are often quoted as those of Zeno Gandía himself, and in most discussions of the book it is assumed that he is the one who defines and embodies its deeper problematic. If he is not identical to the narrative voice, the assumption goes, he is by far the most conscious and articulate figure in the novel, and his ideas, however contradictory, correspond to its broader perspective and meaning.

In terms of the plot and narrative structure, however, it is Silvina who occupies the central role, and Juan del Salto is most conspicuous for his absence. The story begins and ends with her, in precisely the same setting, the young girl's despairing stance on the cliff above the river forming an emblematic frame around the intervening events. More significant, though perhaps less obvious, is Silvina's centrality to the climax of the book. It is Chapter 7, that traumatic "night of crime and love," when the young peasant girl experiences, in blinding succession, a bloody murder and an act of sexual passion. That is the point in the action—evoked in the motto as "the serene summer night"—toward which all the emotional tension gathers, and after which the pace noticeably slackens and the moral and personal knots are unraveled. And through all those middle chapters of the book—during the flood scene, on that crucial summer's night, and at the trial of conscience that ensues—Juan del Salto is hardly even mentioned by name, and he plays no part in the events. He surfaces again only later, after the dust has settled, his aloofness from what transpires all the more blatant.

At times, as in the memorable flood scene immediately preceding the climax, his remoteness from the action seems to be the very point at issue. Torrential rains have caused the river to overflow its banks, and a young boy is about to be carried away in the deluge. Hearing the desperate cry for help, Juan del Salto comes forth to witness the scene. Rather than leaping to the rescue, though, he remains on the sideline, enraptured by the noble humanity of his courageous peasants. Even the language here, with its ironic play on his name, goes to accentuate his physical inactivity, and to underscore the hypocrisy inherent in his fervent idealism:

> Juan del Salto felt wonder, nor surprise. He had witnessed similar things many times before. Inés Marcante, the one who had been whipped by Montesa earlier in the day, jumped into the water from the left shore. Almost simultaneously, six more *campesinos* jumped in. The liquid monster parted, allowing a few shreds of humanity, ennobled by heroism, to penetrate its depths.

Only intellectually, in his chronic mental leaps from lofty ideals to practical self-interest, is Juan del Salto true to his name. When it comes to real life-and-death plunges, like Silvina's *salto mortal* at the end, he is far away, or as in the flood scene, he can only feel and think, immobilized by his own internal rhetoric.

For there, too, in the face of physical danger and heroic humanity, he is encountering Silvina's world, even though she herself is not directly present. The terrified little 14-year-old (a boy of her age) is seen clinging for life, as she does, from the limbs of a tree. Silvina is further associated with the episode through its hero, Inés Marcante, with whom she later comes to spend the last years of her brief life. The whole scene, in fact, which stands out as the only instance of strong moral affirmation in the book, seems to prefigure symbolically the entire course of events. Silvina, of course, ends succumbing to the catastrophe while the young boy is saved; but the same disconnection between the threatened state of the peasant and the aloof world of the *hacendado* is strongly evident again as the story concludes.

The distinctive quality of *La charca* rests on this basic contradiction, represented by the contrasting protagonists, but also engrained throughout in the narrative structure and texture. That is, it is a disconnection not only between Juan del Salto and Silvina, but between the intellectual and dramatic dimensions of the fictional world itself. When ideas are expressed and philosophies expounded, the figure of the educated *hacendado* dominates, and there is relatively little action; while the main events, centering around the experience of Silvina, transpire unaccompanied by the rhetoric of reflection and explanation.

This contrast is also the source of the central irony in *La charca*, for the mute bearers and sufferers of the action actually do more to articulate the moral thrust of the novel than does its apparent spokesman. To refer again to the flood scene, where the two worlds come closest to colliding, the aftermath of that feat of heroism is different for the two main characters. Juan del Salto's ray of optimism and paean to humanity is but a momentary flash, after which he quickly returns to his real interests: he is off with his *mayordomo* Montesa, who had just whipped the heroic laborer Inés Marcante into obedience, to take stock of the damages the flood has brought to his plantation. Typically, the burst of idealism and human sympathy gives way to his more pressing concern for property and, of course, for the security of his son.

For Silvina, on the other hand, the image of the imperiled boy is but another foreboding of her own eventual downfall. The flooding river is to him what the engulfing social reality is to Silvina, for even Inés Marcante turns out to be anything but a hero in his treatment of her. The one-time embodiment of Juan del Salto's ideal is arrogant and abusive, to the point where Silvina, just before her end, chooses to leave him rather than share him, and their bed, with another woman. This final refusal, the act of a young woman—she is about eighteen by the end—rejecting the burden of entrenched sexual oppression, represents an act of real heroism and humanity. Though characteristically mute and unreflected, it raises her moral stature in the book above that of the patriarchal Juan del Salto.

*　*　*

Like its intellectual protagonist, though, the narrator of *La charca* also maintains a distance from the immediate tragedy. For it would be misleading to presume the ideological perspective of the novel to be that of the downtrodden peasantry. It has rightly been viewed, especially in recent studies, as an elitist work, saturated with the prejudices and apologetics of a frustrated colonial ruling class. Though total disdain is reserved for the criminal, inhuman world of "*el negocio*," the portrayal of the peasantry and of women is also by and large a demeaning one: they are an inert, ignorant mass, open game for the corruption and disease that surround them. This class and sexual bias, buttressed as it is by overtones of racial determinism, is explicit and unconcealed. Yet the ironic treatment of Juan del Salto, the very embodiment of these hierarchies, points to greater complexity than would be suggested by such outwardly reactionary associations.

The historical dating of the novel is of interest in approaching its ideological perspective and ambiguities. It is known that Zeno Gandía wrote *La charca* in the early 1890s, the years preceding its publication in 1894. What has not been adequately noted is that the only historical reference in the book places the action much earlier, in the late 1860s and early 1870s.

Later on in the story, Juan del Salto is engaged in a lively dinner conversation with his respected friends Dr. Pintado and Father Esteban. The discussion is spirited and wide-ranging, finally turning to the politics of the day. "The three friends," it is said, "were inspired by the progressive nature of the September revolution." The dramatic events of the "Glorious Revolution" in Spain, which occurred in September of 1868, must have been recent, as the three liberals are still reeling with enthusiasm for the spirit and rhetoric of reforms ushered in at the time. "No more guardianship," they proclaim in unison, thinking of both the Spanish motherland and the colony. "They spoke of rights and duties, of equality, of the need to equalize before the law all sons of the nation, all groups, all people."

Such was the language and tone of the liberal colonial elite at that stage of Puerto Rican history, and it would not be so for long. By 1873 the theme would more likely have been the new constitution and the abolition of slavery, and in the 1880s, closer to when *La charca* was written, it would surely have been the serious economic crisis and political repression that ensued, culminating in the "Terrible Year" of 1887. From his vantage-point in the early 1890s, Zeno Gandía was evidently harkening back a full generation, setting up the span of elapsed time between authorial and narrative present that was typical of much nineteenth-century realist fiction.

Perhaps too much might be made of the coincidences that emerge from this more precise dating of the novel's action, beginning with the fact that as a child of Silvina's age Zeno Gandía himself witnessed the September Revolution first-hand in the streets of Barcelona (an experience which he was to recall vividly much later in life). In the years around 1868 when the novel is set, his other protagonist, Juan del Salto, is somewhere around the author's age when he is writing it. And, in a more political vein, is it not likely that "el Grito de Lares" also passed through the author's mind, that first major political assertion of Puerto Rican nationality which occurred only two weeks after the September events in Spain? And if we bear in mind the words of the motto, "such was the cry that he called out on the serene summer night" and their subtle bearing on Silvina's despairing outcries, *La charca* could be read as a testament to the Puerto Rico of that early outburst of national affirmation.

The very absence of any mention of Lares in a novel so explicitly set in just those years is actually rather remarkable, though it is in line with the silence that long surrounded that event in the island's official culture. Could it be, as the eminent Venezuelan critic César Zumeta (a contemporary of Zeno Gandía) suggested when *La charca* first appeared, that the author "was well aware that the *guardia civil* was reading over his shoulder?" One recent critic, in fact, has gone so far as to see in *La charca* "a tacit desire to create a national consciousness and to foment anti-colonial revolution."

But such deductions are still largely conjectural and better left to future study to either substantiate or discard. The point of specifying dates and time-spans is not to arrive at some telling chronological details, however charged they may seem with symbolical implication. The goal, rather, is to approach more closely the specific socio-historical field of the novel, which encompasses the period between its portrayed action and its eventual composition. *La charca* represents Puerto Rican society—or rather, a certain aspect of that society—in the years between the late 1860s and the early 1890s. On one end of that frame is the four-year period—say 1867 to 1871—during which the fictional action occurs and when major legal and political strides were made toward the formation of Puerto Rican nationhood; the other pole comprises the years just prior to 1894 when Zeno Gandía was writing, on the eve of the transfer of the colonial nation from Spanish to North American hands. A critical interpretation of the novel must obviously have both periods in view and certainly not assume them to be interchangeable. But what is perhaps most important is the relation between them: how is the Puerto Rico of 1867–71 altered by being portrayed from a hindsight of some 25 years? And what form does the ideological and literary viewpoint of a Zeno Gandía in the 1890s assume when it sets out to represent Puerto Rico in those earlier times? Changes and developments occurring in the intervening years, and the extent to which they bear on the fictional rendering, are of central interest.

Another important qualification has to do with the scope of Puerto Rican society represented in *La charca*. Perhaps because of its uncontested stature as the "flower" of the Puerto Rican novel, the work is customarily read as a metaphor for the whole Island society. Zeno Gandía was the first to caution against that assumption, having conceived *La charca* as but one installment in an ambitious novelistic project that originally was to comprise eleven volumes, each intended to focus on a different aspect of social reality. The author of course could not have foreseen that he would never complete his project, nor that his portrait of coffee-growing Puerto Rico would continue to draw greater acclaim than the other "*crónicas*"—*Garduña, El negocio* and *Los redentores*—as the supreme literary achievement.

La charca refers to a specific portion, or aspect, of Puerto Rican society. As has been pointed out—by Francisco Manrique Cabrera and other critics—"*la charca*" and "*el café*" are intricately associated, and the sense of morbid inertia implies first of all life in the coffee regions. The title refers to the whole society only by extension: "*la charca*" is Puerto Rico itself insofar as the country's most stagnant, self-enclosed sector, coffee cultivation, epitomizes the condition of the entire national economy. This generalization must of course take account of the relation of the part to the whole, that is, the extent to which the delimited world of Juan del Salto and Silvina is set against the larger social panorama of Puerto Rico and its colonial status. The novel itself gives us little basis for this contextualization, since the universe surrounding the coffee plantations is presented as such a self-contained unit. For the inhabitants of that world, the author implies, it appeared self-contained and disconnected, which of course contributes to the isolation and inertia to which he is drawing attention. But the novel contains no mention of other economic and social sectors and their active bearing on the world of coffee.

Yet, in addition to coffee, it was sugar production and international commerce that were central, moving forces in Puerto Rican economic life for all those years, from the 1860s through the 1890s. While it is true that coffee claimed the highest monetary value on the world market, especially in the late 1880s when it reached its peak, at no point did it surpass those other areas of economic activity in terms of its defining role in overall social development. As regards both the productive forces and the relations of production, the coffee-producing sector had long been representative not of change and the advent of modern classes, but of the old world of small scale production, servility and patriarchal authority.

The question of the ideological orientation of *La charca*—the subject of widely divergent interpretations—may perhaps be more fruitfully approached with such a guiding framework of the historical field and specified social horizon. Omissions, from this vantage point, turn out to be as revealing as what is actually presented. For one thing, the very isolation of the world of coffee, its virtual disconnection from other forces comprising the totality, indicates an ideological distortion of some magnitude. There are no slaves, no sprawling canefields or sugar mills, no burgeoning commercial establishments, no artisan trades, no movement of rural workers to the coastal towns with its gradual formation of an agricultural proletariat. Even within the system of coffee production, in fact, there is no hint of the widespread and particularly exploitative employment of women and children for all stages of labor on the plantation.

All of these factors, seemingly extraneous in *La charca*, would bear directly on the fictional experience portrayed, perhaps lending some dynamic to the immobile reality thus viewed largely from within. Furthermore, those neglected dimensions were also active tendencies within the historical field. Between 1868 and 1894, the institution of slavery and its aftermath (following abolition in 1873), the continual expansion of sugar holdings, the restricted growth of colonial commerce and the faltering proletarization of the masses all assumed increasing importance in the definition of national life, as did the many political changes to which those processes gave rise. Yet none of these tendencies, of which the author was assuredly aware when writing, comes to figure in the unfolding and outcome of the book.

Zeno Gandía was once characterized as an "aristocrat with liberal tendencies," and the ambivalence suggested in that epithet still seems remarkably apt. His merciless anatomy of "*el Puerto Rico del café*" leads to what sounds like an all-around condemnation and a view of a social world doomed by its own internal corruption and passivity. On the other hand there is a protectiveness, and more than a hint of nostalgia, in the treatment of that threatened world, especially as it is invaded and superseded by the steady awakening of commerce (represented at the end of the novel with the establishment of Andújar & Galante, Inc. off in the coastal city of Ponce). For no matter how sickly and stagnant the "swamp" of rural life may be, it remains morally and spiritually preferable to the scheming, parasitic world of "*el negocio.*"

There are thus many ways to approach a critical understanding of *La charca* and its ideology, and the present round of debate is indeed opening up suggestive new ones. Of particular relevance is the important recent work in nineteenth-century Puerto Rican history by such writers as Fernando Picó, Astrid Cubano and Laird W. Bergad, some of which focuses specifically on the coffee-producing areas during the same period. With all due qualifications, the novel seems to be another example, so prevalent in the tradition of nineteenth-century realism, of a critique of emerging capitalism from the standpoint of earlier, pre-capitalist relations. It may tend to idealize and sentimentalize that antecedent world, but the weight of its narrative force is directed against the impending inhumanity and reification being ushered in by the incipient bourgeoisie. The rural world is condemned, to be sure, but mainly because it is so easily overrun by the corruptive influence of private property and money. Reference to pre-capitalist conditions—including the empathetic treatment of the peasantry—thus conveys a sense of criticism and rejection of bourgeois society. It implies an alternative, though residual and mystified, to the decadence and inhumanity of the social order that is taking its place. For this reason the ideological position of *La charca* evades any simple classification.

It was an historically futile position, though, as was that of the class it represented, which accounts for the defeatism and pessimism of the book's guiding tone and metaphor. The colony's coffee-growing elite, in fact, appears to be the very embodiment of the stagnant social order that surrounds it; though voicing the ideals of autonomy and reform and claiming Zeno Gandía's lifelong allegiance, the *hacendados* prove ultimately ineffectual because of their structural dependence on both the destitution of the peasantry and the vagaries of international commerce. And this sense of hopelessness could only have been reinforced by the nagging colonial bondage under which Puerto Rico continued to languish: direct subjection to metropolitan power constituted the main obstacle to any kind of autonomous national development and independent initiative on the part of the emerging classes.

Through a familiar transfer, of course, it is the servile masses who bear the brunt of this historical frustration. In terms that resonate through much elitist thinking in Puerto Rico, the poor and working people are characterized as pathologically docile and held directly responsible for their own lowly condition. This derogatory attribution defines the main tenor of the novel, being voiced not only by Juan del Salto, Montesa and Dr. Pintado, but by the narrator as well. However, closer reading and attention to the book's thematic composition suggest that the fatalistic title and determinist rhetoric are not all there is to *La charca*. For there can be no denying the undercurrent of sympathy and even admiration for the humble masses, especially as manifest in the implicit moral elevation, however subdued and paternalistic, of the tragic Silvina.

* * *

This political and philosophical ambivalence is further reflected in the complex literary placement of *La charca*. During the same historical span, 1870-1890, a major shift occurred in Puerto Rican literature. The years in which the novel is set saw the height of romanticism, with its Edenic exhaltation of the Puerto Rican landscape expressed in elegiac tones and styles. In the ensuing decades came the gradual ascendancy of literary realism aimed at providing an objective representation of colonial society. Zeno Gandía and Alejandro Tapia y Rivera, the two major figures in late nineteenth-century Puerto Rican literature, both exemplify in their own careers this transition from a romantic to a realist mode of writing.

Some writers, like Zeno Gandía, carried the realistic project even further, seeking not only a description of social forces but their clinical anatomy: the society was regarded as "sick" ("*un mundo enfermo*") and the task of literature was to get to the root of this pathological state in order to "cure" it; as the motto begins, "to tell everything so as to know everything, so as to cure everything." This quote from Zola announces a program of naturalism, and *La charca* is readily identified as an example of the "roman experimental." Much has been made of the influence of Zola in Latin America, an influence which was particularly strong and direct in the case of Zeno Gandía because of his career as a medical scientist and his extensive familiarity with French literature. Those words from the motto of *La charca* are from *Dr. Pascal* (1893), the last and summary novel of the Rougon-Macquart series after which Zeno Gandía obviously fashioned his "chronicles of a sick world." (The motto, I would argue, forms an integral part of *La charca*, both in terms of its literary identification with Zola and because of its subtle, poetic anticipation of the story to follow. It should continue to be included even though the author evidently authorized its omission from the last edition published during his lifetime in 1930.)

Still greater critical attention has gone to the many deviations from the naturalist model, evidence of countervailing movements coming to the author from Spain and the other Latin American countries. The general consensus is that *La charca* actually evidences a hybrid, eclectic naturalism whose theoretical program is modified in practice by prominent shades of Spanish realism, lingering romanticism and anticipations of prose *modernismo*. This tracing of influences and movements is of value in its own right in the case of a country like Puerto Rico, whose whole literary life has been so diminished and distorted by uninterrupted colonial rule. It is important to ascertain that *La charca* is not just the "great Puerto Rican novel," springing sui generis from native traditions and not inspired by promising new developments in other countries. It is also necessary to recognize that Zeno Gandía's work is not merely an imitation or offshoot of a European source but has its own distinctive qualities, deriving from its precise historical and cultural context.

But literary classification should also serve to shed light on political processes and to deepen our understanding of the work itself. Zeno Gandía and many other Latin American writers of his day saw in naturalism a way of rigorously exposing social conditions in their totality, and particularly the "lower depths" of those societies, the peasantry. They were no longer satisfied with the superficial, folkloric populism of the "cuadros de costumbres," nor with the rhapsodic idealism of the romantic mode. They wanted to go deeper, and their clinical sight was usually riveted on those most victimized by the social pathology, the rural laborers.

In this sense, *La charca* must be read in relation to other works of naturalist fiction in Latin America. *La charca*, in fact, was not the first example of that genre to appear in Puerto Rico, nor did its publication in 1894 usher in a new movement. Naturalist ideas were introduced in 1882 in *El Buscapié*, a prominent literary journal edited by Manuel Fernández Juncos. As in most Latin American countries, the movement caught on in Puerto Rico, and in the ensuing years there appeared a spate of second-rate naturalist novels by Zeno Gandía's precursors and immediate contemporaries, such lesser-known authors as Francisco del Valle Atiles, Matías González García, Camela Eulute Sanjurjo and Federico Degetau. Naturalist writing continued on into the early twentieth century in occasionally interesting works by Ramón Juliá Marín, José Pérez Lozada and José Elías Levis. All of this literature had in common a focus on the social world of the Puerto Rican peasantry, and that emphasis would remain central to Puerto Rican fiction through the 1940s, long after the naturalist fever subsided.

More pertinent still is the work of Salvador Brau, a figure more of Zeno Gandía's intellectual stature. Brau's short naturalist novel *¿Pecadora?* (1890) and especially his important sociological essays, *Las clases jornaleras en Puerto Rico* (1882) and *La campesina* (1886), were instrumental in drawing the attention of the Island's liberal intelligentsia to the pitiable conditions of the peasant masses. The very vocabulary and political tone contained in those observations on the situation of peasant women seem to resonate in many passages of *La charca*.

The turn from romanticism to realism and naturalism was thus more than a matter of changing literary fashions. Rather, it was representative of a larger reorientation of the educated elite, away from the aloofness and subjective idealism of an earlier stage and toward a more concrete, objective assessment of the national problematic. Not that there was a total abandonment of the romantic temper, nor that the authors suddenly took up the interest of the impoverished classes and saw the historical project from their perspective. But there was a new dynamic at work, the critical focus of realism and awakened concern for the peasantry going to deflate the rhetorical excesses and evasions of the romantic vision. It is important to mention that this tendency toward realism and naturalism in the national literature was also prevalent in the emerging artisan and working-class fiction in the 1890s and especially in the first two decades of the twentieth century.

The dynamic interplay between contending literary and social orientations is directly present in *La charca*, and in fact corresponds to that distinctive narrative tension between the book's protagonists. For Juan del Salto and Silvina view the world, and particularly the natural setting, in different ways—one typically romantic, the other realist and social. The *hacendado's* experience of nature, in his own words and as attributed to him by the narrator, is elegiac: the aesthetic exterior of the landscape sends him into a state of mystical enthusiasm, and the language is charged with poetic cadences and metaphysical correspondences. Such passages are directly reminiscent of the rhapsodic writings of José Gautier Benítez, the young Hostos and the earlier verse and prose of Zeno Gandía himself.

But the opening scene of the novel, where we encounter nature from the viewpoint of Silvina, explicitly contraverts this familiar romantic optic. The young peasant girl is left cold and unmoved by that beautiful spring sunset, which the narrator has just presented to us in all its enchanting splendor: "The trees, ever alive, wore pink vestments and red trappings; the landscape was like a dream-world, fashioned by the hand of Spring." But Silvina, we are immediately told, "looked, but did not see. That poetic scene, so familiar to her, offered no distraction. The peaceful sunset was of no interest to the fourteen-year-old girl."

What Silvina "discovers" in observing the natural setting, behind and beneath its outer surface, is the world of people who inhabit it. The very lay of the landscape, which she surveys as though through the lens of a movie camera, reveals to her and to the reader the full range of hierarchies and contradictions in the surrounding society. The long paragraphs which follow, presenting nature through Silvina's eyes and on the basis of her social experience, serve as a convenient introduction to the cast of characters. More than merely a literary device, though, they also provide a detailed map of the prevailing structure of class and sexual power. Silvina's own subordinate, precarious place in that social panorama, even more than her epileptic condition, already implies her final end. For she sees all of this, after all, while leaning against the branches of a tree "so as not to fall," the passive verbs "*asida*" and "*sujeta*" somehow epithetic of her dependent, defenseless position.

This collision of class perceptions could hardly be more dramatic, and the importance attached to it is stressed by its occurrence at the outset of the story. It serves as an initial cue that we are to witness sharply contrasting human experiences of the same social and natural reality. And this difference, embodied in the main characters and representative of their divergent class perspectives, is also expressive of differing literary styles and philosophical imaginations. Romanticism and realism, the main tendencies prevailing in Puerto Rican letters, are thus set into dynamic counterpoint in *La charca*. Rather than merely external influences or contending alternatives, they are woven into the poetic and thematic fabric of the book.

True to its naturalist credo, the outcome and overriding tenor of *La charca* seem fatalistic—the guiding metaphor of the title indicates that it is a world pathologically doomed to stagnation and moral pollution. But, significantly, it is not naturalism in any doctrinaire, deterministic sense that goes to expose and satirize the romantic tone and posture. *La charca* may be most appropriately considered a work of critical realism, since the forces impinging on the course of events are overwhelmingly social and not biological or ecological. The role of race, heredity and climate—which prevail in strict naturalist terms—is marginal when compared with the decisive weight of lived social experience. The fate of Silvina, to take the most obvious instance, is not haunted by any "ghosts" inherited from her mother Leandra. On the contrary, her character is one of refusal and rebellion which, though ending in futility, is diametrically opposed to that of her grotesquely submissive parent.

This placement of *La charca* in the realist tradition should help to over-come its facile identification with the naturalist school and the prescriptions of Zola. At the same time, it also serves to counteract the common tendency of highlighting examples of romantic and modernist writing as poetic ex-ceptions to the mechanical laws of naturalism. Rather, *La charca* may be seen to range freely yet cautiously between those stylistic poles, activating both but yielding to the excesses of neither. It is this balance, this interplay of contrasting human possibilities, that lends the novel its enduring fascina-tion, making it still today such a penetrating literary portrayal we have of nineteenth-century Puerto Rican society.

But the interest of *La charca* to contemporary readers goes beyond the insights it provides as a social document, or even its place at the threshold of modern Puerto Rican fiction. For in that book, and in the other installments of the "crónicas de un mundo enfermo," Zeno Gandía lent profound literary representation to a key stage in a protracted historical process which we are still living through in the present day. The final third of the nineteenth century saw the decisive formation of Puerto Rico as a colonial nation. It was the time when the emerging social classes first arrived at a collective—and then a differentiated—political and cultural expression. And it was the time when the whole society was entering into its new position in the international economic system.

Since then, of course, the whole colonial orbit has changed from Spain to the United States, and all of Puerto Rican life has been altered by sweeping industrialization and mass emigration. But the world of *La charca* is still with us today in the pervasive and unrelenting affliction of imperialist rule. Zeno Gandía diagnosed it as "sick," and sought in vain for a "cure." Or rather, as the author would have it, the cure is the novel itself—the endlessly flowing river—which goes on "telling it all" even after the sad story has been told. Bearing witness to colonial misery in its deeper psychological dimensions, the novelist also uncovers rays of hope and change. Despite his pessimism, Zeno Gandía always detected this glimmer of affirmation. This was true in *La charca* and it was also evident toward the end of his life, when he again took stock of his country's pitiable condition. Writing in 1929, Zeno Gandía concluded his gloomy account by reminding us that for all of the oppression endured by Puerto Rico, "there is some reaction. At times a latent fire flares up, efforts in the right direction are made—utterings that could perhaps lead our mother island to a better future."

We would thus do well to keep returning to *La charca*. For what it says, and leaves unsaid, still illuminates our present struggle.

"Bumbún" and the Beginnings of *Plena* Music

Mon, Rafa and Maelo are gone. The death of those three master *plene-ros*—Mon Rivera, Rafael Cortijo and Ismael Rivera—in recent years marks the end of an era in the history of the Puerto Rican *plena*, that form of popular music which arose at the beginning of the century in the sugar-growing areas along the southern coast of the Island, and which within a generation, by the 1930s, came to be recognized by many as an authentic and representative music of the Puerto Rican people. Despite the unfavorable odds dictated by its evidently African-based features and its origins among the most downtrodden sectors of the population, *plena* rapidly supplanted the traditions of both *bomba* and *música jíbara* as the favored sound among many poor and working people. *Plena* even superseded the *danza* as the acknowledged "national music" of Puerto Rico. Tomás Blanco's 1935 essay "Elogio de la plena" was a landmark in this process of intellectual and cultural vindication, which is itself part of a larger project aimed at acknowledging the fundamental role of African and working-class expression in the history of Puerto Rican national culture.

The story of the *plena* comprises three chapters, each spanning a period of about twenty-five years.[1] The first quarter-century, which extends to the earliest recordings of *plena* around 1926, saw the emergence and consolidation of the distinctive form and its spread to all regions of the Island. Between 1925 and 1950, when Canario and then César Concepción were at their peak, *plena* continued to extend its popularity, reaching the salons and ballrooms, gaining intellectual recognition by sectors of the cultural elite, and establishing itself among Puerto Ricans in New York. In this period the onset of recording and radio were of key importance, and involved the commercialization of the music with an attendant departure from *plena* roots. The third stage, spanning the 1950s and 1960s, constitutes a return to

First published in *Centro Boletín*, 2/2 (Spring, 1988): 16–25. It also appears in *Salsiology*, Vernon W. Boggs, Ed. (New York: Excelsior, 1992): 59–67.

those roots, both in the working-class point of reference and in the renewed moorings in *bomba* and Afro-Caribbean rhythms. Mon Rivera, Rafael Cortijo and Ismael Rivera, while making full use of recording technology and contributing ingenious innovations to the style, brought *plena* back to the streets and among the poor workers and unemployed masses from whom it had sprung. The social world of *plena*, and the monumental significance of Cortijo, has been captured memorably in the testimonial account of Cortijo's funeral by Edgardo Rodríguez Juliá.

Though the story of the *plena* since the days of Canario is familiar to many, very little is known of that first, prerecording stage, when *plena* was first emerging from its folk roots and establishing itself as the most popular and typical genre of Puerto Rican popular music. Here the towering practitioner was the semi-legendary Joselino "Bumbún" Oppenheimer (1884–1929), whose very name suggests his place in *plena* history: Oppenheimer, an unlikely surname for a black Puerto Rican worker, was adopted from that of German immigrant *hacendados* and attests to his direct slave ancestry, while the nickname "Bumbún" echoes the thudding beat of his *pandereta*, the tamborine-like hand drum which was idiosyncratic of the *plena*, especially in its beginnings. "Bumbún" Oppenheimer, a distant memory to the few remaining survivors of his times, was the pioneer of the whole tradition, the first "king" of *plena*, the forger of the style and creator of some of the all-time favorites of Puerto Rican song.

Bumbún was a plowman. For years in the early decades of the century he drove oxen and tilled the fields of the huge sugar plantations outside of his home city of Ponce. In the mornings he would leave La Joya del Castillo, the Ponce neighborhood where he lived, and be off along the paths and byways leading to Hacienda Estrella. He hitched up the plow and prepared the oxen for the day's work. Then he was joined by the *cuarteros*, the young laborers hired daily to help the plowmen by walking ahead to keep the oxen moving and by clearing the furrows of stones and cane stubble. Bumbún's *cuarteros* were always in earshot, though, for they also served as his chorus in the *coplas* (couplets) and *plenas* he sang to the beat of ox and mule hooves and the rhythmic thrust of the plow:

> No canto porque me oigan
> Ni porque mi dicha es buena.
> Yo canto por divertirme
> y darle alivio a mis penas.

Bumbún composed many *plenas* while tilling the fields of Hacienda Estrella. Patiently he would teach the song choruses to his plowboys, who would repeat them in energetic response to the "musician-plowman" as he went on to sing the solo verses of his new song. After work, Bumbún would make his way back to La Joya del Castillo where, at night, he would introduce his latest compositions to the many *pleneros* and fans who gathered in the homes and storefronts of his neighborhood in those years. Thus the *plenas* of Bumbún Oppenheimer, rather than falling into quick oblivion, have endured as treasures of the *plena* repertoire.

The plowman Joselino Oppenheimer was king, "Rey de la Plena." In a history boasting such better-known royalty as Cortijo, Canario and César Concepción, Bumbún stands at the threshold. In addition to his countless original compositions and performances of *plena* standards like "Cuando las mujeres quieren a los hombres," "Tanta vanidad" and "Los muchachos de Cataño," Bumbún led the first *plena* band and became the first professional *plenero* when he decided to set down his plow and dedicate full time and energy to music. He was also one of the earliest masters, some would say unsurpassed, of the *pandereta*. Though he could also play accordion or *güiro* as the occasion demanded, Bumbún was a virtuoso *panderetero*. In the midst of a vibrant improvisation he would rest it suddenly on his shoulder, bounce it off his head, or roll it along the floor, all the while twisting and jerking his body in a wild frenzy.

And La Joya del Castillo, Bumbún's neighborhood in Ponce, is the recognized birthplace of the Puerto Rican *plena*. There in the small wooden houses, bars and supply stores is where the *pleneros* would gather for their nightly *tertulias*, sharing their latest compositions and renditions to the pleasure of an appreciative, bustling public. In the first decades of the century, musicians and enthusiasts from the surrounding areas, and eventually from all parts of the Island, had to go to Ponce to find out about the *plena*, and La Joya del Castillo was the renowned hub of the action. The regal name, by the way, should fool no one; hardly a "jewel of the castle," La Joya del Castillo is actually a euphemism, in true *plena* spirit, for la "hoya" del Castillo: it was the "hole" occupying the ravine beneath the mansion fortress of the famous rum-baron Serrallés. Expectedly, La Joya del Castillo suffered the fate of so many working class barrios in twentieth-century Puerto Rico: it was eventually razed without a trace by the forces of progress and replaced by "modern" buildings and thoroughfares.

Most important to the birth of the *plena*, it was to that neighborhood, around the turn of the century, that families of former slaves from the British Caribbean islands of St. Kitts, Nevins, Barbados and Jamaica began to arrive and settle, bringing with them musical styles and practices which were different and exciting to the native Ponceños. Among these new arrivals was a couple named John Clark and Catherine George. Mr. Clark and Doña Catín sang and played music in the streets of La Joya del Castillo and came to be known as *los ingleses*, the English people. Their daughter Carolina Clark, usually called Carola, was a foremost *panderetera* in those dawning years, and she and her husband, the popular *plenero* Julio Mora ("La Perla"), helped to fuse the novel strains introduced by *los ingleses* with traditions and styles native to Puerto Rico. Though it is not known how or why, it is clear that the "English" sound caught on in Ponce and sparked the emergence of a new genre of Puerto Rican popular music. Some theories of *plena* origins even contend that the very word "plena" derives from the English exclamations "Play Ana" or "Play now" which accompanied those early street performances.

However that may be, the historical significance of this "English" influence is paramount. After abolition the former slaves were set adrift throughout the Caribbean. They moved toward coastal cities and plantations and, increasingly as the century neared its end, abroad to other islands or neighboring regions on the continent. Venezuela, Cuba and of course Panama were common destinations, but Puerto Rico also drew contingents of immigrants, especially from the English-speaking Caribbean islands whose economies had been languishing since British imperial interests turned emphatically to India and Africa. The southern coastal city of Ponce was the main port of entry for these "free" laborers, particularly as of 1898 when that whole part of the Island became blanketed by huge capitalist plantations in the hands of U.S. and creole-owned sugar corporations.

The Clarks and Georges and the other *ingleses* who settled in La Joya del Castillo were part of this migratory movement. The infusion of their musical expression into the popular music of Puerto Rico, though a mystery in its specifics, illustrates the multiple intersections and blending of cultures as working people scatter and relocate. New, "foreign" styles, instruments and practices arrive, attract attention for their newness and find imitations. The role of external sources in the beginnings of *plena* history, which has been ignored in most accounts of the tradition, deserves attention because it points up the regional, Caribbean context for the emergence of twentieth century song forms in all nations of the area: *son*, calypso, *merengue* and many other examples of the "national popular" music of their respective countries were all inspired by the presence of musical elements introduced from other islands.

As the case of the *plena* shows, the foreign influence served as catalyst. The real roots of *plena*, as is universally acknowledged, are in the *bomba*: all of the early *pleneros*, including Bumbún, were originally *bomberos*, and the most basic features of *plena* derive directly or indirectly from *bomba*. Moreover, the historical development of *plena* proceeded primarily in its interaction with other genres of the "national," Puerto Rican tradition, notably

the *seis* and the *danza*. The varied musical expression of the slave population, the peasantry from the mountainous inland and the national elite make
up the direct context for the birth and growth of *plena*, while the "imported"
elements brought by *los ingleses* constituted a spark igniting the appearance
of a new genre at a time when the regional, racial and class divisions underlying the relative separation of those traditions were in the throes of abrupt
change.

The emergence of the *plena* coincided with the consolidation of the
Puerto Rican working class; it accompanied and lent idiosyncratic musical
expression to that historical process. The first two decades of the century,
when *plena* was evolving from its earliest traces and disparate components
into a distinct, coherent form, saw the gravitation of all sectors of the Puerto
Rican working population—former slaves, peasants and artisans—toward
conditions of wage-labor, primarily in large-scale agricultural production
set up along capitalist lines. More and more workers, formerly inhabiting
worlds separated by place and occupation, came into direct association,
both at the workplace and in their neighborhoods; their life experience and
social interests were converging, and assumed organized articulation with
the founding of unions, labor federations and political parties.

Many of the best-known *plenas*, from the earliest times on, tell of strikes,
working conditions and events of working-class life; they give voice, usually
in sharp ironic tones and imagery, to the experience of working people in all
its aspects. Topical events, seized upon in all their specificity, take on general, emblematic meaning to Puerto Rican working people of varied stations,
places and times because of their shared social world and perspectives. Even
the musical features of the *plena*, with its boisterous syncopated rhythms,
improvised instrumentation and vigorous call-and-response vocal cadences,
testify to this working-class base, as becomes clear in the derogatory outrage
voiced so often by the cultured elites when reacting to the "primitive" and
"vulgar noise" of *plena*.

Integral to the qualitative change in employment conditions, of course,
was unemployment and the presence of a reserve of poor people without
work. Working-class neighborhoods like La Joya del Castillo housed not
only the regularly employed but also, perhaps in still greater numbers, those
living hand-to-mouth on earnings from a range of other sources—from odd
jobs, street vending and occasional or seasonal work to ragpicking, hustling
and prostitution. It was this sector, largely descendant from slave backgrounds, that figured preponderantly in defining the flavor and texture of
cultural life in the community. And it was among them, those most hard-
pressed and forced to the margins of the new socio-economic order, that
plena found its earliest and most characteristic social base. As one com-

mentator has it, writing in 1929 when the *plena* was taking all classes of Puerto Rican society by storm, "The *plena* arose in the brothels; it was born in the most pestilent centers of the underworld, where harlots hobnob with the playboys of the bureaucracy. But the *plena*, after all, stands for the conception of art held by the common people, by the illiterate masses. The *plena* reviews the public events of the day with irony, and interprets them according to the effect they have on the lower classes."

The same conditions that engendered this structural excess of unemployed workers also propelled the emigration of growing numbers of Puerto Ricans from the Island in search of work and opportunity. Migration, primarily to the United States, has been an inescapable fact of life for Puerto Rican workers since the first years of the century. It has also been a recurrent theme of *plenas* since early on. The notorious expedition of hundreds of workers to Arizona in 1926, arranged under contract and ending in dismal failure, occasioned several songs and versions, including one attributed to Bumbún: "Dime si tú no has pasado / por el Canal de la Mona / Ahora tú pasarás / cuando vayas pa' Arizona." And when he learned of the support shown the destitute survivors of that voyage as they returned to the Island, Bumbún composed "Los emigrantes": "Llegaron los emigrantes / pidiendo la caridad / Unos venían en el Cherokee / y otros en el Savannah." The well-known standard "La Metrópoli," also from those early years, is one of many *plenas* about the arrival in New York, treating the migration experience in more sanguine terms, though an undertone of irony is still present: "En esta metrópoli / se critica la vida / pero si nos vamos / volvemos en seguida."

Thus the *plena* tells of emigration, and it also emigrates, taking root in New York and enthusing audiences from all sectors of the Puerto Rican community by the late 1920s. The migration of some of the foremost *pleneros* and *plena* groups to New York, and the lure of recording possibilities, were decisive in this shift, as the metropolis itself became the center for the further popularization of the *plena* for the ensuing decades. The figure of Canario looms large in this new stage of the tradition, as recording and commercial incentives resulted in major changes in the sound and social function of the form. The hugely influential presence of Canario and his group in New York during the 1930s, and a decade or so later that of César Concepción, conditioned the development of the *plena* through mid-century. But already by 1929, when that early commentary appeared in the New York weekly *El Nuevo Mundo*, the *plena* had struck firm roots in the emigrant community: "accompanying the continual stream of Puerto Ricans to this city of the dollar," it says there, "like a ghost, or like some left-over that it's impossible to get rid of, there sound the chords of the *plena*. And at night in our Latin 'Barrio,' oozing out of the cracks in the windows and blasting from the music stores, there is the sound of the Puerto Rican *plena*, which has taken over everywhere, from the poorest and filthiest tenements of East Harlem to the most comfortable middle-class apartments on the West Side."

Despite the many changes marking the history of the *plena*—diffusion to all regions and social strata of Puerto Rican society, expanded and altered instrumentation and thematics, the influence of recording and commercialization, migration of its principal center of evolution to New York, continual intermingling with other musical styles—the humble beginnings of that story need to be called continually to mind. When Bumbún Oppenheimer composed his enduring songs while driving an ox-drawn plow across the canefields of Hacienda Estrella, rehearsing his newly-invented verses with his chorus of plowboys, he established the source of the *plena* in the process of human labor and interaction with nature. It was work and the life-experience of Puerto Rican working people that made for the substance and social context of the *plena* in the streets and bars of La Joya del Castillo where it was born, and it is that same reality which has remained the most basic reference-point for *plena* music down to the present.

Cortijo's Revenge: New Mappings of Puerto Rican Culture

It was the best joke of the week. Imagine, naming the Centro de Bellas Artes after Rafael Cortijo. *El Centro Rafael Cortijo para las Bellas Artes*, the Cortijo Center for Fine Arts! The very idea of it, our country's cultural palace, its halls bearing the venerable names of Antonio Paolí, Rene Marqués, Carlos Marichal and Sylvia Rexach, baptized in honor of the street musician par excellence, the unlettered, untutored promulgator of *bomba y plena*! And yet, far-fetched as it might seem, people began treating as fact what was only a proposal by an aspiring political candidate, or actually not even a proposal but the threat of a proposal. "Vote for me and I'll propose it" was the message. And though within a few days the whole issue passed into hasty oblivion, for that week in mid-August 1988 el Centro Rafael Cortijo was the talk of Puerto Rico, filling the newspapers with rumors and recriminations in all directions and generating a debate which would have made not only Cortijo but Antonio S. Pedreira turn over in his grave.

And many, indeed, were the echoes of Pedreira's lofty concerns. As one commentator wrote in *El Mundo*, "This event makes us ask ourselves, once again, who we are—that philosophical exercise which has so long been a constant in our daily lives. If we can clear away all the triviality, opportunism and back-biting it has generated, this move to honor Rafael Cortijo serves to transform the Palace of Fine Arts from a majestic architectural structure into an ongoing metaphor and reminder of the path to take when it is clear exactly where we stand."[1] Here we are, back again to that historic questionnaire initiated by the journal *Índice* in 1929, the provocative "who are we and how

This essay was originally presented in Spanish on April 26, 1990, at the "Fiesta de la Lengua: Dedicada a Antonio S. Pedreira," sponsored by the Departamento de Estudios Hispánicos, University of Puerto Rico. It was published in *Centro Boletín* 3/2 (Spring, 1991): 8–21 and in *On Edge: The Crisis of Latin American Culture*, George Yúdice, Jean Franco and Juan Flores, Eds. (Minneapolis: University of Minnesota Press, 1992) are we?" (*¿qué somos y cómo somos?*) that led, after a flurry of responses from some of the Island's leading intellectuals and some years of gestation, to that most extended and influential of all reflections, Pedreira's *Insularismo* (1934). Not that we are just returning to that existential preoccupation some sixty years later, with the comfortable advantage of hindsight. For as dated and derivative as Pedreira's thinking may strike us today, the groping search which he undertook has never really abated and has remained with us, in modified versions and with changing emphasis, through the decades. Whether it was Vicente Géigel Polanco, Tomás Blanco, René Marqués, José Luis González, Luis Rafael Sánchez or Rosario Ferré, writers of each subsequent generation have addressed the same issues as inhabited the pages of *Insularismo*, and have ultimately met with similar frustrations.

But the hubbub over the appropriate legacy of Rafael Cortijo signals the continuing relevance of *Insularismo* in especially sharp relief, and at a time when the very interrogation of culture and identity, the "master narrative" of any collective cultural history, has come under grave suspicion. It took the towering presence and symbolic passing of a black popular musician of the uncontested stature of Cortijo to force the questions of African and working-class culture onto the agenda of every-day Puerto Rican life. It may have occasioned laughs and irony at the time, and exemplified partisan opportunism at its most cynical, but the threat to sanctify the name of Cortijo and the ensuing reactions from all quarters of the cultural establishment bring into rare focus the still unfinished business involved in exposing the theoretical confines of *Insularismo*.

And the rejoinders in the Cortijo crossfire were as telling as the seemingly outlandish suggestion itself. What about the other stellar figures in the history of Puerto Rican music, the first line of argument went, as the names of Juan Morel Campos and Rafael Hernández were quick to surface; isn't it after all, as Pedreira had claimed, the *danza* and the international standard *boleros* and *canciones* that represent the backbone of the national music? And if it's about memorializing illustrious black Puerto Rican artists, what about the great eighteenth-century *mulato* painter José Campeche, or what about the renowned black singer Ruth Fernández, who has the added asset, in "affirmative action" terms, of being a woman, and is even alive to perform at the inaugural? And then, if the occasion is one of acknowledging the *plena* as the authentically national popular music, what about Manuel Jiménez ("Canario"), the first to extend the *plena*'s popularity through recording, or what about John Clark and Catherine George, those children of immigrants from the English-speaking islands who were the first known practitioners of *plena*? Or, we might add, since his name went unmentioned, what about Joselino "Bumbún" Oppenheimer, who was instrumental in establishing the *plena* as a musical form and practice?

But the cries of "why Cortijo" went further than the unveiling of other names, which extended from Manuel Alonso to Enrique Laguerre, and included Luis Palés Matos, Julia de Burgos, Juan Tizol, Felipe Rosario Goyco ("Don Felo"), Rafael Ithier, Juano Hernández, Carmelo Díaz Soler and Francisco Arriví. Beyond the catalogue of just-as-deserving, and of greater theoretical interest, objections were raised as to the anomaly of naming a center of "fine arts" after an exponent of the "popular arts," no matter how unequalled a master. The "Centro de Bellas Artes," the thinking goes, "was built because of the need for theaters in which to hold concerts, drama, ballet, opera and *zarzuela*."[2] Of course there may also be a need for a center for popular art, especially since "we now have to hold salsa and rock concerts in coliseums and stadiums with poor acoustics, unbearable heat, foul smells and a host of other inconveniences." But to appropriate the space intended for the fine arts is not the answer. After all, and here the reasoning gets interesting, presentations of the fine arts tend to be very expensive, and because they are absolutely needed "for the greatest cultural good of the people," they require subsidy from the government and the public sector, "so as to keep prices reasonable for the audience." Sites catering to the popular arts, on the other hand, are generally "private businesses that can only cover their expenses by enjoying the affluence of the public." The commentator ends by acknowledging that "it's often not possible to draw a clear line between popular and fine arts," but his final thought, following from this rather convoluted account, is that "there's a right place for everything." The bottom line, it seems, and ultimate justification for assigning the popular arts to the business sector, is "quality"; as the then director of the Instituto de Cultura Puertorriqueña, Elías López Sobá, reminded us, "this is a place of the fine arts. It is for those who have a contribution to make in the field of dance, theater, music, plastic arts, mime and pantomime."[3]

Behind the aesthetic and fiscal objections, of course, lurk the moral ones. It is interesting that on these grounds the strongest position was voiced not so much by the upholders of the "high arts," but by the prominent folklorist Marcelino Canino. In Prof. Canino's view, "though musicians of the stature of Mozart found inspiration in the dances and tunes of the common folk," Cortijo's music can only be described as "vulgar" and "lumpen."[4] Rather than exalt the black race, he said, Cortijo's songs only denigrated it further. "It was music for the masses which never became folkloric because it has not lived on in the memory of the people." Such language has a sadly familiar ring to it, being typical of the early reaction to most forms of twentieth-century popular music, from jazz and the blues to samba, *son* and calypso. The epithets "vulgar" and "lumpen" accompanied the *plena* for the first three decades of its existence, and here they are once again, in 1988, in the assessment of Cortijo. Not only is he excluded from the ranks of the country's fine arts, and even of the national folklore, but he is also rejected ad hominem: the noted constitutional lawyer Federico A. Cordero, who spoke out immediately and vehemently against the renaming of the Centro, argued that Cortijo set a bad example for the country. "Puerto Rican society is today deeply concerned over the problem of drugs, so that to speak under these conditions of Cortijo, who was part of the drug subculture, is not a good example to follow."[5]

The objections to the idea of a "Centro Rafael Cortijo para las Bellas Artes" thus amounted to a broadside, coming from many political and social quarters and especially from among the prevailing voices of the cultural elite. Which is indeed why they won out, squelching the threat long before it could become a proposal on the floor. When the dust settled, a position prevailed which, despite all the disclaimers and quite beyond the issue of renaming the Centro de Bellas Artes, continues to deny the constitutive role of African and popular expression in the national culture. In other words, it was a victory for racism, as members of the Cortijo family and countless other Puerto Ricans, including many intellectuals and musicians, were quick to point out. Not only did they clear the record of personal defamations, but they directly identified the racist motives behind the political opportunism of the Popular Democratic Party (PPD). It seems that the Populares were trying to save face in the wake of an infamous remark made a few months earlier by Rafael Hernández Colón on a visit to Spain. There in the Hispanic "madre patria" the PPD governor took the occasion to refer to the African contribution to Puerto Rican culture as a "mere rhetorical adscription" ("una mera adscripción retórica"). Floating the idle threat of honoring Cortijo was thus a defensive maneuver which, ironically, could only result in still another mandate for that familiar Eurocentric mentality. Just how Eurocentric is clear even from Hernández Colón's effort to answer the resounding criticism of his comments. By considering Puerto Rican culture "essentially Spanish," he only meant to refer to "the racial integration of our people around its common Hispanic roots."[6]

It was against this still dominant mentality—the mentality, we might add, of Pedreira in his time—that the most vocal proponents of Cortijo spoke out. While not necessarily bemoaning the defeat of the effort to rename the Centro, Cortijo's long-time friend and fellow musician Tite Curet Alonso argued strongly for the immense stature of Cortijo in Puerto Rican music. In direct response to the charges of Marcelino Canino, Curet Alonso states the key point: "Rafael Cortijo made our most vernacular rhythms, the *bomba* and *plena*, known throughout the world ... And if nobody remembers Rafael

Cortijo, why such concern over him and why the idea of lending his name to the Center for Fine Arts according to law? No, my dear professor, no sir! Cortijo was great and continues to be great, as you well know beyond the shadow of a doubt."[7] Curet Alonso ends by calling attention to the seamy aftermath of the whole Cortijo affair: they actually went so far as to dig up his body, six years in the grave, for an autopsy. "Our poor friend! And after so many of our civic and political leaders come to mourn for you, with tears in their eyes, at the Cemetery of Villas Palmeras!"

In true *plena* tradition, it was Rafael Cortijo's funeral on October 6, 1982 as much as his musical breakthroughs in the mid-fifties which marked a turning-point in Puerto Rican culture and its theoretical reflection. Thanks, in large measure, to Edgardo Rodríguez Juliá, whose brilliant chronicle, *El entierro de Cortijo*, 1983 (Cortijo's Funeral), anticipated in almost uncanny ways the whole uproar over Cortijo in 1988. At one point his narrator even fantasizes whimsically about the eventual admission of Cortijo into the hallowed halls of the country's high culture: "Maybe some Leticia del Rosario will come along one day, in twenty years or so, and establish a Rafael Cortijo Theater, under the administration of González Oliver's son, and thereby enact a grotesque kind of poetic class justice."[8] "La venganza de Cangrejos" ("the revenge of Cangrejos") is what this same inversion of the class hierarchy was called in 1988. (Santurce, where the Bellas Artes is located, was called Cangrejos in Cortijo's time, and the deepest irony of the whole case is that Cortijo was born and raised in a house at the very address where the Centro de Bellas Artes now stands.) On the occasion of his funeral, Rodríguez Juliá built a real memorial to Cortijo while his narrator reflected on the meaning of immortality in the age of mediated popular culture: "But you will live on, Cortijo," he wrote, "even if nobody listens to you anymore; there will stand your monumental work, silent but patient, and always ready to spring back to life. To be immortal is not so much to go on living as to be sure of resurrection. Cortijo is for the 'cocolos' and the salsa lovers what Canario is for me: a daring leap over two decades. But don't worry, my dear little Cortijo, you'll see that we won't forsake you, even though this damned historical memory of ours only extends back as far as what we have forgotten" (37).

Generation after generation, stage after stage in the history of the country, the concept of the national culture penetrates progressively deeper to its black, working-class roots. "This idea of class revenge," one commentator noted in 1988, "evokes a sense of pride in Puerto Rico. Here every one of us has a secret ancestor in the closet."[9] The very idea of a "Centro Rafael Cortijo para las Bellas Artes" is part of "a long voyage toward the integration of our Puerto Rican identity in view of that key link which is our African heritage," another step in the unveiling of that ancestral secret.

* * *

The path out of and beyond "insularismo" has been first of all this extended journey inward, and deeper than Pedreira could have imagined in 1934. It began back in the nineteenth century, in the writings of Salvador Brau, Alejandro Tapia y Rivera and others, and gained further impetus from the lesser-known working-class writer Ramón Romero Rosa in his 1903 article "A los negros puertorriqueños."[10]

In Pedreira's times it proceeded forward in the essays of Tomás Blanco, especially his *Elogio de La Plena*, 1935 (In Praise of the Plena) and in the poetry and poetics of Luis Palés Matos. A new juncture was marked off in 1954 with the release of Cortijo's "El Bombón de Elena" and the publication of José Luis González's story "En el fondo del caño hay un negrito" ("At the Bottom of the Ditch There's a Little Black Boy"). The mid-seventies saw the publication of Isabelo Zenón's two-volume *Narciso descubre su tracero* (Narciso Discovers His Behind), the first extended exposé of racism in Puerto Rican culture and politics. But it was in the 1980s, most prominently in *El entierro de Cortijo* and in José Luis González's controversial essay "El país de cuatro pisos" ("The Four-Storey Country," 1984, originally 1979), that the balance finally tipped, and the new, Afro-Caribbean horizon has come into full view.

For the long quest inward leads not so much to some hidden "essence" of our identity, some primordial "¿qué somos?", but to a sharper understanding of the dynamic within Puerto Rican culture and its place among the cultures with which it most directly interacts. If it is to be more than a "mere rhetorical adscription," the recognition of blackness necessarily points beyond the shores of the Island to the rest of the Caribbean and Latin America and to the cultural dynamic in the United States. In this respect, the Eurocentric, elitist view in the manner of Pedreira constituted the very intellectual insularity which his book called upon his compatriots to overcome. Discovering and valorizing African "roots" has comprised a second stage, after the first one marked off by *Insularismo*, in the theoretical definition of Puerto Rican culture, and that stage has only come to full articulation over the past decade. Yes, there is a national culture, as Pedreira did after all affirm with all his gloomy reluctance, but it is grounded on the popular, African-based traditions of that culture.

The eighties, though, has also been the decade of wariness, in much contemporary cultural theory, over the dangers of essentialism in defining "identities" of any kind, be they class, national, racial-ethnic or sexual.

And here, I think, we might see a stretch of the voyage ahead. On this count the writings of Rodríguez Juliá, and of other contemporaries like Ana Lydia Vega, Rosario Ferré and Luis Rafael Sánchez, seem more helpful than José Luis González's architectural construct in "El país de cuatro pisos," though that essay would certainly best qualify as the most direct sequel to *Insularismo* in recent years. For despite its often welcome strokes of historical revisionism, González ultimately has recourse to an essentialist stance, most evident in his explosive claim that the "first Puerto Ricans were black Puerto Ricans." Rather than originary, authentic "roots" of a cultural tree, or the ground floor of a cultural building, our African background needs to be assessed as a guide to the culture's dynamically changing placement in the surrounding cultural geography. Maybe Pedreira's navegational image of the "brújula del tema" (thematic compass) is useful after all in countering the still prestigious metaphors of organic growth and the contructivist blueprints designed to replace them.

The most characteristic contemporary response both to Eurocentric, elitist privileging and to the relativism of the syncretist model seems to be what we might call a relational one, which would aim to identify not some originary identity but the contacts and crossings experienced by the culture as social practice. It is not the popular, African component in itself that goes to define the "real" Puerto Rican culture, but its interplay with the non-African, elite and folkloric components. Similarly, with respect to the national culture, it is not the shores of the Island that demarcate the "¿qué somos y cómo somos?", but the expanses of sea, land and air which conjoin our cultural territory with the other(s). Even the history of *bomba* and *plena*, which especially after Tomás Blanco's landmark essay has gained wide recognition as the most distinctively Puerto Rican musical tradition, attests to the need for such a situational approach: at key stages in that history the influence of Haitian, Anglophone Caribbean and Cuban and Dominican styles and practices have been of signal importance. A promising recent example of this method as applied to the interaction of European elite and black artisan cultures within the Puerto Rican tradition is Angel Quintero Rivera's work on the *danza*.[11]

But I find that Rodríguez Juliá's writing goes especially far in the direction of a relational, non-essentialist presentation of Puerto Rican culture in its contemporary dynamic. *El entierro de Cortijo*, far from merely paying celebratory homage to the great *plenero* and to African roots, chronicles the multiple intersections which actually characterize the culture at any given point in time and place. The evocation of the fallen cultural hero gains its particular poignancy from the account given to the simultaneously interacting presence at his funeral of sharply contrasting cultural worlds. The most obvious of these interplays is the running contrast between Cortijo and the early-century *criollo* poet Luis Lloréns Torres, and between that poet himself and the "Caserío Lloréns Torres," the working-class projects where the funeral procession begins. Here is how the mischievous chronicler captures that irreverent collision between signifier and signified: "The name of the poet (who is actually second-rate, though an ingenious versifier) has undergone an ironic transposition: the projects, that anti-utopia created by the welfare state of Muñoz Marín, shares with the myth the virtue of a meaning which is both blurred and perfectly clear . . . Fuck, as they say in the Motherland, and to think that all this is a whole lot more than the name of a poet. If we leave behind the courses in Puerto Rican literature and the standard manual of Manuel Manrique Cabrera, Lloréns Torres signifies smack, set-ups, salsa beats à la Marvin Santiago, drug busts, joints, blow and needle tracks. My God, this place sure has a bad rep, as my mother would say" (13). Class and racial differences are thus analyzed by their concrete enactment in the participatory observations of the chronicler, who is himself of course very much implicated in the cultural drama: "a white boy with chubby cheeks, a handle-bar mustache and eyeglasses is a disturbing presence in Lloréns" (13).

The narrative form appropriate to this relational method of cultural analysis is the chronicle, while the texture of the story is a kind of stylistic pastiche. The diverse, interacting cultural voices and idioms are not defined, but are contextualized and given utterance. This pastiche effect is evident not only in the language but also in the historical perspectivism, where the narrative present is set into striking proportional relation with earlier cultural stages. (It is interesting that the chronicler here points to the year 1934 as a benchmark of a preceding cultural stage, the 1934 not of Pedreira's *Insularismo* but of the hey-day of Canario.) That acute retrospective sense only heightens our awareness that we were in the mid-1980s when the story happens and is told. "1954 . . . Cortijo is not only the last of the great *pleneros*; Cortijo is the very flavor of the *plena* of those years, the 1950s, that seem so long ago to us living today, closer in fact to the 1930s of Canario than to these apocalyptic 1980s. But let's figure it out . . . In 1954 you were twenty years from 1934; in 1984 you'll be thirty fatal years from those shows when Cortijo's group performed at the Taberna India, featuring Reguerete and Floripondia. I was born in 1946, just ten years after the beginning of the Spanish Civil War . . . On October 9, I'll be 36, and I'll have to explain to my son, who's a rock fan, that Cortijo's very first group still wore ruffle-sleeve shirts" (30). With that patchwork of chronological measurements as a starting-point, the chronicler goes on to set forth, in what must be the most sparkling five pages on the topic, the revolutionary importance of Cortijo in the history of Puerto Rican popular music.

Rodríguez Juliá does not ignore the question "¿qué somos y cómo somos?", the agonizing problem of cultural "definition." True to his relational, non-essentialist approach, though, he insists the real challenge is not definition but description, not a claim to the idiosyncratic and originary but an account of diversity and complexity. Making no presumption of "objectivity," he relies time and again on the subjective reference so as to bring the historical and cultural Other closer, not only to the narrator himself but to all who co-habit the same or adjacent cultural chronicles. "How to define our people?" he ponders, just at the moment when he catches a glimpse of "the matriarchal presence of Ruth Fernandez" among the throngs of mourners. "To define is easy, but how difficult it is to describe! They're down-home people people (pueblo pueblo), my Puerto Rican people, with all their contradictory diversity, like that sickly-looking lady with her hair in a bun and wearing sneakers because of her bunions, you know, like the bunions in the *plena* 'Los juanetes de Juana'; the little beads of greasy sweat remind me of those self-sacrificing ironing-women and cooks who used to pass by every Saturday on the streets of my childhood and head off to their working-class places of evangelical worship" (18).

The chronicler defines by way of describing, and describes his "pueblo pueblo" by invoking, through association and memory, an emblem of Puerto Rican nationality. And just at this point, when the narrator directly poses the issue of identity, it is women who inspire and embody the cultural collectivity, black working-class women. Here the dimension of gender supplements and perhaps even underlies the more commonly emphasized factors of class and race. We need only call to mind a few of Pedreira's unflattering words about women to appreciate how far we have come on this issue as well as that of class and race. Women are characterized in *Insularismo* as weak and frivolous, and it is clearly the men who are suited to take firm command of the educational and cultural tasks of the country and lead the way out of collective insularity.[12]

As Rodríguez Juliá's emblem of identity indicates, it is women who are seen to comprise the most representative and potentially most emancipatory force in the whole cultural pastiche. At the present stage of thinking about Puerto Rican culture, women's perspectives and experience are coming to be recognized as still another path beyond the elitist, ethnocentric and patriarchal confines of *Insularismo*. The feminist standpoint in Puerto Rican cultural theory and practice is most clearly and forcefully set forth, of course, by women writers and artists themselves, though it also appears in works by male authors, such as Juan Antonio Ramos and Manuel Ramos Otero. Rather than replacing or superceding the dimensions of Africanism and popular culture, women's perspectives typically complement them and foster a critical awareness of their basic importance in the culture.

This interplay of gender, class and racial-ethnic awakenings is perhaps most evident in the writings of Rosario Ferré. Her *Papeles de Pandora* (Pandora's Papers), *Maldito amor* (Cursed Love), *Sitio a Eros* (The Seige of Eros) and other fiction, poetry and essays constitute an extended evocation of black, popular Puerto Rican culture from the experiential vantage-point of a woman, and a woman from the white elite at that. She brings the world of *plena* culture to life in her own lyrical voice, summoning its energy in the very cadence of her prose.

* * *

Toward the end of *Insularismo*, in a rare personal aside, Pedreira remarks that he first really became aware of being Puerto Rican, and of a distinctively Puerto Rican way of acting and speaking, when he was a student at Columbia University in the early 1920s. In New York, he recalls, "I met many Latin Americans who would easily notice in me traits that are typical of us as a people."[13] It was abroad, away from the Island, and in the perception of others, that the particular features and contours of the native culture came into view. This experiential paradox, the sense of moving closer because of physical and cultural distance, has recurred among so many Puerto Ricans before and since Pedreira's student days in New York that it is almost archetypal of the emigrant consciousness. For its sheer scale and duration, and because of the obvious psychic impact of this inside-outside paradox, the migration and resettlement process has assumed definitive importance in Puerto Rican culture and its theorization. I once commented that what is most conspicuously missing in José Luis González's rather shaky "four-story country" are the cellar (*el sótano*) and the roof (*el rufo*).[14] What is the Puerto Rican cultural edifice without its Taíno foundation? And, as González himself dramatized so well in his story "La noche que volvimos a ser gente" (The Night We Became Human Again), what is a tenement ("un buildin") without a "rufo," what is Puerto Rico in our times without the Nuyorican community?

"En el fondo del nuyorican hay un puertorriqueño" ("At the bottom of every Nuyorican there is a Puerto Rican") the young New York poet Tato Laviera recently proclaimed, thus paraphrasing González's best known story. And in another poem, entitled "Nuyorican," Laviera openly berates his beloved island homeland for being less Puerto Rican than El Barrio:

> yo soy tu hijo,
> de una migración,
> pecado forzado,

> me mandaste a nacer nativo en otras tierras,
> por qué, porque éramos pobres, ¿verdad?
> porque tú querías vaciarte de tu gente pobre,
> ahora regreso, con un corazón boricua, y tú,
> me desprecias, me miras mal, me atacas mi hablar,
> mientras comes mcdonalds en discotecas americanas,
> y no pude bailar la salsa en san juan, la que yo
> bailo en mis barrios llenos de todas tus costumbres,
> así que, si tú no me quieres, pues yo tengo
> un puerto rico sabrosísimo en que buscar refugio
> en nueva york, y en muchos otros callejones
> que honran tu presencia, preservando todos
> tus valores, así que, por favor, no me
> hagas sufrir, ¿sabes?[15]

With this playfully earnest inversion of perspectives, the assessment of Puerto Rican "insularism" has come full circle. For the Nuyorican Puerto Rico is not "insular" enough, having been overrun by continental values and flavors even more than has been permitted by the Puerto Rican "enclave" on the continent.

The dynamic relation between the Island and the "enclave," the title of another book by the same poet, has held an intense fascination among Puerto Ricans, including its writers and artists, since the 1950s, when the New York community began to assume its immense proportions and when the Island's major writers took it up as a central theme in their work. Of equal intensity have been the discussions, and the distortions, of the emigration experience, reflective of the various angles from which it has been viewed. Beyond dispute, though, is that the migration and emigrant community have been the main historical disclaimer of the notion of Puerto Rican culture "insulated" within its territorial confines. The relation of Puerto Ricans to places removed from the Island has had a very different effect than was envisioned by Pedreira in *Insularismo*. Responding to a comment, which he cites in English, from a 1930 issue of a U.S. monthly to the effect that Puerto Rican schoolchildren "have an unusual interest in far away places and like to go to the map," Pedreira only sensed "a melancholy process of perpetual isolation." "The map which we study with such care and affection," he concluded, "is but an escape-valve which unconsciously helps to ease some of the pressure to emigrate."[16]

Of course, that process was still only a trickle in those years, and its mushrooming in the ensuing decades has fortunately engendered more creditable analyses of the relation of Puerto Ricans to geography lessons. What has been emerging in recent years is the understanding that it is not a question of division or unity, but of circulation and reciprocity. This new, relational concept, articulated most memorably by Luis Rafael Sánchez in his story "La guagua aérea" ("The Air Bus"), derives in part from the increasingly circulatory nature of the migration process itself, and the simultaneous physical and spiritual access of so many Puerto Ricans to both cultural worlds. Under the present conditions of transportation and communication, Puerto Rico is part of New York, and like it or not, New York is present in Puerto Rico.

But another source of this advance beyond earlier dilemmas and distortions is the new direction of thinking about cultural change and contact developed in recent years. Contemporary, "post-modern" cultural theory, with its guiding concepts of decentering, deterritorialization and the crisis of representation, has been busy refiguring the whole problematic of "borders" and "bridges" which so preoccupied Pedreira and later thinkers. Even the models of "mainstream" and tributary cultures, of cores and peripheries, primary and subcultures—yes, even dominant and subordinate—which have been so influential since the sixties, have begun to recede in favor of more interactional and more carefully delineated paradigms. And Puerto Rican culture, which had long been such an exemplary case in point for those earlier dualities, is today once again a particularly rich field for remapping cultural theory and testing its new vocabulary.

"Somos una generación fronteriza" ("We are a border generation"), Pedreira moaned, regarding as he did Puerto Rico's situation at the crossroads of two discordant cultures as the origin of its collective disorientation and isolation. The overbearing presence of both has made for a condition of pertaining to neither, a state of cultural "anomie" as that term is deployed by later diagnosticians like René Marqués and Eduardo Seda Bonilla. The "frontier" is an outpost, far removed from the hub of any identifiable and rooted cultural expression.

Recent cultural theory among Chicano writers, whose history revolves around the existence of "la frontera," allows us to think in a new way about cultural collisions, interfaces and navegable crossings. The border, that site of mutually intruding differences, may be perceived not as a kind of no-man's-land, but as a well-spring of cultural innovation and identification. For the Chicano writer and performance artist Guillermo Gómez-Peña, "la cultura fronteriza" (border culture) signifies not exclusion and denial, but inclusion and discovery. "I opt for 'borderness,'" he says, "and assume my role: My generation, the *chilangos*, who came to 'el norte' fleeing the imminent ecological and social catastrophe of Mexico City, gradually integrated itself into otherness ... And one day, the border became our house, laboratory, and ministry of culture."[17]   The same positive account of the border situation is voiced by the Chicana poet Gloria Anzaldúa in her book *Borderlands/La Frontera*; from a strong feminist perspective she speaks of a "new mestiza consciousness," a migratory spiritual homeland in which "continual creative motion keeps breaking down the unitary aspect of each new paradigm."[18]

Aboard our "air bus," Puerto Ricans have come to inhabit the same fertile borderlands. In his entertaining little tale of the late-night flight from San Juan to New York, Luis Rafael Sánchez notes that the very historical ambivalence of his fellow passengers opens up a new space of creativity and cultural referentiality. "Puerto Ricans," he comments, "who want to be there but must remain here; Puerto Ricans who want to be there but cannot remain there; Puerto Ricans who live hanging from the hooks of the question marks *¿allá? ¿acá?*, Hamletian disjunctives that ooze their lifeblood through both adverbs. Puerto Ricans installed in permanent errancy between 'being there' and 'being here' and who, because of it, deflate all the adventurous formality of the voyage until it becomes a 'mere ride on a bus' ... however aerial, so it may lift them filled with assurances over the blue pond ... the blue pond, the Puerto Rican metaphor for the Atlantic Ocean."[19] Puerto Rican culture today is a culture of commuting, of a constant back-and-forth transfer between two intertwining zones. "I cannot live in Puerto Rico because there's no life for me there," one passenger remarks, "so I'll bring it with me bit by bit; on this trip, four crabs from Vacía Talega, on the trip before, two fighting cocks, on my next, all of Cortijo's records." As the story ends, "It is the imposing flow of reality with its hallucinating proposal of newer, furiously conquered spaces. It is the relentless flow of a people who float between two ports, licensed for the smuggling of human hopes."

The Nuyorican experience is showing how it is possible to struggle through the quandary of biculturalism and affirm the straddling position. Not with the claim to be both, but as the title of a poem by Sandra María Esteves words it, with a pride in being "not neither." In "Not Neither," the Nuyorican woman poet enacts this drama of confusion and self-discovery: "Being Puertorriqueña Americana Born in the Bronx, not really jíbara Not really hablando bien But yet, not gringa either, Pero ni portorra, pero sí portorra too Pero ni que what am I? ... Yet not being, pero soy, and not really Y somos, y como somos Bueno, eso si es algo lindo Algo lindo."[20] In a beautiful little poem Tato Laviera also gives voice to this new sense of beauty and freedom as it erupts from the interstices and neglected enclave of Nuyorican life. Here, in "tight touch," the cultural rhythms engender a self-confidence and dignity which dispel all lingering traces of the proverbial Puerto Rican "insularism" and "docility":

inside the crevice
deeply hidden in a basement land
inside an abandoned building
the scratching rhythm of dice
percussion like two little bongos
in a fast mambo
quivering inside this tiny ray
of sun struggling to sneak in
the echo of the scent attracted
a new freedom which said, "we are
beautiful anywhere, you dig?"[21]

* * *

Pedreira's closing thoughts in *Insularismo* are about music; the last of the many deficiencies in Puerto Rican culture which he chooses to mention is "an acute shortage of composers" and a general lack of musical creativity. "We must help in this effort with a sense of generosity and patriotism," he announces, "and with the sincere hope of filling, in our own times, this gap we may notice today in one area of our nation's culture."[22] This alarm was sounded in the early 1930s, when Canario's and Rafael Hernández's songs were playing everywhere, and but a few years before Tomás Blanco's "Elogio de la Plena."

But Pedreira's views on Puerto Rican music are well-known. The *plena* was for him another form of our folkloric music, along with the *seis*, which in its instrumentation and style incorporates "elements from the three main roots forming our cultural trunk." But despite its deep cultural origins, this kind of music was for Pedreira "nuestra nerviosa música brava" ("our nervous savage music"), which he considered to be basically out of tune with our cultural "climate." In pronouncing the *danza* the national music of Puerto Rico, Pedreira fused Hispanophilia with that geographical and atmospheric determinism that lies at the heart of his guiding metaphor. The line of thinking here illustrates, perhaps more clearly than anywhere else in *Insularismo*, the openly repressive strategy of cultural elitism. The *danza* arose, he claims, because "our climate could not bear such constant agitation" as that of the "música brava," and we had to find "more intimate and relaxed forms of expression." "The *danza* is for us what the fox-trot is for the North Americans, that sporting, active and strong people who needed a choreographic exercise consonant with their athletic constitution, gymnastic prowess and hygienic, Alpine character. Puerto Rico, by contrast, being a tropical, anemic country, needed a dance rhythm which was slow and reserved ... Our *danza*, unlike the fox, lends itself to light amusement and conversation. Its calm movements, with extended intervals which have a relaxing effect, respond appropriately to the demands of the climate. The *danza* serves as a respite from our wild music."[23] Thus, in this view, the *danza* arose, and must persist, in order to counteract and hold down the intense cultural energy of "la música brava."

Pedreira of course did not live to witness how "wild" our music could get by the time Rafael Cortijo got hold of it. What he referred to repeatedly as a period of "transition" and "intermezzo" in the country's cultural history turns out to have been the threshold of a new economic and political order. Industrialization, a refurbished colonial status and mass emigration have transformed the geography of Puerto Rican culture and ushered what had been the "repressed," silenced and discarded cultural actors and voices to the foreground of the entire cultural field. As in North America, where the fox-trot has been eclipsed many times by even "wilder" steps and rhythms, in Puerto Rico the national culture has been impelled to let down its elitist defenses and make way for the explosive ascendancy of our "nervous," overly agitated forms of popular expression. While the leisurely grace of the *danza* has itself come to assume an antiquarian, folkloric stature, the tradition of *bomba* and *plena*, in league with its cousins *la rumba, el son, la guaracha, el mambo* and *el merengue*, and with North American jazz and rhythm and blues, has become an integral strain of the popular Latin American music of our times, *la salsa.*

Rafael Cortijo, along with Ismael Rivera and Mon Rivera, were catalytic in this protracted subversion of the cultural hierarchy, a process that took hold a generation ago, in the 1950s, and which by our times has assumed definitive importance in all thinking about Puerto Rican culture and identity. It may be some time yet before we have a *Centro Rafael Cortijo para las Bellas Artes*, and perhaps even longer before this new popular, Afro-Caribbean and feminist cultural subject can emerge as a revolutionary agent in the face of our ongoing colonial condition. But what was the joke of the week in August 1988 was also a landmark, of sorts, in the rewriting of our national history, another advance in our collective defiance of *insularismo*. It is in this spirit that the Nuyorican poet Tato Laviera, at the request of Cortijo himself, wrote his poem "rafa"; the closing stanzas give eloquent voice to the momentous energy of Cortijo's revenge:

> as he finally exploded 1960
> ismael rivera sounds puerto
> rican charts creating music
> the world over;

as we search through plena history
there's a godfather-padrino-figure
humble but stubborn to his traditions;

as we detail contributions
so we must all stand
gracious ovation
rafael cortijo
general consensus
Puerto Rican people.[24]

III

Members of the National Committee of Lodge No. 4792 (Mutualista Obrera Puertorriqueña) of the International Workers Order, ca. 1940. Jesús Colón is seated, third from the left, directly beneath banner. The Jesús Colón Papers, Centro de Estudios Puertorriqueños, Hunter College, CUNY; Benigno Giboyeaux, for the Estate of Jesús Colón and the Communist Party of the United States of America.

National Culture and Migration: Perspectives from the Puerto Rican Working Class

Going on 500 years now, the history of Puerto Rico has been the history of colonial oppression. Ever since the landing of Christopher Columbus and the heralded exploits of Ponce de León, the Caribbean island has been in the direct political grip of foreign empires—for four centuries that of Spain, and since 1898, with the sunset of European colonialism, that of the United States. This background of uninterrupted colonial bondage serves to crystallize the search for Puerto Rican national identity. Whatever stands to defy or deny the norms imposed by the reigning colonial power, or acts to transform them beyond obvious recognition, emerges as a definitive and distinctive feature of the national culture. Such, in a broad stroke, is the assumption underlying the many bold and pronounced efforts to differentiate an essentially Puerto Rican experience in the face of prolonged foreign domination.

Such a monolithic view of the opposition between colonizers and colonized, however, has also helped to obscure the subtle shadings of this political and cultural process, since it divorces the struggle for national self-definition from the dynamic at work within the colonial society itself. At every point in Puerto Rican history, the details of real life point out a cleavage in interests and motivation between the anti-colonial aspirations of the owning classes and those of the producing majority. Even the late-nineteenth century calls for national unity against Spain issued by the progressive *criollo* elite rested on a pretense of social cohesion which their artisan and freedmen compatriots were less and less ready to accept. By the first years of the twentieth century,

Co-authored with Ricardo Campos. First presented on April 10, 1978, as a paper at the Colloquium on "Caribbean Identity: Puerto Rico and Haiti," sponsored by the Department of Romance Languages and the Latin American Studies Program, Princeton University. Published in English, Centro Working Paper, 1979, and in Spanish in *Puerto Rico: Identidad nacional y clases sociales* (Río Piedras: Ediciones Huracán, 1979): 81–146.

this class division of the national culture became articulate and dramatic in proportion. What is more, because philosophical differences have reference to physical survival and well-being, the antagonism appeared irreconcilable.

The following pages are intended as an introductory discussion of some of the most prominent aspects of this rapidly altered cultural context. The point of departure is the sharply diverging conception of patriotism, national liberation and human freedom which were being voiced by leaders of the national elite and of the Puerto Rican working class, an ideological discordance bearing directly on central themes in the tradition of the national culture. In the second part, attention is turned to the related opposition in these two classes' understanding of migration and its impact on national cohesion and identity. The third part is an interpretation of the cultural expression of Puerto Ricans in the United States as it contrasts with official policies and institutions developed under the Commonwealth to explain and orient this growing emigrant community.

I

In 1905, there occurred the largest and most militant agricultural strike in Puerto Rican history until that time. In the same year, delegates representing the newly-formed workers' organizations—the *Federación Libre de Trabajadores* and the *Partido Obrero Socialista*—presented a set of one hundred seventy reform proposals and resolutions, aimed at improving the conditions of the Puerto Rican working class, to the session of the Legislative Chamber. One of these demands, known as House Bill 14, called for a limit to the load a worker should be expected to carry on his shoulders. At that time, dock-workers and *braceros* in all fields of production were being forced to carry three-hundred-pound cargo, or twice their own bodily weight, as this was the standard packaging volume for export produce.

The legislature, of course, was controlled by the incumbent Unionista Party, which represented the interests of the Puerto Rican landowners and the budding bourgeoisie. These interests were threatened not only by the organized workers, whose demands had to be continually tabled or watered down, but by the United States Congress, which maintained ultimate veto power over any and all local legislation. Because of the tenuous position of the class they represented, the *Unionistas* were typically obliged to sacrifice the life-blood of the Puerto Rican workers in their desperate scramble for a niche in the mammoth imperialist market.

House Bill 14, hardly an unreasonable request to save the straining backs of the Puerto Rican *bracero*, met just such a fate. Its most vocal opponent in the Legislature was the majority speaker, none other than the famed orator and poet, José de Diego. It is of some interest to recount the impassioned argument of José de Diego, who is still revered in recent, progressive histories of Puerto Rico as the spiritual father of the *independentista* movement against United States imperialism. Dismissing the proposal as more appropriate to labor organizations than to national legislation, De Diego went on to reflect on the philosophical nature of human labor: "I believe that a man's work ought not be regulated, as this is contingent to the freedom of contract. A man can work and bear on his shoulders the weight that he can sustain according to his physical constitution and energy." Besides, he continued, betraying his most heart-felt class concern, "to institute a law of this kind would be tantamount to forcing our commercial enterprises and factories to pack their goods according to a specified amount of weight, which would of course be unrealizable."[1] His consoling advice to the working man, in promising to help him attain a "brilliant future," is that he "should not expect everything from the State. He can and ought manage to raise himself up by his own force and, if need be, make the climb with one-, two- or three-hundred weights until, like Sisyphus, he reaches the heights of the rock. In Germany, in England and in the United States workers have labored for their own dignity, and have created respectable organizations with the aid of nothing but their own initiative and their own honest efforts."

The response of the working class to the illustrious poet-patriot José de Diego was presented by their elected spokesman, Ramón Romero Rosa. Denouncing the "horrible crime" at which House Bill 14 was directed, Romero Rosa reminded the delegates of the miserable, anemic physical condition of the Puerto Rican peasantry, and of the widespread illiteracy which prevents the majority of the population from participating in political life, including the workers' organizations themselves. "As they are denied all the benefits of education, deprived of bread for their stomach and of bread for their minds, I understood that we, as representatives of the Puerto Rican people, should come to their rescue by seeing to their assistance." Romero Rosa agreed that "misery has always existed. But the misery of ancient times was attributable to the natural order, while that of today is artificial, and fostered by overproduction of a mechanized economy." As political representatives of the society, "we who never stop talking of our Puerto Rican homeland are obliged to take action in favor of the deprived class."[2]

In mentioning the word *patria*, Romero Rosa was striking at the heart of José de Diego's most sacred historical mission. "If we want to build a *patria*," Romero Rosa concluded, "let us apply all our intelligence and our utmost powers to elevate the hard-working peasant class so that the Puerto Rican *patria* begins to have meaning for them. Let us see to the benefit of the peasant class so that tomorrow we may say that we have built a worthy, honest, intelligent and industrious *patria*."

José de Diego belongs to the pantheon of Puerto Rican intellectual heroes. The esteem in which he was held by the national and international elite was boundless, as is reflected in the many important official positions he held: for years he was president of the Chamber of Delegates, the *Ateneo Puertorriqueño*, the Association of Writers and Artists, the *Unión Antillana* and the Latin American Association of Puerto Rico; he held the chair of the University Institute for Roman Law founded in his name; he was associated with the Antillean Academy of Language, the Institute for Social Reforms of Puerto Rico, the Royal Hispano-American Academy of Science and the Arts of Cádiz; and was Member of Honor of the Universal Cervantes League, the Ibero-American Union, the Center for Hispano-American Culture, the International Academy of History, and the Latin American Association of Paris. Sporting his authorized pseudonyms, "Caballero de la Raza" ("Knight of the Race") and "León Americano" ("American Lion"), he won general acclaim as the national poet of Puerto Rico. Many of his poems, which uphold the classical nineteenth-century heritage while drawing cautiously on the linguistic and rhythmic innovations of Latin American *modernista* poetry, entered smoothly into the treasury of Puerto Rican verse. Since his death in 1918, he has enjoyed sustained appreciation from the spectrum of cultural and political opinion on the Island.

None of the many homages to his impressive spiritual achievements, however, such as Concha Meléndez's *José de Diego en mi memoria*, account for his long-standing career as principal attorney for the infamous *Guánica Central*, the largest sugar refinery in Puerto Rico and the cardinal exploiter of the Puerto Rican working class.[3] In such a capacity, and because of the stances he assumed in the government, he was singled out as the butt of attack by the workers and their spokesmen. Despite his lengthy apologetic discourse to parliament on "Cuestiones obreras" (1913),[4] his blocking of House Bill 14 and countless other such demands proves that he carried the obligations of his legal profession directly into political chambers. For the workers, his poetic and philosophical eloquence was but a thin veil camouflaging his very interested defense of the *hacendado* class.

De Diego's ardent patriotism and clamor for national sovereignty relegated the democratic aspirations of the working majority, and were often pronounced at their expense. His ideal of political liberty, centered as it was on a defense of Hispanic cultural integrity and of the Castilian language, was hopelessly spiritualized and detached from the most pressing social realities of his time. What is more, it was equivocal and opportunist at key moments, as in his call for postponing discussion of the proposed national plebiscite on political status in deference to the United States cause in World War I. It is worth reconsidering the anti-imperialist renown of a figure like De Diego, who could speak in these terms before a jubilant Puerto Rican legislature in 1917:

> We are citizens of the United States, we live and twenty thousand of our soldiers will fight and die under its glorious flag . . . We should wait until Puerto Rican blood brightens the splendor of the flag of the Unites States, so that our spilled blood enriches our rights and speaks for us to the American people in those jubilant and triumphant days of world peace.[5]

Even his renowned Hispanophile disdain for United States cultural aggression was tempered by what seemed an intrinsic awe before the prowess of North American expansion; the same timely speech began with a torrent of praise for the superiority of the Anglo-Saxon race.

De Diego was not without adversaries among the contemporary political elite. Rosendo Matienzo Cintrón, for example, gave him a quite different nickname—the Latin-babbling "Tijelino"—in his satirical dialogues on events in parliament.[6] Matienzo Cintrón's break with the Unión and founding of the Independencia Party in 1912, along with the forthright socialist lawyer for the Federación Libre, Rafael López Landrón, represented a rejection of the colonial politics styled by both De Diego and Muñoz Rivera.[7] López Landrón's lengthy treatise of 1907, *Los ideales socialistas* (Socialist Ideals), still buried in the archives of working-class publications, constitutes one of the most important statements on social theory in Puerto Rican political writing of the time.[8] On every count, it stands in sharp contrast to the outlook of José de Diego.

But the most thorough, antagonistic opposition to De Diego were the working-class leaders themselves. Ramón Romero Rosa was a typesetter by trade; under the pseudonym R. de Romeral, he was a prolific writer and outspoken organizer of the workers for the ten years until his death in 1907. As early as 1899 he authored a powerful manifesto entitled *Socialismo y política* (Socialism and Politics) which circulated widely in the working-class movement. There he proclaimed himself a "revolutionary socialist," and stated, "I shall forever uphold with utmost zeal the sacred axiom of the immortal Karl Marx: 'The emancipation of the workers must be the task of the workers themselves.'" Among his many journalistic articles and dramatic pamphlets of the following years, he also contributed his significant essay, "La cuestión social y Puerto Rico" (The Social Question and Puerto Rico), in which he applied the major currents of socialist thought to the immediate and long-term problems facing the colonial society.[9]

For the working-class intellectual like Romero Rosa, love of one's home country and the fight for its freedom from the colonial yoke take on practical meaning only when viewed as part of the worldwide struggle for the liberation of human labor from capitalist exploitation. In eloquent tones worthy of De Diego's finest oratory, Romero Rosa proclaimed in 1899:

> I shall never be a regionalist in the sense of believing that this beautiful piece of earth is my unique and exclusive center of life, even though I bear within my soul profound feelings of love and endearment for Puerto Rico, and a world of poetry which could resound like a holocaust for all its natural splendors. With fullest conviction I say that wherever man moves his arms in fruitful productive labor, and enjoys the rewards and pride of consuming his flesh in carrying out his daily chores—there, I say, is his homeland, his honor and his life ... [10]

Romero Rosa's iconoclastic patriotism did have its forebears in Puerto Rican culture, most notably in the figure of another revolutionary typographer, "Pachín" Marín. The memorable poems of "Pachín" Marín were a biting, ironic retraction of the mystical patriotic visions of nineteenth-century romantic poets like José Gautier Benítez, whom De Diego repeatedly acknowledged as his esteemed spiritual predecessor. In fact, "Pachín" Marín's famous sonnet "El Trapo" (The Rag)[11] —in which the very rhythmic structure of the poem goes to show how any scrap of old rag can serve as a national flag as long as it is used in the fight for freedom—seems to anticipate, critically, the stanza of De Diego's catechismic "Bandera antillana" (Antillean Flag):

> La santa bandera de Borinquen tiene el ojo de Dios,
> en el triángulo eterno, que mira
> y enciende y azula el espacio de una creación ...
> y sus listas rojas son caminos de ardientes anhelos
> y las blancas, caminos de llanto y dolor ...
>
> (The holy flag of Borinquen has an eye of God,
> within an eternal triangle, which watches
> and inflames and gives blue tones to the space of a creation ...
> and its red stripes are paths of ardent yearning
> and its white stripes paths of weaping and pain ...)[12]

The very life-struggle of "Pachín" Marín, who was present among the Puerto Rican and Cuban revolutionaries in authorizing the Puerto Rican flag and who died in the midst of military battle in Cuba in 1895, is a standing refutation of De Diego's ethereal concept of Antillean unity as expressed in the same poem:

> De un daltonismo el misterio simbólico subvierte el color
> y la lejanía; Cuba y Puerto Rico
> tienen una sola bandera en las dos ...
> ¡La unidad perpetua del Dios de la vida!
> ¡La unidad fecunda del Dios del amor!
>
> (As though by daltonism the symbolic mystery subverts the color
> and the distance; Cuba and Puerto Rico
> have a single flag made into two ...
> Perpetual unity of the God of life!
> Fertile unity of the God of love!)

Within a few years of "Pachín" Marín's death, the organized working-class movement provided the social foundation for his scathing political critique. Romero Rosa and his fellow socialists recognized that religious, symbolical patriotism in the manner of Gautier Benítez and José de Diego constitutes an ideological pillar to maintain the economic and political servitude of the workers. Romero Rosa warned explicitly that "the worker should not be a patriot in the mystical sense of the word nor allow himself to be swayed by the fanaticism involved in all religion."[13] Religions, he went on, are invented by the ruling classes "to fill the minds of the unhappy producers with fantasies and dreams of artificial paradises, and to prepare them for submission, docility and blind obedience so that they will not rebel against the injustices of the owners and their governments." Likewise, the complementary ideology of narrow patriotism, "from the moment that it is introduced to the worker, begins to engender in him hatred for other races and nations in order to blunt his longing for universal brotherhood and world peace."

The early socialist leaders of the Puerto Rican working class were alarmed neither at the religious nationalism of a figure like De Diego nor at its practical manifestation in the polemic over House Bill 14. Nor, in fact, were they particularly hopeful or intent to persuade the political elite otherwise.

Their main objective was to expose the propagandistic interests behind official politics and culture, and to win the working-class majority of Puerto Rico away from the ideological influence of their overlords. The authority of this influence was seductive and pervasive, voiced as it was in commanding rhetoric and resting on age-old customs of dominance and acceptance. The most challenging task of the class-conscious workers was to subvert the sanctified cultural symbols of national cohesion, many of which the popular masses have come to perceive and cherish as their own.

One of Ramón Romero Rosa's staunchest comrades, another prolific Puerto Rican intellectual condemned to historical oblivion, was a worker named Eduardo Conde. Also involved in labor organizing efforts since the late 1890s, Conde was a merchant marine, a house painter, a favorite "reader" in the cigar factories, and a long-time correspondent for the main working-class newspaper, *Unión Obrera*. He outlived Romero Rosa, took part in the founding of the Partido Socialista in 1915 and published his forceful polemical essay, *Acusación y Protesta*, in 1919. On January 8, 1905, two days after the Epiphany (Día de Reyes), Conde printed a short discourse in *Unión Obrera* entitled "Los Reyes Magos."

There is, it may be assumed, no need to emphasize the importance of *Día de Reyes* as an annual holiday observed for centuries by all Puerto Ricans, and by all countries in the domain of Spanish Catholicism. As is known, an entire cultural repertory surrounds the beneficent yearly visit of the three Wise Men and, especially in colonial countries like Puerto Rico, the feast day came to represent the holy conjunction of clerical and secular royalty and magnanimous authority. January 6, like December 25 in Protestant societies, is the time to unveil all the binding myths of expectation and reward, to rekindle the songs and rituals of generalized sacrifice and gratitude.

It is interesting to evoke what was to become of this sanctified custom in the hands of a revolutionary Puerto Rican worker like Eduardo Conde writing in 1905. What hypocrisy, what a vicious delusion, his message reads, to perpetuate this fantasy that all children are rewarded according to the hospitality they show the weary sacred travelers!

> All the children of rich parents have to do is put a tiny little box (or none at all) with a few blades of grass on their balcony or under their beds and the next day they find the floor covered with toys and goodies. But, poor children, really poor children, who walk around without any clothes or without shoes on their feet, who have nothing to eat and who sleep on the hard ground in hallways or on park benches, children who are abandoned by their parents because they can't afford to feed them—oh yes, children can leave all the boxes of hay they want, but they won't find a dammed thing because the Three Kings don't pass through hallways or alleys, they wander *On High*, they pass along the rooftops and leave gifts for the sons of the wealthy, to children who in two minutes destroy a toy that cost ten dollars, ten dollars that could buy food and clothing for ten children

who need it because they don't have any.[14]

Eduardo Conde goes on to explain why this is so, why this festival of happiness and generosity brings so much sadness to poor mothers, fathers and children—and he warns:

> Because the miserable worker is exploited by the boss in an abusive and cruel way; because what is wasted on luxuries today will make it impossible to attend to the just needs of the poor children; because those who have their cupboards full of food need it in order to extract 500 percent according to their calculations . . .

Charity and philantrophy in this kind of society, Conde remarks in the same biting tones, does not extend to the hallways and the streets, because there the children are filthy and sickly and might contaminate any benevolent sharer from among the more fortunate and blessed. And, of course, it is all the poor peoples' fault, since everyone knows they throw away their money on useless work and at all the parties they have all year long. "Mankind," he concludes, "is made that way" ("porque . . . la humanidad está así constituida").

The most interesting device used by Conde in this sardonic outburst of working-class logic is his framing of the exposure with references to a popular song dedicated to the visit of the Three Kings. He begins by quoting, in the form of a motto, the opening lines of the well-known ditty: "Now the kings are leaving, / Blessed be to God . . . " ("Ya se van los reyes / Bendito sea Dios . . . "). At the end of his bitter tirade, he repeats the same folkloric motto, providing this time the third verse—which contains the promise of the Kings' return year after year—and subjecting it to the rigor of his social diagnosis:

The rich children, they may well sing:

> "Now the Kings are leaving,
> Blessed be to God,
> They're gone and they'll be back" . . .

> Yes, they'll be back, because they love you so much,
> they'll be back to bring you more and more whistles,
> drums and little cars to play with.[15]

Poor children, too, will sing:

"Now, the Kings are leaving ... "
They're gone, yes, and here's hoping they'll never be
back again!

In this way, Eduardo Conde has managed to carry his demystification
of religious traditions to the level of their familiar expression in the hearts
of the popular classes. He confronts the workers and peasants with their
own spontaneous and internalized complicity in the very mythology which
serves to perpetuate their social oppression.

Ramón Romero Rosa's political confrontation with the outlook of José
de Diego and Eduardo Conde's sarcastic subversion of popular customs
represent parallel events in the same historical process. The emergence of
proletarian consciousness introduces a qualitatively new content to what
seemed a harmoniously cohesive national culture; it brings into play a new
world-view which stands in radical antagonism to both the treasured ideals
of the educated elite and the fatalistic folklore of the servile masses. This
momentous event constitutes a key juncture in Puerto Rican cultural history.

II

On March 21, 1915, in the town of Cayey, hundreds of Puerto Rican
workers came together to found the Puerto Rican Socialist Party. The
keynote message of that historic convention was delivered by the newly
elected Secretary General and long-time leader of the Federación Libre
de Trabajadores, Manuel F. Rojas. "Economic independence," Rojas said,
"cannot be won through the economic struggle alone. As long as the capitalist can secure power which derives from the people, and can convert it into
an adulterated, concocted law of which capitalism is the only beneficiary, it
will not be possible, comrades, to think of economic independence without
laws to guarantee its implementation ... Here, at this first convention of the
party we represent, we must resolve to unite all the forces of the people to
struggle for the social, economic *and political* emancipation of the people
themselves."[16] Within two years, in the elections of 1917, the young party
gained control in seven municipalities, had two representatives elected to
the legislature, and won 14 percent of the popular vote. To accompany
these local successes, Puerto Rican workers from all over the Island were
composing hymns of praise to the triumph of the Bolshevik Revolution.

One of the delegates to the founding convention in 1915 was a young
tabaquero who was born and grew up right there in Cayey: Bernardo Vega.
Bernardo was filled with enthusiasm at the birth of the new party, and influenced deeply by the many inspired working-class leaders who gathered

in his home town. But he was not to continue his organizing activities in Cayey, nor to enjoy directly the first fruits of the party's political campaigns. In August, 1916, Bernardo Vega left Cayey and Puerto Rico behind him, taking the course of migration to New York City in which he would be followed by so many of his countrymen in the fifty years that ensued.

Bernardo recounts his departure and voyage to the United States in the opening chapter of his memoirs—*Memorias de Bernardo Vega*—which were edited and published by César Andreu Iglesias in 1975.[17] This book, written during the late 1940s but not to see the light of day until ten years after the author's death, stimulates a radical rethinking of modern Puerto Rican history, and particularly the momentous migratory experience of the Puerto Rican working class. For behind Bernardo's seemingly voluntary decision to leave his beloved home town and homeland were the pressures of economic necessity and the dictates of imperialist planning policies that propelled entire contingents of his compatriots into waves of migratory motion. In the course of his narrative, he clearly identifies his emigration and decades of tribulation in New York as illustrative of a collective national and class reality. The opening pages of his memoirs, entitled "De su pueblito de Cayey a San Juan y de como Bernardo llegó a Nueva York sin reloj" ("From his little town of Cayey to San Juan and how Bernardo arrived in New York without a watch"), provide a personal account of the migration which has brought nearly half the Puerto Rican working class to the United States in the twentieth century.

To appreciate the special quality of this first chapter, and the historical value of the entire book, it is important to bear in mind the ambiguities of a ruling-class and colonialist understanding of the same emigration process. In 1914, the Governor of Puerto Rico, Arthur F. Yager, submitted to the President and War Department of the United States a proposal advocating the planned emigration of Puerto Ricans as a solution to the pressing social problems on the Island, problems which stemmed—in the Governor's view—from rampant unemployment and acute "overpopulation." This proposal, eventually accepted and implemented many times in the following decades, inspired a clamorous and conflicting response among the Puerto Rican elite. The owning class itself was sharply divided on the issue basically between those who threw their lot directly with the interests of the imperialists, and the "national" *hacendados*, who sensed a need on their own part to retain a ready labor reserve. It was the latter sector which took the most vocal stand, and the argument behind their opposition, with all its equivocation, provides the dominant perspective for years to come. Their most articulate spokesman was, once again, José de Diego.

De Diego expressed his indignant reaction to Governor Yager's proposal in an eloquent, short essay, "El desplazamiento" ("Displacement," 1914).[18] The patriotic poet is outraged at the very idea, which he considers beneath the dignity of any "civilized government," of "impelling emigration, of *negotiating* the emigration of Puerto Ricans" like any other business deal. To legislate such a process by treaty, contract or policy is for him unheard of "in the history of international law and in the history of colonization, even under the cruel system of the ancient Asiatic conquerors!" For an educated intellectual and renowned political lawyer, De Diego gives evidence of a short historical memory even here. But to come to his main argument: he is worried about the miserable condition of the Puerto Rican workers and intransigent over the cruel inhumanity of the prospect of transporting people like cargo or cattle. He places the blame for the existence of an unsupportable population excess and an abysmal standard of living squarely on the imperialists; he implies, at least, that independence is the only long-term solution.

Such is the surface level of De Diego's anti-imperialist fury. The undercurrent of his rationale runs much deeper. The most disastrous consequence of "negotiated" emigration, for him, is that it would "destroy the density of our population, the wall which resists the destruction of our personality and our race." "Displacement," he exclaims, "displacement in all forms, up to and including that brand-new version of diplomatic arrangement with foreign countries: displacement of Puerto Rican citizens by North Americans, of the Castillian language by English, of *jíbaros* by Yankees."[19] At such a thought, De Diego is swept into the realm of sheer fantasy: "Couldn't they just as well displace our geographical latitude, our entire Island, with its mountains, plains, rivers and trees, carry us with the wind to another location less persecuted by cyclones and colonial governments?"

De Diego found the scheme put forth by Governor Yager so scandalous that he did not seriously believe it could be put into effect, or so he says. But if it should, he warns his countrymen, "no Puerto Rican should leave Puerto Rico, no patriot should abandon his *Patria*, so that his place be taken by an invader. Everyone should stay here, right here ("aquí dentro"), firm, locked in by hunger and protest but not denying our motherland our resistance in life and our bones in death!"

Now, as mentioned, José de Diego acted on many fronts as a legal representative of the "national" *criollo* bourgeoisie, that sector which opposed large-scale emigration because it threatened to drain the country of the labor reserve they needed to maintain their largely seasonal, servile relations of production. Be it recalled that in Parliament De Diego took a stand not only against House Bill 14, but against the eight-hour working day, a minimum wage law and wage payment in hard currency as well. As Eduardo Conde repeatedly reminded his fellow workers, it was De Diego who said, "The worker should earn what is needed for his subsistence, and nothing more."[20] In his rhetorical essay "El Desplazamiento," De Diego is providing the imaginative, philosophical expression of this economic stance. His fears for the unity of the nation and the purity of the race and culture, as humanitarian and anti-colonial as they may sound, stem from definite class motivation. His call for patriotic resistance to cultural aggression and planned emigration amounts to sheer rhetoric and is blatantly disdainful of the real needs of the Puerto Rican masses.

Nor was De Diego consistent in his repugnance for the North Americans and glorification of the Puerto Rican or, rather, "Hispanic" race. By 1917, all sectors of the colonial bourgeoisie coalesced in support of the United States war effort, and the *independentista* elite postponed their calls for a plebiscite on the issue of national status. On November 6 of that year, to the thunderous applause of his fellow politicians, President of the House De Diego spoke of the North American "race" in very different terms. Based on his readings of Italian anthropological literature, and especially Cesare Lombroso's book *L'Uomo Delinquente*, the national poet discovered "in the North American type the superman of the modern age, with his extended neck, long legs, broad chest, physiologically provided with the strongest arms for facing up to the struggle for survival, and psychologically gifted with an aggressive, tenacious will to undertake the struggle for progress."[21] He spoke out in praise of the lofty moral values of people of the United States, "descendant as they are from one of the superior races of Europe, and fortified by cross-breeding with other races of analogous origin, situated in a colossal portion of the World, and reaping the prolific gifts of the soil, subsoil and skies." With this new, "scientific" understanding, his admiration and sympathy could only grow, as did his faith in the eminent justice which was awaiting the Puerto Rican people, "and in the efficacy of our insistent demand for the welfare and freedom of our people."

On his way from Cayey to New York, Bernardo Vega made a stop-over in San Juan. There he had occasion to take leave of his comrades from the *Partido*: Manuel F. Rojas, Santiago Iglesias, Prudencio Rivera Martínez and Rafael Alonso Torres. "All of them," he recalls, "regretted my decision to leave because of the loss they said it would mean for our nascent workers' movement. But they did not try hard to dissuade me. As socialists, we dig our trenches everywhere in the world."[22] Bernardo, of course, was no typical emigrant: his departure was in large measure voluntary, and, what is more, his perspective derived from an uncommonly high level of class consciousness. Bernardo and his comrades recognized that a person's "identity" is distinguished not so much by his particular ethnic makeup, but by his historical role in the social struggle, and by the culture of his people in its struggle for equality and independence.

Not that Bernardo Vega ignores his own distinctive physiological traits; on the contrary:

> In those days I was a man of larger stature than was common among Puerto Ricans. I was white, a *jíbaro* from the mountains, and there was that waxen hue to my face so characteristic of men from the heart of our country. I had a round face with high cheekbones, a wide flat nose, and small blue eyes. As for my lips, well I'd say they were rather sensual, and I had a good set of strong, straight teeth. I had a full head of clear chestnut hair, and in contrast to the roundness of my face I seem to have had square jaws. All in all I felt pretty ugly, though there was never a lack of women that took me for the contrary.[23]

Immediately following this graphic description, which would seem to lend Bernardo an almost typological *jíbaro* significance, he goes on to place himself and his physical appearance into the social context where it belongs. This delightful passage is of utmost interest to anyone studying the experience of Puerto Rican "identity" in the United States setting:

> I did not inspire much sympathy at first sight, I'm sure of that. I have never been a man of easy friendship. No doubt my physical appearance had a lot to do with it. I hadn't been living in New York for long before I realized how hard it was for people to tell where I came from. Time and again I was taken for a Polish Jew, or a Tartar, or even a Japanese ... God forgive my dear parents for this humanity, which was after all the only thing they handed down to me."[24]

Bernardo's message is clear: the only "race" that really counts is the human race, which is composed of many different nationalities and ethnic groups. The "humanity" inherited by Bernardo from his parents is not merely his relatively indistinguishable human countenance, but his ingrained instinct for human fraternity and equality. It is important to add that Bernardo Vega did not accept his light-skinned *jíbaro* features as in any way typical or distinctly representative of the Puerto Rican people. He recognized the multi-ethnic composition of the nation from which he had departed, as his powerful political homage to Arturo Alfonso Schomburgh, a black Puerto Rican, illustrates unequivocally; in his memoirs, he spoke of Schomburgh's accomplishments in the following terms: "He arrived here as an emigrant

and has left a rich legacy to our countrymen and to North American Black
people: magnificent example of the identity of oppressed peoples!"[25]

The emotional and psychological aspects of the emigration experience
also find masterful treatment in these opening pages of his semi-fictional
autobiography. Bernardo gets no sleep the night before his departure, his
mind swarming with nostalgic fantasies of his beloved Cayey, his friends
and family, and of the beautiful hills and rivers of his homeland. As the boat
is about to sail, he finds himself up on deck with all the other passengers
who are, like himself, soaking in their last glimpse of San Juan. "I did not
want to lose a single breath of those final minutes in my country, final for
me anyway."[26]

But even in this shared and innocent sentimentality, Bernardo finds himself at odds with many of his fellow passengers, and again the distinction
refers to a difference in class perspective. For as soon as the boat hit the
high seas and began to pitch, most of the passengers headed for their cab-
ins, where some of them stayed cooped up for the entire four-day voyage.
"Not I," says Bernardo, "I stayed up on deck until the island was lost from
sight in the first shades of nightfall."[27] Upon arriving in New York, two
classes of Puerto Ricans disembark: first those traveling first-class, "businessmen, well-to-do families and students. In second-class, which is where
I was, there were the emigrants, most of us *tabaqueros.*" Metaphorically,
the seasickness which forces the "first-class" passengers to flee to their cabin
bunks stands for their insulation from the world outside, their confinement
within the narrow comforts of their familiar provincial domain. The Puerto
Rican worker, it is suggested, does not necessarily share this *insularismo,*
an infamous attribute stamped by Antonio Pedreira on the entire national
psyche. Rather, his horizons are open to the world; he is anxious and willing
to experience other lives, other places.

Much of this revolutionary vision, of course, is imputed to his original
experience by a Bernardo Vega looking back from a point much later in life,
and after many intervening experiences. But this narrative retrospection
detracts nothing from the validity of his observations. During the voyage,
for example, Bernardo admits that he shared in the common wish-dreams of
his fellow passengers as to their plans and hopes for life in New York. "First
savings could go to sending for close family. Later, after a few years, time
would come to return home with good means. Whoever it was, sight was
set on the farm to be purchased or the little store to be set up in town ... All
of us built our own little castle in the sky." The tone of these sentences is
ironic; Bernardo knows, in hindsight, that a very different fate awaited those
Puerto Rican workers in East Harlem, the South Bronx and Williamsburg.
As a class, and no matter how ardent their patriotic longing, they would not

be returning to Puerto Rico, nor would they be scraping together enough savings to do much but stay alive. Bernardo understands now, when writing his memoirs, if he did not realize them, that he and the other second-class emigrants imagined themselves to be first-class passengers in even dreaming such a future.

Perhaps the most intriguing aspect of these pages from Bernardo Vega is his treatment of the initial cultural shock of the arriving emigrants. He recalls that all of them seemed overdressed and curiously out of style.

> I mean, we had on our Sunday best. I myself was dressed in a navy blue cheviot sportjacket, or "flus," as they would say back home. I was wearing a borsalino hat made of Italian straw. I had on my black shoes with long, pointy toes. I was sporting a white vest and a red tie. I would have arrived with a dazzling wrist-watch, but a traveling companion warned me that it was considered effeminate to wear things like that in New York. So as soon as the city was in sight and the boat got into the harbor, I tossed my watch to the sea ... And just to think, it wasn't long before those wrist-watches came into style and ended up becoming all the rage. So, I arrived in New York without a watch.[28]

Despite the many variations created by changes in styles and times, this little scene rings with familiarity for the many larger and frequent waves of newly-arrived Puerto Rican immigrants to New York. Anxiety over feeling out-of-place in a foreign habitat, dictated by the ridiculous yet painfully real clash of contrasting norms; the arbitrary and bewildering interplay of transitory tastes and preferences; the affectation and display forced on a people coming onto a scene with unwarranted expectations—all of these personal and cultural traumas have continued to haunt the migrant Puerto Rican workers, and are evoked here in the very stylistic mannerisms of the text. Even the notorious "Latin" masculine instinct comes into play; but Bernardo places this trait in proper historical perspective by confronting it with the unacknowledged but equally insidious sexual prejudice of the modern, "liberal" metropolis.

The anecdote of the discarded wrist-watch carries a larger metaphorical connotation. For unlike the other cultural baggage, this object is not primarily aesthetic, but functional: it tells the time of day. While still in Puerto Rico, Bernardo was continually locating himself in time. The chapter begins on August 2, 1916 early in the morning; he arrives in San Juan at 10:00 A.M. He spends the next few hours visiting an old teacher, the afternoon with his socialist comrades, and the evening with the heirs of a prestigious Cayey family living in the capital. He spends his sleepless night walking the streets of San Juan and ends up at dawn in the Plaza de Armas, "seated on a bench, looking up now and then at the clock of the City Hall."[29] The tropical sun, the first trolley and the hustle of men and women leaving for work announce his last morning in Puerto Rico. At 2:00 that afternoon he boards the *Coamo*. From that moment on, aside from the passing of four days at sea, no further indication is given as to the time.

When Bernardo throws his wrist-watch to the sea, it is more than a submission to prevailing cultural prejudices. His arrival in New York "without a watch" represents a loss, or rejection, of temporal bonds, of familiarity, of personal and social bearings. As a loss, it is a disorientation and implies a sense of bewilderment and uprootedness which contrasts abruptly with the solace he had gained from the big clock on the San Juan City Hall and from the well-known streets and trails of his native Cayey. But as a rejection—and Bernardo does discard the watch of his own choosing—it means entering a new life with a new time-frame, taking up new habits and engaging in new struggles in a new and different context.

Again, the fictional and biographical Bernardo Vega was both typical and atypical of Puerto Rican working-class emigrants. Unlike the vast majority of them, he was a revolutionary socialist and went through the migration experience understanding the economic necessities and political supervision that set it in motion. To this extent, he appears to downplay much of the brutal hardship that emigration has meant for thousands of working-class families over the years. But he was, after all, a worker, and his book goes on to tell of the abuses and tribulations he shared with the masses of his exiled compatriots. It is his heightened social consciousness that makes it possible for him not only to document, but to analyze critically his life as a Puerto Rican worker in New York.

After he throws his watch to sea, Bernardo's life goes on to new chapters: "Trials and tribulations of an emigrant in the Iron Babel on the eve of World War I"; "Proletarians lend a hand, but hunger pinches and there is no remedy but to work in a munitions factory"; "Customs and traditions of the *tabaqueros* and how work got done in the cigar factories of New York"; and so forth. Chapters in Bernardo Vega's life, all of them are lessons for the people of Puerto Rico and the United States, and most of all for Puerto Rican people living in the United States.

III

Who says I must be sweet soft barefoot and helpless, when stepped upon I will scream be hard and
cold break bottles and windows Rage with revenge.

—Sandy Esteves, "Who says I can't"

In 1924 a leaflet was circulating in El Barrio. The Alianza Obrera Puertorriqueña, a newly-formed organization of Puerto Rican workers in New
York City, was calling upon its membership and all interested compatriots
to attend an important meeting that Sunday at the "Hall Socialista" on East
107th Street between Park and Madison. The occasion was a major address
on the latest developments in Puerto Rican politics; the speaker was Luis
Muñoz Marín. "Sensational political declarations," the leaflet read, "will be
made by this intelligent young man concerning the manifesto recently issued in Puerto Rico by Mr. Tous Soto and Mr. Antonio Barceló, in our effort
to keep the Puerto Rican colony residing in New York abreast of reliable,
up-to-date information."[30] The leaflet was signed by Jesús Colón, Secretary
of the Alianza, which included among its most active members Bernardo
Vega.

It is not certain what "sensational political declarations" the young Muñoz
Marín made to his audience of Puerto Rican emigrants about the imminent
"alliance" between Puerto Rico's two established parties—the "Unionist"
and the "Republicans"—to counteract the growing successes of the Socialist Party. But from earlier statements it can be assumed that he was warning
the workers of the treachery of bourgeois parties. At the Socialist Convention of October 6, 1920, Muñoz Marín had spoken out in firm opposition to
a proposed electoral pact with the Republicans. "In the name of our country,
of Puerto Rico, and of pure *criollismo*," he pronounced at that time, "I ask
that this convention vote unanimously against any unity with the Republicans, which is a bourgeois party, a party of infamy and shamelessness. Its
President, after all, is José Tous Soto, who is chief attorney for the Guánica
Central, the most powerful corporation in Puerto Rico and one of those that
brutally exploits the proletariat of our country."[31] Referring in such terms
to José de Diego's professional successor, Muñoz Marín emphasized that
it was a "decisive moment in the history of Puerto Rican socialism," and
that no one can uphold the principles of socialism and the working-class
movement and at the same time sanction a pact "with any bourgeois party
in the world." Following the convention, he reaffirmed his position in an
interview with *El Mundo*. He added that although such tactical alliances
may have been necessary in the past, and Karl Marx had spoken of them "in

his *Communist Manifesto*," these had only been entered into in "despotic, militarist countries, where the bourgeois party had as much revolutionary fervor as the proletarian party."[32] "I have said many times," he concluded, "that capitalism is like a huge raven, of which the right wing is the Union Party and the left wing the Republican Party. I see no use in uniting with one in order to sever the other."

Muñoz Marín had joined the socialist movement at the end of World War I, upon returning to Puerto Rico from Washington, D.C., where his father—Luis Muñoz Rivera—had been Resident Commissioner since 1904. After youthful years of prestige, educational privilege and budding literary recognition, he embraced the cause of freedom and justice for his suffering countrymen. He met Santiago Iglesias and other socialist leaders and promoted enthusiastically their impressive electoral campaigns. He even tried his poetic hand at proletarian literature: in 1918 he co-authored—with Evaristo Ribera Chevremont and Antonio Coll Vidal—a book of stories, *Madre haraposa* (Mother in Rags), which bore the subtitle *Páginas rojas* (Red Pages).[33] Throughout those early years, his vision was filled with the dream of social redemption and proletarian revolution, as in his agitational poem "The Pamphlet":[34]

> The dream that sleeps in breasts stifled by tuberculosis
> (A little air, a little sunshine!);
> the dream that dreams in stomachs strangled by hunger
> (A bit of bread, a bit of white bread!);
> the dream of bare feet
> (Fewer stones on the road, Lord, fewer broken bottles!);
> the dream of calloused hands
> (Moss ... clean cambric ... things smooth, soft, soothing!);
> (Love ... Life ... Life!)
> I am the pamphleteer of God,
> God's agitator,
> and I go with the mob of stars and hungry men
> toward the great dawn ...

What was to become of Muñoz Marín's staunch political principles and revolutionary dreams is too familiar to require retelling. His countless coalitions and compromises with bourgeois parties and "New Deal" imperialists came to define the course of Puerto Rican politics for decades and, in many ways, down to the present day. Yet the opportunist maneuvers cultivated in the Popular Democratic Party, Commonwealth Status and Operation Bootstrap were foreshadowed by the entry of Muñoz Marín into the Puerto Rican working-class movement around 1920. The slogan of the *Populares*—

"Bread, Land and Liberty," in that order—was but the continuation of a trend within Puerto Rican socialism from its inception—the trend of economism, of relegation of the issue of national independence to the short-term, bread-and-butter demands of the "popular masses." Among the workers, this position had been a characteristic, and understandable, response to the nationalism of the colonial *hacendado* capitalists and their spokesmen who did not provide any solutions to the economic problems of the workers. But when linked to the pro-Americanism of Santiago Iglesias, especially in his partnership with Samuel Gompers and the vigilant influence of the A.F. of L., this democratic appeal for economic justice fell easy prey to economism and reformism. The Socialist Party vote of 1919 with Santiago Iglesias, and against the resolution on national independence introduced by Manuel F. Rojas, signaled a major ideological setback for revolutionary socialism in Puerto Rico.[35]

Muñoz Marín could not have successfully engineered this conversion of independent, working-class politics and organization into populist coalitions and reformism without revamping the coordinates of Puerto Rican culture. To this end, he was forced to reinstate the hegemony of the patrimonial heritage. In his many pronouncements over the decades, Muñoz Marín continually emphasized the situation of Puerto Rico as a "member of the great Western civilization," and its distinctive "personality" and national characteristics as variants and contributions to this binding legacy. The perspectives of indigenous, African and of course working-class expression were treated, when at all, as folkloric remnants and subcultural appendages to this defining strain of Spanish, Occidental culture.

But the key to Muñoz Marín's successful cultural policy, was that he framed his Occidentalism in such a way as to incorporate the ultimate harmony of "Latin" and Anglo-American culture. Within this framework, and because of the particular political and geographical context of Puerto Rico, the culture of Puerto Rico became a "bridge," or "frontier," between two cultures. In a major address on "The Puerto Rican Personality in the Free Associated State" held in 1953, Muñoz Marín announced this convenient amalgam of cultural nationalism and colonial assimilation:

> We know that Puerto Rican culture, like that of the United States, is and has to be part of the great tradition of Western culture. But there is no such thing as a Western man who is not a man from some place in the Western world. If we are not Western with Puerto Rican roots, we will be Westerners without roots at all. And the vitality of a people has a great need for roots. We are a Western people in the manner of our own roots. We are

Americans of the United States and Americans of America and
Westerners of the West. And we are all this as Puerto Ricans
from Puerto Rico.[36]

This was an appealing message, to which Puerto Ricans of all classes could
rally. Behind its high-sounding internationalist claim, however, was a rationale for disclaiming any historical responsibility for the "surplus" Puerto
Rican population who had been turned loose from the nation over the course
of planned migration currents.

By 1953, when the first elected Governor of Puerto Rico delivered this
speech to the Teachers' Association, hundreds of thousands of Puerto Ricans
were living in the United States. Muñoz Marín had surprisingly little to say,
in his official, public statements, about this huge exodus of his countrymen,
nor of their situation in the United States. He considered migration a natural,
rational and beneficial process, as it had the effect of alleviating the seemingly incurable unemployment and alleged over-population on the Island,
while providing job opportunities for thousands of working-class families.[37]
And he hailed the right which Puerto Ricans share with "citizens from any
state in the Union" to move to places where there is more employment; the
Puerto Rican migration, for him, was "as normal as the flow of any other
citizens" of the United States.[38]

The Puerto Rican living in the United States, it was recognized, brings
a different national culture, different "roots," than those prevalent in his
new place of residence. "Of people like him," Muñoz Marín was to say,
consolingly, "the United States has been built—people who voluntarily left
their homeland, adapting themselves to the culture they found there and
contributing to it and enriching it. The Puerto Rican who takes up residence
in the United States should adapt himself to his new community, as the Irish,
Polish, Italian and Scandinavian people did before him."[39] Culturally, then,
if not politically, Puerto Ricans move to the United States not as citizens
from any state in the "Union," but as immigrants from a foreign country.
Puerto Rican culture, in the new setting, is another ingredient in the pluralist
melting-pot.

Such, then, is the official policy toward the cultural situation of Puerto
Ricans in the United States. It rests on the ideological complementarity
of assimilationism and cultural nationalism—assimilation based on the harmonious contribution of the dominant culture of the arriving peoples, and
nationalism based in the distinctive but assimilable "roots" originating in
the spiritual fatherland. In these terms, the cultural position of the Puerto
Rican emigrant can preserve two points of reference at once—the elite cultural patrimony of the Island and mainstream, institutionalized United States

culture—without evoking any real polarity whatsoever. What must go unmentioned, of course, for this paradigm to remain convincing, is the per-
sisting imperialist oppression of Puerto Rico, and the colonial position and
largely working-class composition of the Puerto Rican population in the
United States.

One of the most influential transmitters of the cultural trappings put together under the Commonwealth to the setting of Puerto Ricans in the United
States has been María Teresa Babín, long-standing professor of Spanish literature at the City University of New York. Among her many activities,
associations and writings—including *Introducción a la cultura hispánica*
(1949), *Jornadas literarias* (1964), *Panorama de la cultura puertorriqueña*
(1958) and *The Puerto Ricans' Spirit* (1971)—she edited one of the few anthologies of Puerto Rican literature available in English, *Borinquen* (1974).
The arbitrary selection and organization of that reader—it contains, in fact, a
separate chapter entitled "The Muñoz Dream: Father and Son"—is matched
only by the eclecticism and nostalgic, romantic tenor of the introduction.
This criticism is intended not to deny the value of the anthology in making
many historically important texts accessible to English-language readers for
the first time.

In her introduction, Babín manages to conjure up the entire mystique of
the "cultural heritage," while carefully circumventing every salient contradiction in the unfolding of the national culture. Fanfares of tribute are paid
to the usual monuments, like the founding of the Ateneo and the Institute of
Puerto Rican Culture, José de Diego's poetic vision and Pedreira's *Insularismo*, while the trappings of popular folklore and progressive events, such
as the Taíno resistance and "El Grito de Lares," receive mention as well.

Even "the Puerto Rican exiles, as we may call the thousands of compatriots living in New York and other places," are represented and discussed in
Borinquen.[40] In the writings of Piri Thomas, Pedro Pietri, Victor Hernández
Cruz and other examples of the "Neo-Rican modality," the editor finds "a
sampling of moving and beautiful things created with pain and sorrow, in
a flash of anger as victims of repression and discrimination on foreign soil,
witnesses of a system of life and death that has left its Carimbo mark in
their flesh and in their souls." Yet she is quick to qualify her praise when
contemplating, again, the grandeur of the national tradition:

> Although the literature of Puerto Rico far surpasses that of the
> Neo-Rican, or self-styled Rican, in the United States, the latter
> represents a continuity of the island heritage. Since it is so much
> older and richer, it is naturally more complex and sophisticated.
> El Barrio or Los Barrios selections, no matter how crude and

young, in a cultural sense, have a vitality that demands recognition; for it is a literature in the process of creation, whose forms and goals have already begun to affect those of the Mother Culture on the Island.

Even a cursory reading of a poet like Pedro Pietri, of course, shows how far removed much of the "Neo-Rican modality" is from the lofty cultural ideals of María Teresa Babín and her "Muñoz Dream." Puerto Rican writers and artists in the United States grew up in homes wracked by poverty and illiteracy; their families for generations back had been victimized by intense capitalist exploitation and national oppression. At their best, their works lash out against these inhuman conditions, and burst all the broken promises and artificial idealizations which go to perpetuate them. They draw on and topple myths from both Puerto Rican and United States cultural idioms, and express themselves in English or Spanish, and not uncommonly in rapid switching between the two.

How far from the museums, institutes and academies is that stammer of working-class obedience and frustration which opens Pietri's "Puerto Rican Obituary":

They worked
They were always on time
They were never late
They never spoke back
when they were insulted
They worked
They never took days off
that were not on the calendar
They never went on strike
without permission
They worked
ten days a week
and were only paid for five
They worked
They worked
They worked
and they died
They died broke
They died owing
They died never knowing
what the front entrance
of the first national city bank looks like.[41]

In these poems, Pedro Pietri is totally scornful of every sign and symbol of the "land of opportunity" and has no mind to contribute affirmatively to the cultural "enrichment" of the United States. In "Broken English Dream" he arrives with his fellow Puerto Rican immigrants: "We follow the sign / that says welcome to america / but keep your hands / off the property / violators will be electrocuted / follow the garbage truck / to the welfare department / if you cannot speak english."

And Pietri is just as wary of the familiar old Puerto Rican signs that only convey the same, corrupt message in a different language: "So this is america / where they keep you / busy singing / en mi casa toman bustelo / en mi casa toman bustelo." In "Beware of Signs" he warns of "smiling faces that do not smile / and bill collectors who are well trained / to forget how to habla español / when you fall back on those weekly payments." "What they talk," the poem ends, "no es español / what they talk is allotta BULLSHIT." An even more direct repudiation of elitist cultural nationalism like that of María Teresa Babín may be seen in the paintings and sketches of Jorge Soto.[42] One of these works is an adaptation of the official seal of the Institute of Puerto Rican Culture praised by Babín as illustrative of "that balance of ethnic components—Indian, African and Spaniard—the spiritual domain of the 'cosmic race,' proclaimed by the Mexican thinker José Vasconcelos as the epitome of the cultural amalgam in Latin America." The seal, which was conceived at the founding of the Institute in 1955, actually places the Spanish *conquistador* in the center, bearing a sacred book and flanked on either side by the naked Taíno with armfuls of fruit and the bare-chested slave armed with a machete. In his sketch, the "Neo-Rican" Jorge Soto illustrates graphically the insidious meaning of this official image of Puerto Rican ethnic balance.

It is clear that the most vocal artistic expression of Puerto Ricans in the United States did not accept the "Muñoz Dream" or María Teresa Babín's version of "Borinquen," but characteristically unmasked them as still another subterfuge. They have drawn their energy and resources from their own experience, and from other rebellious currents in North American culture—especially the cultural expression of U.S. Blacks—rather than from any spiritualized mythology rooted in the Puerto Rican "Mother Culture." To this extent, their outcry represents not a continuity, but a rupture, with the dominant national tradition.

Yet it is important to assess this "Neo-Rican modality" against alternative historical backdrops, and in particular its relation to the development of Puerto Rican working-class culture. For despite its origins in proletarian misery, and its forceful protest against abusive conditions, this art rarely suggests any specific revolutionary project. Typically, the tone is one of prolonged sarcasm, and the outcome of any emotional movement is existential desperation or individualized brooding. When Puerto Rico is evoked, it is not as a society with a history of struggle to build on, but as a fantasized paradise having little to do with contemporary reality. Piri Thomas's chapter "Puerto Rican Paradise" from *Down These Mean Streets* is an example, as is the closing stanza of "Puerto Rican Obituary": "where beautiful people sing / and dance and work together / where the wind is a stranger to miserable weather conditions / . . . Aqui you salute your flag first / Aqui there are no dial soap commercials / Aqui everybody smells good," etc. Even when the homeland is taken to be the streets of El Barrio, and the historical colony is not evoked, the range of possibilities does not include any hint of political strategy. As Miguel Algarín and Miguel Piñero put it in their anthology, *Nuyorican Poetry* (1975): "For the poor New York Puerto Rican there are three survival possibilities. The first is to labor for money and exist in eternal debt. The second is to refuse to trade hours for dollars and to live by your will and 'hustle.' The third possibility is to create alternative behavioral habits."[43] Aside from wage-slavery and lumpen hustling, then, there remains the special role of the prophetic street poet who survives, presumably, by force of his own creative energy.

The rebellious young Puerto Rican artists in New York had no way of recognizing their continuity with the working-class traditions of Puerto Rican culture, since it is precisely this component of the national history which imperialist relations are most urgently obliged to suppress. The Puerto Rican cultural outburst of the 1960s could not possibly have been aware of a Puerto Rico as seen by Ramón Romero Rosa, Luisa Capetillo or Eduardo Conde, nor even of the earlier class struggle of Puerto Ricans in New York as narrated by Bernardo Vega or Jesús Colón. All of these figures, and above all the political and cultural relations they established between the revolutionary movement in the United States and in Puerto Rico, have been cast into oblivion by the subsequent course of history.

And yet, in spite of this disconnection, the closest thematic precedent for New York-based Puerto Rican writing in the last decade were set by books like *Memorias de Bernardo Vega* and *A Puerto Rican in New York* by Jesús Colón. Literary expression of the life and struggles of Puerto Ricans in the metropolis, tossed from job to menial job to unemployment and welfare lines, and subject to abuse and discrimination at every turn, did not spring up new-born in the 1960s. The new wave, of course, has had its own authenticity, vitality and diversity, since it responds to rapidly changing conditions and cultural influences, and is clearly the voice of a second- and third-generation presence. But the background to this production, even of the more personal, modulated lyrics of Victor Hernández Cruz and Sandra

María Esteves, is situated in earlier decades of reflection on the same social experience.

Jesús Colón is one of the few available links of this kind, though there are surely many more still to be unearthed. Like Bernardo Vega, he grew up in Cayey, and emigrated to New York in the late teens. Raised in the culture of the *tabaqueros*—his book begins with a proud description of the daily "readings" in the hometown cigar factory—Colón did not cling as tenaciously as did Vega to that trade. The best of his sketches, in fact, relate the sordid details of his experience as a bottle-washer in the lower East Side and as a dockworker in Hoboken. Politically, Jesús Colón was one of the founding members, at the age of seventeen, of the first New York Committee of the Puerto Rican Socialist Party in 1918. While Secretary of the Alianza Obrera Puertorriqueña in the early 1920s, he was a New York correspondent to the socialist newspaper *La Justicia*, published in Puerto Rico. He later joined the Communist Party U.S.A., which in the 1930s and 1940s was no rarity among Puerto Rican workers: in those years, the Party had some of its most active branches in the Spanish-speaking communities of Manhattan and Brooklyn. Colón ran several times for local office as an American Labor party candidate, and was for many years head of the thirty Spanish-speaking lodges of the International Workers Order. The last twenty years of his life (1955–74), he spent as a regular columnist for *The Daily Worker.*

As in the case of Bernardo Vega, much of his political attention went to the Spanish-speaking workers in New York, and he remained a steady link to the struggle in Puerto Rico and Latin America. But Jesús Colón devoted more thinking and writing to his relation, as a Puerto Rican, to North American workers of other nationalities. He wrote in English about such topics as "How to Know the Puerto Ricans" and "The Library Looks at the Puerto Ricans," and some of his most moving and politically instructive pages capture the differing reception of Puerto Ricans by Black and white working-class families. In short, he identified himself as a Puerto Rican and as a worker: as a Puerto Rican standing for independence from colonialism, and as a worker in the United States fighting for economic and political change. The final, title article of *A Puerto Rican in New York* gives cogent expression to this sense of historical identity:

> Colonialism made me leave Puerto Rico about forty years ago. Colonialism with its concomitants, agricultural slavery, mono-culture, absentee ownership and rank human exploitation are making the young Puerto Ricans of today come in floods to the United States, if only for a few months to work in the equally exploited agricultural fields.

For the ones that are here in greater New York—six hundred thousand strong—let us show them that there are millions of people that are struggling to take the country away from the trusts that exploit Puerto Rico and the United States alike. Yes, that there are millions of persons to whom that phrase I read many years ago—"We the people"—means what it says, that we are ready to fight for lower prices, more housing, for a progressive people's government and for peace for "We the people of the United States in order to form a more perfect union ... "

As I see things moving in the whole world, among the broad masses and socialist-minded forces in the United States, and among the Puerto Rican nation, including potential forces within all its political parties, independence for Puerto Rico will come sooner than you think.[44]

It seems a far cry indeed from this revolutionary internationalism to the rebellious defiance and ethnic pride of the younger writers. But there are signs that the cultural and political history of the Puerto Rican working class, in the United States and on the Island, may prove an invaluable resource in breaking the ideological impasse in which the "Nuyorican modality" now seems to find itself. Some such indications are evident in the recent poems and skits of Sandra María Esteves, the popular songs of Conjunto Libre and the dance experiments of Betti García. An even stronger example is the work of the Brooklyn-born poet, Louis Reyes Rivera. Generally in the tenor of contemporary Black verse, Reyes Rivera's poems only started appearing in print in 1976, and not in the usual anthologies or journals of Puerto Rican writings: he is founder and editor of Shamal Books, a publishing effort dedicated to printing and distributing the texts of young, aspiring poets like himself.

Along with personal impressions and love poems, Reyes Rivera has composed some outstanding monologues of sympathy and identification with the working class. Consider, for instance, the stanza from "For Tom and Judy":

My heels click
    along quiet hallways
where Tom's son,
    Junior,
used to mop and dry.

My heels click
    against the corridors

Junior used to mop and dry.
Junior had his wine jug
         to wash the splinters
      from his mop handle.
Junior used his wine jug
         to wash the splinters
      from his mop handle
swinging his mop
      picking up nerves—
Junior used his wine jug
         to pick up his nerves
and I don't even know
      who
he even was.[45]

Another impressive example is the concluding section of the title poem from *Who Pays the Cost* (1977); here he opposes the presumptions of street fashion to the reality of working-class oppression:

Who breaks those mine / shaft
         ore deposits day by day
for a tenth of a slice
      from the whole of a loaf
that should have been all
his?
Who sleeps
      with trenches in the mud
         on an acre of oblivion
that used to be his mother's
stream?
Who plucks the grape
      pulls the peach
curses callouses inside wine vats
changing jelly into cream
      so you might yet appear
         to look a little softer
than the other someone else?

TELL ME THIS:
      How much is the price
      to call yourself
         COOL

and who pays the cost
                after you got over?[46]

Reyes Rivera has also written poems which more directly reflect on and adapt Puerto Rican historical experience, such as "Marianita" and "Grito de Lares."[47] He expresses an awareness of the role of the poet—or, in his terms, the "cultural worker"—which is markedly different from that of the "Nuyorican poets." "Too many artists," he says, "ignore the connection between what they have to offer and what the people need ... Cultural workers don't have that choice. I have to earn my way into each person's awareness. I can't shoot for the pockets of a producer. I am the janitor of a history who has to work for his due ... We need the worker in order to arm and protect ourselves with strong, sharp images. We have to be clear about our love. And our only choice is to be persistent!"

Much history, then, is left to be recouped. Today's Puerto Rican cultural workers, grappling to lend contours to a collective identity that has been battered and twisted by colonialism, have many lessons to learn from their working-class forebears in the United States and in Puerto Rico. It is this legacy, more than the inflated visions of José de Diego and the pretentious "national heritage" of the Institute of Puerto Rican Culture, that has long offered a countervailing perspective on the historical position of the Puerto Rican people.

By way of conclusion, it is worth turning again to the pages of *Unión Obrera* in 1906. On December 10 of that year, another forgotten Puerto Rican workers' leader, Eugenio Sánchez López, contributed an article entitled "Cuestión palpitante" ("The Burning Question"). In a few paragraphs, Sánchez López laid to rest the notion that the politicized workers, in opposing the nationalism of the colonial elite, failed to understand the nature of modern imperialism. In calling for an army of labor to match up to the international force of capital, he asked of his fellow-workers:

> Haven't you come to see the professional elements, the bankers, businessmen and industrialists uniting with their counterparts in the Nation? Of course, and these are the same elements who are so intent on redeeming what they call their patrimony, and in so doing feel no need to cling together stubbornly in some kind of debilitating regionalism.[48]

"Even if we should live to see an 'independent republic,' " he continued, "it would be naive not to organize ourselves in unity with our comrades from the United States, for with all our political independence we would still be confronted with the American colossus and its even more dreadful trusts."

Sánchez López recognized the identity of interests between the Puerto Rican workers and the working people in the United States. He understood that not even national independence harbored any inherent guarantee to an improved lot for the great majority of Puerto Rican people. Now, if the analysis of Sánchez López was valid in 1906, when United States imperialism was first setting up shop in the colonial nation, is it not all the more so today, when every aspect of life on the Island is saturated with the earmarks of foreign control, when the Puerto Rican capitalists are operating in open league with Wall Street and the Pentagon, and when a third of the Puerto Rican population has taken up permanent residence in the United States? "Are we going to deny the undeniable fact," he ended by asking, "that the more abundant our forces, the more effective our resistance? Are we going to be such Quixotes that our lances and shields are no stronger than those of the knight-errant dreaming pathetically of his Dulcinea?"

There are answers, then, to the question of political alliances, and to the even more vexed issue of national and cultural "identity" so integrally bound up with it. What the emergence and evolution of conscious working-class expression shows is that national culture cannot be understood as an essentially psychological, religious, anthropological, biological or ethnic entity, fixed in time and attached ineradicably to a group of people in some monolithic totality. It is in such terms—or, most often, in one of many per-mutations of these categories—that the ruling classes of all nations stamp and circumscribe the "psyche" of those within the national economic unit at their command; "national culture" is defined and fashioned after their historically dominant image so as to serve their historically governing inter-ests. The national "soul" which is presumed to reside within each and every member of the nationality, is either immutable or malleable according to the contingencies of the international marketplace, as the very sequence from José de Diego to Antonio Pedreira to Luis Muñoz Marín makes abundantly clear in the case of twentieth-century Puerto Rican theory.

Depending on historical circumstances, and where the ideological ac-cent is placed at any given stage, one of two classical bogeys will surface as dominant. One is the "nationalist bogey of assimilation"—to use Lenin's phrase[49]—and of "cultural genocide," according to which national culture is treated as an ahistorical archetype capable of some pure, ideal manifestation and therefore chronically threatened by contamination and extermination as a result of contact with other cultures. Characteristically, the idea of "preserving" the culture is invoked in order to camouflage the real effect of isolating and extracting it from its ongoing process of transformation and interaction. Needless to say, no class distinctions are drawn either within the culture under attack, or within that genocidal culture into which it is being assimilated. The other typical position might be called the assimilationist, universalist bogey of "separatism," which would minimize the element of coercion and privilege in the relation between imperialist and colonial cultures and deny the culture of colonial peoples any distinctive lines of historical, national development. This taboo is manifest in Muñoz Marín's vehement condemnation of all signs of practical struggle for national liberation. When referring to the situation of Puerto Ricans in the United States, it is epitomized in what has been called the danger of forming an "unassimilated ethnic cyst,"[50] that is, the tendency of Puerto Ricans to group together and seal themselves off from the larger society. This resistance to the "mainstream," it is argued, must be overcome as earlier immigrants came to overcome it, as it "will always be the source of discord and friction."

The alternative outlook of grounding an approach to culture on the dynamic of the class struggle does not deny the need for national liberation from imperialism, nor the direct ramifications of colonial oppression of the Island within United States society. Rather, it asserts as a strategic principle and historical reality that the working class is the only force capable of carrying the anti-colonial struggle through to its completion. Puerto Rican national culture, then, if it is to be viewed as the ascendant culture standing in most radical opposition to that being imposed by imperialism, should correspond largely to the developing cultural manifestation, and "identity," of the working class.

From this vantage-point, the answer to the danger of "assimilation," especially in the United States context, is transformation of the national culture in the direction of unity and equality with the working-class cultures of other nationalities. This kind of "integration" is different, qualitatively, from contribution to the "enrichment of the culture of the (North) American nation," for unlike that slogan it is grounded on a recognition of the colonial position of Puerto Rico, and of the national oppression of Puerto Rican people in the United States. Furthermore, it rests on the differentiated concept of the cultures of both nations. And the answer to what is feared as "separatism" and "ethnic cysts" is affirmation of the national culture, in all its psychological, spiritual and aesthetic qualities, as the expression of a people's resistance to imperialism. Over the course of Puerto Rican history, it is the class division of the national culture as of the turn of the century, and the large-scale emigration of Puerto Ricans to working-class settings in the United States since World War II, which represent the main events conditioning the contemporary redefinition of Puerto Rican identity.

Puerto Rican Literature in the United States: Stages and Perspectives

Can anyone name the great Puerto Rican novel? It is *La charca* by Manuel Zeno Gandía, published in 1894 and first available to American readers in English translation in 1984. The lapse, of course, is symptomatic. After nearly a century of intense economic and political association, endless official pledges of cultural kinship, and the wholesale importation of nearly half the Puerto Rican people to the United States, Puerto Rican literature still draws a blank among American readers and students of literature. Major writers and authors are unknown and, with a handful of exceptions, untranslated; English-language and bilingual anthologies are few and unsystematic, and there is still not a single introduction to the literature's history available in English. Even the writing of Puerto Ricans living in the Unites States, mostly in English and all expressive of life in this country, has remained marginal to any literary canon, mainstream or otherwise. Among the "ethnic" or "minority" literatures, it has probably drawn the least critical interest and the fewest readers.

Yet, as a young Puerto Rican friend once put it, "Puerto Rico is this country's 'jacket.'" In no other national history are twentieth-century American social values and priorities more visibly imprinted than in Puerto Rico's. Puerto Rico, in fact, or at least its treatment at the hands of the United States, is part of American history. Its occupation in 1898 after four centuries of Spanish colonialism, the decades of imposition of English, the unilateral decreeing of American citizenship in 1917, economic and social crisis during the Depression years, externally controlled industrialization, unprecedented migration of the work force and sterilization of the women,

First published in the *ADE Bulletin* (Association of Departments of English), 91 (Winter, 1988): 39–44. Republished in *Redefining American Literary History*, A. LaVonne Brown Ruoff and Jerry W. Ward, Jr., Eds. (New York: Modern Language Association, 1990): 210–18.

ecological depletion and contamination, relentless cultural saturation—all these events pertain not only to Puerto Rican historical reality but to the recent American past as well. And in no foreign national literature is this seamy, repressed side of the "American century" captured at closer range than in the novels of Zeno Gandía and Enrique Laguerre, the stories of José Luis González and Pedro Juan Soto, the poetry of Luis Palés Matos and Julia de Burgos, or the plays of René Marqués and Jaime Carrero. Understandably, Puerto Rican literature in the twentieth century has been obsessed with the United States, whose presence not only lurks, allegorically, as the awesome colossus to the north but is manifest in every aspect of national life. Those intent on reworking literary curricula and boundaries would thus do well to heed this telling record of United States politics and culture as they bear on neighboring peoples and nationalities.

Closer still, of course, and more directly pertinent to a "new" American literary history, is the Puerto Rican literature produced in the United States. Not until the late 1960s, when distinctly Nuyorican voices emerged on the American literary landscape, did it occur to anyone to speak of a Puerto Rican literature emanating from life in this country. How, indeed, could such an uprooted and downtrodden community even be expected to produce a literature? Such relative newcomers, many lacking in basic literacy skills in either English or Spanish, were assumed to be still caught up in the immigrant syndrome, or worse, to be languishing in what Oscar Lewis termed the "culture of poverty." But in books like Piri Thomas's *Down These Mean Streets* and Pedro Pietri's *Puerto Rican Obituary*, there was suddenly a literature by Puerto Ricans, in English and decidedly in—and against—the American grain.

This initial impetus has since grown into a varied but coherent literary movement, and over the past decade the Nuyoricans have come to make up an identifiable current in North American literature. That this movement also retains its association to Puerto Rico's national literature and, by extension, to Latin American literary concerns is a crucial though more complex matter. In fact, it is Nuyorican literature's position straddling two national literatures and hemispheric perspectives that most significantly distinguishes it among the American minority literatures. In any case, those years of cultural and political awakening in the late 1960s generated an active literary practice among Puerto Ricans born and raised in the United States, who have managed to expound a distinctive problematic and language with a bare minimum of institutional or infrastructural support.

Critical and historical interest in this new literature has also grown. Journal articles and introductions to books and anthologies, although scattered, have helped provide some context and approaches. Along with critics like

Edna Acosta-Belén, Efraín Barradas, Francis Aparicio and John Miller, Wolfgang Binder, professor of American studies at the University of Erlangen, deserves special mention. His substantial work on contemporary Puerto Rican literature is based on an ample knowledge of the material and close familiarity with many of the authors. Further study of this kind has ascertained with increasing clarity that Puerto Rican literature in the United States was not born, sui generis, in the late 1960s and that its scope, like that of other emerging literatures, cannot be properly accounted for if analysis is limited by the reigning norms of genre, fictionality, language or national demarcation.

In 1982 there appeared the first, and still the only, book on Puerto Rican literature in the United States, Eugene Mohr's *The Nuyorican Experience*. Mohr, professor of English at the University of Puerto Rico, offers a helpful overview of many of the works and authors and suggests some lines of historical periodization. I will therefore refer to Mohr's book, and especially to some of its omissions, in reviewing briefly the contours of Puerto Rican literature in the United States. How far back does it go, and what were the major stages leading to the present Nuyorican style and sensibility? To what extent does its very existence challenge the notion of literary and cultural canons, and how does this literature relate to other noncanonical and anti-canonical literatures in the United States?

*   *   *

The first Puerto Ricans to write about life in the United States were political exiles from the independence struggle against Spain who came to New York in the late decades of the nineteenth century to escape the clutches of the colonial authorities. Some of Puerto Rico's most prominent intellectual and revolutionary leaders, such as Eugenio María de Hostos, Ramón Emeterio Betances, Lola Rodríguez de Tío and Sotero Figueroa, spent more or less extended periods in New York, where along with fellow exiles from Cuba they charted further steps to free their countries from Spanish rule. The lofty ideals of "Antillean unity" found concrete expression in the establishment of the Cuban and Puerto Rican Revolutionary Party under the leadership of the eminent Cuban patriot Jose Martí. This early community was largely composed of the radical patriotic elite, but there was already a solid base of artisans and laborers who lent support to the many organizational activities. It should also be mentioned that one of these first settlers from Puerto Rico was Arturo Alfonso Schomburg, a founder of the Club Dos Antillas and, in later years, a scholar of the African experience.

The writings that give testimonial accounts and impressions of those years in New York are scattered in diaries, correspondences and the often

short-lived revolutionary newspapers that still await compilation and pe-
rusal. Perhaps the most extended and revealing text to have been uncovered
thus far is a personal article by the Puerto Rican poet and revolutionary martyr Francisco Gonzalo Marín. "Pachín" Marín, a typesetter by trade who
died in combat in the mountains of Cuba, figures significantly in the history
of Puerto Rican poetry because of his emphatic break with the stale, airy
clichés of romantic verse and his introduction of an ironic, conversational
tone and language. In "Nueva York por dentro: Una faz de su vida bohemia,"
he offers a pointed critical reflection on New York City as experienced by
the hopeful but destitute Puerto Rican immigrant.

In *The Nuyorican Experience*, Eugene Mohr makes no mention of "Pachín" Marín or of these first, nineteenth-century samples of Puerto Rican
writing in New York, though the Cuban critic Emilio Jorge Rodríguez has
drawn proper attention to them. The sources are of course still scarce,
and that period of political exile was clearly distinct in character from the
later stages, which were conditioned by the labor immigration under direct
colonial supervision. Nevertheless, writings like that of "Pachín" Marín
and some of the diary entries and letters of Hostos and others carry immense
prognostic power in view of subsequent historical and literary developments.
In a history of Puerto Rican literature in the United States they provide an
invaluable antecedent perspective, a prelude of foreboding, even before the
fateful events of 1898. When read along with the essays and sketches of José
Martí on New York and the United States, these materials offer the earliest
"inside" view of American society by Caribbean writers and intellectuals.

Mohr dates the origins of "the Nuyorican experience" from Bernardo
Vega's arrival in New York in 1916, as recounted in the opening chapter
of Vega's memoirs. While the *Memorias de Bernardo Vega* (Memoirs of
Bernardo Vega) is a logical starting point, since it chronicles the Puerto
Rican community from the earliest period, the book was actually written in
the late 1940s and was not published until 1977. (An English translation
appeared in 1984.) Despite the book's belated appearance, though, Bernardo
Vega was definitely one of the "pioneers." He and his work belong to and
stand for that period from the First through the Second World War (1917–
1945), which saw the growth and consolidation of the immigrant community
following the Jones Act that decreed citizenship (1917), and preceding the
mass migration after 1945. In contrast to the political exiles and other
temporary or occasional sojourners to New York, Bernardo Vega was also,
in Mohr's terms, a "proto-Nuyorican": although he eventually returned to
Puerto Rico late in life (he lived there in the late 1950s and the 1960s), Vega
was among the first Puerto Ricans to write about New York as one who was
here to stay.

Puerto Rican literature of this first stage showed many of the signs of an immigrant literature, just as the community itself, still relatively modest in size, resembled that of earlier immigrant groups in social status, hopes for advancement and civic participation. The published writing was overwhelmingly of a journalistic and autobiographical kind: personal sketches and anecdotes, jokes and *relatos* printed in the scores of Spanish-language newspapers and magazines that cropped up and died out over the years. It is a first-person testimonial literature: the recent arrivals capturing, in the home language, the jarring changes and first adjustments as they undergo them.

Yet the analogy to the European immigrant experience was elusive even then, long before the momentous changes of mid-century made it clear that something other than upward mobility and eventual assimilation awaited Puerto Ricans on the mainland. The most important difference, which has conditioned the entire migration and settlement, is the abiding colonial relationship between Puerto Rico and the United States. Puerto Ricans came here as foreign nationals, a fact that American citizenship and accommodationist ideology tend to obscure; but they also arrived as a subject people. The testimonial and journalistic literature of the early period illustrate that Puerto Ricans entering this country, even those most blinded by illusions of success and fortune, tended to be aware of this discrepant, disadvantageous status.

For that reason, concern for the home country and attachment to national cultural traditions remained highly active, as did the sense of particular social vulnerability in the United States. The discrimination met by the "newcomers" was compounded by racial and cultural prejudice, as the black Puerto Rican writer and political leader Jesús Colón portrays so poignantly in his book of autobiographical sketches set in those earlier decades, *A Puerto Rican in New York*. In both of these senses—the strong base in a distinct and maligned cultural heritage and the attentiveness and resistance to social inequality—Puerto Rican writing in the United States, even in this initial testimonial stage, needs to be read as a colonial literature. Its deeper problematic makes it more akin to the minority literatures of oppressed groups than to the literary practice and purposes of "ethnic" immigrants.

Another sign of this kinship, and of the direct colonial context, has to do with the boundaries of literary expression established by the norms of print culture. For in spite of the abundant periodical literature, with its wealth of narrative and poetic samples in that period and in subsequent periods of Puerto Rican immigrant life, surely the most widespread and influential form of verbal culture has been transmitted, not through publication, but through oral testimony and through the music. The work of oral historians in gathering the reminiscences of surviving "pioneers" will be indispensable in supplementing the study of printed texts. Also of foremost importance in this regard is the collection and analysis of the popular songs of the migration, the hundreds of *boleros, plenas,* and examples of *jíbaro* or peasant music dealing with Puerto Rican life in the United States, which enjoyed immense popularity throughout the emigrant community. Starting in the 1920s, when many folk musicians joined the migration from the Island to New York, the popular song has played a central role in the cultural life of Puerto Ricans in this country. It needs to be recognized as an integral part of the people's "literary" production. Only in recent years, and mainly in reference to the "salsa" style of the present generation, have there been any attempts to cull these sources for broader cultural and theoretical meanings (see Duany). But it was in those earlier decades, when favorites like Rafael Hernández, Pedro Flores, Ramito, Mon Rivera, Cortijo, and Tito Rodríguez were in New York composing and performing songs about Puerto Rican life here, that this tradition of the popular song began.

*   *   *

A turning point in Puerto Rican literature, before the advent of the Nu-yoricans in the late 1960s, came around 1950. This second stage covers the years 1945–65. Those two decades after World War II saw the rapid industrialization of Puerto Rico under Operation Bootstrap, and hundreds of thousands of Puerto Rican workers migrated to New York and other United States cities. This avalanche of newly arriving families, a significant part of the country's displaced agricultural proletariat, drastically changed the character of the Puerto Rican immigrant community, distancing it still further from the familiar immigrant experience. The "Puerto Rican problem" became more urgent than ever for official and mainstream America, as did the infusion of drugs, criminality and the forces of incrimination into the crowded Puerto Rican neighborhoods. It should be remembered that *West Side Story*, written and first performed in the mid-1950s, was intended to ease this explosive situation, though it actually has had the long-term effect of reinforcing some of the very stereotypes, so rampant in the dominant culture, that it sought to dispel. The same must be said of Oscar Lewis's book *La vida* and its infamous notion of the "culture of poverty."

It was in this period and because of these conditions that the migration and the emigrant community in the United States became major themes in Puerto Rican national literature. In prior decades some authors from the Island had of course shown an interest in their uprooted compatriots, setting their works in New York and choosing immigrants as their protagonists: parts of *El negocio* and *Los redentores*, the later novels of Manuel Zeno Gandía, take place in the United States, and frequent bibliographical reference is made to still another unpublished novel by Zeno Gandía entitled *Hubo un escándalo* (or *En Nueva York*), though it has not yet been possible to study that manuscript. José de Diego Padró, an interesting but neglected writer active between 1910 and 1930, set much of his long bizarre novel *En Babia* in New York, as did the dramatist Fernando Sierra Berdecía in his comedy *Esta noche juega el jóker*. But these are random and rare exceptions and still do not indicate any inclusion of the emigrant experience in the thematic preoccupations of the national literature.

By mid-century, though, accompanying the more general shift in the literature from a rural to an urban focus, the attention of Island authors turned decisively to the reality of mass migration and the emigrant barrio. Many writers, such as René Marqués, Enrique Laguerre, José Luis González, and Emilio Díaz Valcárcel, came here in those years to witness it directly, while a writer like Pedro Juan Soto, later identified more with the Island literature, actually lived through the emigration firsthand. The result was a flurry of narrative and theatrical works, all appearing in the 1950s and early 1960s, some of which still stand today as powerful fictional renditions of Puerto Rican life in the United States. In contrast to the primarily testimonial writings of the previous period, this was the first "literature," in the narrow sense, about the community here, in which imaginative invention, dramatic structure and stylistic technique are used to heighten the impact of historical and autobiographical experience.

Despite the undeniable artistic merit of some of this work—I would single out the stories of José Luis González, Soto's *Spiks*, and, for historical reasons, René Marqués's *La carreta*—it is also clearly a literature *about* Puerto Ricans in the United States rather than *of* that community. Mohr aptly entitles his second chapter, "Views from an Island." That these are the "views" of visiting or temporary sojourners is evident in various ways but is not necessarily a detriment to their literary value. The tendency is to present the arrival and settlement experience in strict existential and instantaneous terms; instead of process and interaction, there is above all culture shock and intense personal dislocation. What these glimpses and miniatures gain in emotional intensity they often lose in their reduction of a complex, collective and unfolding reality to a snapshot of individual behavior. Another sign of the unfamiliarity and distance between the writer and the New York community is the language: though an occasional English or "Spanglish" usage appears for authenticating purposes, there is a general reliance on standard literary Spanish or, as in *La carreta*, a naturalistic transcription of Puerto Rican dialect. What is missing is any resonance of the community's own language practice, which even then, in the 1950s, was already tending toward the intricate mixing and code switching characteristic of Puerto Rican speech in the United States.

But despite such problems, these "views from an island" rightly remain some of the best-known works of Puerto Rican literature in the United States, their literary impact generally strengthened by the critical, anti-colonial standpoint of the authors. The pitiable condition of the authors' compatriots in United States cities is attributed and linked to the status of Puerto Rico as a direct colony. This perspective, and the constant focus on working-class characters, helps dispel the tone of naive optimism and accommodationism that had characterized the writings of such earlier middle-class observers of the emigrant community as Juan B. Huyke and Pedro Juan Labarthe. The writings of Soto, González and others, because of their quality and the authors' grounding in the national literature of the Island, form an important link to Latin American literature. A story like González's "La noche que volvimos a ser gente," for example, is clearly a work of contemporary Latin American fiction, even though it is set in New York and its attention focuses on the subways and streets of the urban United States. The same is true of Díaz Valcárcel's novel *Harlem todos los días* and many more of these works.

It should be emphasized that during the 1950s there was also a "view from within" the Puerto Rican community, a far less-known literature by Puerto Ricans who had been here all along and who, lovingly or not, considered the barrio home. Here again Bernardo Vega and Jesús Colón come to mind, for although the *Memorias* and *A Puerto Rican in New York* chronicle the arrival and settlement over the decades, they were not written until the late 1940s and 1950s. There were also a number of Puerto Rican poets who had been living in New York for decades and who by the 1950s began to see themselves as a distinctive voice within the national poetry; among them were Juan Avilés, Emilio Delgado, Clemente Solo Vélez, Pedro Carrasquillo, Jorge Brandon and José Dávila Semprít. Back in the 1940s this group had included as well Puerto Rico's foremost woman poet, Julia de Burgos. What little is available of this material shows it to be largely conventional Spanish-language verse making little reference to the migration or to life in New York, much less anticipating in any way the complex bilingual situation of the generation to come. But much more of interest may still be found with further study, and it is important to refer to Pedro Carrasquillo for his popular *décimas* about a *jíbaro* in New York, to Dávila Semprít for his forceful political poetry and to Solo Vélez and Brandon for the examples they set for many of the younger poets.

Perhaps the best example of literature from within the community at mid-century is the novel *Trópico en Manhattan* by Guillermo Cotto-Thorner. The contrast with the Island authors' treatment of the emigrant experience is striking: the shock of arrival and first transitions is extended and lent historical depth; individual traumas and tribulations are woven into a more elaborate interpersonal and social context. Most interesting of all as a sign of the author's proximity to and involvement in the community is, once again, the language. The Spanish of *Trópico en Manhattan*, especially in certain dialogue passages, is at times interspersed with bilingual neologisms of various kinds. And at the end of the book there is a lengthy glossary of what Cotto-Thorner calls "Neorkismos."

The contrast between the observers' and the participants' views in Puerto Rican literature of this period does not reflect so much the literary quality as the relation of the writers to the literature's historical development. A novel like *Trópico en Manhattan* may not surpass the stories of José Luis González and Pedro Juan Soto, but it does more extensively reveal the social contradictions internal to the community and give them a sense of epic duration and process. With regard to literary history, that relatively unknown and forgotten novel, with its early sensitivity to "Neorkismos," may more directly prefigure the voice and vantage point of the Nuyoricans than does *La carreta*, or even *Spiks*.

Another such transitional author of the period 1945–65 is Jaime Carrero, who also seeks to clarify that the "outsider-insider" contrast refers not only to place of residence but to cultural perspective. Carrero, whose bilingual poetry volume *Jet Neorriqueño: Neo-Rican Jet Liner* directly foreshadowed the onset of Nuyorican literature in New York, is from the Island, having been to New York for college and other visits. As Eugene Mohr points out, what distinguishes Carrero from those other Island-based writers is "the persistence of his interest in the *colonia* and his sympathy with the Nuyorican viewpoint" (116). His attempts at bilingual verse and especially his plays, from *Pipo subway no sabe reír* to *El lucky seven*, give vivid literary expression to this internal, participants' perspective. Carrero has also written a novel (*Raquelo tiene un mensaje*) about the trauma of Nuyorican return migration to the Island, but Pedro Juan Soto's *Ardiente suelo fría estación* is as yet unequaled in its treatment of that experience.

*   *   *

The third, Nuyorican stage in emigrant Puerto Rican literature arose with no direct reference to or evident knowledge of the writings of either earlier period. Yet despite this apparent disconnection, Nuyorican creative expression effectively draws together the firsthand testimonial stance of the "pioneer" stage and the fictional, imaginative approach of writers of the 1950s and 1960s. This combining of autobiographical and imaginative modes of community portrayal is clearest perhaps in the prose fiction: *Down These Mean Streets*. Nicholasa Mohr's *Nilda* and Edward Rivera's *Family Installments* are all closer to the testimonial novel than to any of the narrative "views from an Island."

This sense of culminating and synthesizing of the earlier phases indicates that with the Nuyoricans, the Puerto Rican community in the United States has arrived at a modality of literary expression corresponding to its position as a non-assimilating colonial minority. The most obvious mark of this new literature emanating from the community is the language: the switch from Spanish to English and bilingual writing. This language transfer should not be mistaken for assimilation in a wide cultural sense. As the content of the literature indicates, using English is a sign of being here, not necessarily of liking it here or of belonging.

By now, the Nuyorican period of United States-based Puerto Rican literature is already unfolding a history of its own. The sensationalist tenor of the initial outburst has given way to a greater concern for the everyday lives of Puerto Rican working people. The growing diversity and sophistication of the movement is evident in the emergence of women writers and female perspectives, as in such books as Sandra María Esteves's *Bluestown Mockingbird Mambo* and Nicholasa Mohr's *Rituals of Survival*, and in the appearance of writers in other parts of the United States. Also of key importance is the ongoing use of an actively bilingual literary field. For it becomes clear that, in the literature as in the community, the switch from Spanish to English is by no means complete or smooth, and it certainly is not a sign of cultural accommodation. For all the young writers Spanish remains a key language-culture of reference even when not used, and some, like Tato Laviera, demonstrate full bilingual capacity in their writing. There also continues to be a Spanish-language literature by Puerto Ricans living here, some of which hovers between Nuyorican concerns and styles and those of contemporary Island literature. Such writers as Iván Silén and Victor Fragoso, like Jaime Carrero and Guillermo Cotto-Thorner before them, have served as important bridges between the two language poles of present-day Puerto Rican writing.

Thus, rather than abandoning one language in favor of another, contemporary Puerto Rican literature in the United States actually exhibits the full range of bilingual and interlingual use. Like Mexican-American and other minority literatures, it cannot be understood and assessed on the basis of a strict English-language conceptualization of "American" literature, or of literary practice in general. Some of the best Nuyorican texts require knowledge of Spanish and English, which does not make them any less a part of American, or Puerto Rican, literature. And the choice and inclusiveness of a literary language is but one aspect of a broader process of cultural interaction between Puerto Ricans and the various nationalities they encounter in the United States.

By its Nuyorican stage, Puerto Rican literature in the United States comes to share the features of "minority" or noncanonical literatures of the United States. Like them, it is a literature of recovery and collective affirmation, and it is a literature of "mingling and sharing," of interaction and exchange with neighboring, complementary cultures (see Gelfant). What stronger source, after all, for the emergence of Nuyorican literature than Afro-American literature and political culture? What more comparable a context of literary expression than Chicano writing of the same period?

Perhaps most distinctly among these literatures, though, Puerto Rican writing today is a literature of straddling, a literature operative within and between two national literatures and marginal in both. In this respect Nuyorican writing may well come to serve as a model or paradigm for emerging literatures by other Caribbean groups in the United States, such as Dominicans, Haitians and Jamaicans. Despite the sharp disconnections between Island- and United States-based traditions, and between stages of the literary history here, it is still necessary to talk about modern Puerto Rican literature as a whole and of the emigrant literature—including the Nuyorican—as an extension or manifestation of that national literature. This inclusion within, or integral association with, a different and in some ways opposing national culture stretches the notion of a pluralist American canon to the limit. Ethnic, religious and racial diversity is one thing, but a plurality of nations and national languages within the American canon–that is a different and more serious issue. After all, if Tato Laviera and Nicholasa Mohr are eligible for canonical status, why not José Luis González or Julia de Burgos, or, for that matter, Manuel Zeno Gandía, the author of the great Puerto Rican novel *La charca*?

Yes, what about *La charca*? It's a fine novel; in fact, if it had been written by an author from a "big" country, say France or Russia, or even Argentina or Mexico, it would probably be more widely admired and even held up as an example of late nineteenth-century realism. It was published in 1894, before the United States acquired the Island, and its plot is set several decades earlier, long before any significant relations had developed between the two countries. And yet, though it does not mention or refer to the United States, *La charca* is still, somehow, about America, a literary pre-sentiment of what contact with North American society had in store for Puerto Rico. The isolated mountain coffee plantation issues into the wider world of commerce and international dealings, represented in Puerto Rican history, and in Zeno Gandía's later novels, by the United States. Like

Jose Martí, "Pachín" Marín and other Latin American intellectuals of the time, Zeno Gandía anticipated the coming of the Unites States' values and power. Even at such a remove, with America's presence still but a metaphor, *La charca* touches the American canon and contributes impressively to the larger task of American literature.

IV

Plena street musicians, including Nelly and Sammy Tanko (sister and brother), making music at The Fiesta de Loiza, Wards Island, New York City, July, 1979. Photographer Máximo Colón. Courtesy Máximo Colón.

"La Carreta Made a U-Turn": Puerto Rican Language and Culture in the United States

Are Puerto Ricans becoming Americanized? Are familiar national life-ways, traditions and markers of identity being assimilated to mainstream U.S. culture? Most observers agree that such a process is taking place, that indeed it could hardly be otherwise, given the degree of economic and political absorption that has long accompanied "culture contact" between the two societies. Particularly when discussion focuses on Puerto Ricans in the United States—and they are frequently the real case in point—no one can deny that the distinctive signs and qualities of Puerto Rican culture, including the Spanish language, are giving way to the seemingly inexorable sweep of Yankee pluralism.

Here, though, the consensus ends, for directly after observing and recording the signs of cultural assimilation come the vexing tasks of analyzing and evaluating them. Is the process desirable or undesirable? Should it be facilitated or denounced? How far along is it, and are there limits to its full realization? Is it inevitable or reversible? Is the main obstacle to total Americanization to be found in national, or "ethnic," resistance, or in the very structural relationship between the United States and Puerto Rico?

More fundamental, perhaps, is the question of what it means for Puerto Ricans to be "Americanized." Which of the most essential features of Puerto Rican cultural life are being integrated? Which are being obliterated by pervasive colonial influences? Which aspects of North American culture are seen as the most potent forces promoting assimilation among Puerto Ricans,

Co-authored with John Attinasi and Pedro Pedraza, Jr. Published in *Daedalus*, 110/3 (Spring, 1981): 193–217. This essay represents the collective efforts of the Culture and Language Policy Task Forces (LPTF) of the Centro de Estudios Puertorriqueños, City University of New York. In addition, the manuscript has benefited from close reading by Ricardo Campos and Frank Bonilla.

especially those living in the United States? Which other U.S. historical experiences of conquest, domination or absorption through migration are most pertinent for Puerto Ricans? Is the issue of Puerto Rican cultural identity best posed as that of an immigrant group, or of an ethnic or racial minority? Are Hispanics set off by language of origin, or are they Third World victims of internal colonialism or perhaps participants in the "culture of poverty?" There is some validity in each of these approaches, and interpretations thus far have generally been based on one or a combination of such models. But to what extent can such partial analogies measure the nature and degree of Puerto Rican acculturation? Finally, if the assimilation process is considered neither desirable nor inevitable—not the inherent aspiration nor the conclusive undoing of Puerto Rican culture—what alternatives remain? Might the persistent affirmation of a discrete national culture, and particularly its tradition of anti-colonial resistance, be somehow consonant with an ever more deep immersion in the cultural life of the United States?

Such an eventuality is rarely, if ever, addressed by commentators on the Americanization of Puerto Ricans in the United States, despite agreement that assimilation is far from complete and in fact highly problematic. Clearly, something other than fluid cultural integration is at work. Although Puerto Ricans are gaining command of English, they are by no means abandoning their native Spanish. But the debate invariably falters at this point; such a seemingly anomalous cultural and linguistic juncture defies the terms of assimilation theory that underlie most intellectual discourse about the issue.

Within the framework set by Milton Gordon in *Assimilation in American Life*[1] and in subsequent discussions, North American sociologists and anthropologists have generally considered Puerto Ricans in the United States as problematic "newcomers," the most recent in the long line of ethnic immigrants, including blacks from the South, to occupy the lowest rung on the ladder of social mobility. Puerto Rican observers, on the other hand, emphasize the distinctiveness of Puerto Rican migrants; unlike their European predecessors, Puerto Ricans come from a nearby colonial nation, and their national ties remain more active. But assimilation theory provides the theoretical context here also, and commentators inside the Puerto Rican community and those outside have come full circle in the prognosis of an eventual incorporation of "Puerto Rican Americans" into the pluralist mainstream. The most basic problem, then, is the method common to both approaches, since it accommodates two divergent currents of interpretation, both of which are glaringly inadequate—that of American social scientists, because it omits or minimizes the colonial dimension of the relationship between the United States and all Puerto Ricans, and that of Puerto Rican writers, because it lacks a consideration of class relations and the cultural dynamic in the United States. Any effort to fuse these miscast tendencies on their own terms, or to build a more satisfactory synthesis by combining the valid insights of both, leads only to further and ever more bewildering dilemmas.

This complex theoretical debate and corollary ethnographic assertions rarely refer to one obvious source of evidence: the firsthand cultural production of Puerto Ricans in the United States and their linguistic practices. The case against cultural imperialism and the data base of urban anthropology have all but ignored the explicit testimony of the community as expressed in its daily verbal interactions, not to mention its painting, drama, music, poetry and dance. Pathologies are extensively documented, the "requiem" is pronounced, proofs and disclaimers are raised on such telling issues as group intermarriage, the relative successes of bilingual education and patterns of upward mobility—while the practical communicative and creative experiences of Puerto Ricans in the United States go largely unanalyzed. Matters of cultural representation, for the most part, are left to the artistic circles themselves. In the galleries, workshops and ensembles, and among the painters, poets and musicians, "Puerto Rican culture" is the substance and product of everyday work, not merely an intellectual issue or category, but a directly and creatively reexpressed reality. Similarly, policymakers and scholars speculate extensively on the Puerto Rican language predicament and its implications for public policy, without ever taking as a point of departure the virtuosity of speech resources in the context of home, workplace, and social interchange.

In this essay we will attempt to tap these active currents by turning to specific instances of Puerto Rican expression in the United States. The conclusions drawn from a long-term study of linguistic practice and attitudes on a single block in El Barrio point up the particular complexity of socio-linguistic change in the Puerto Rican case. These conclusions challenge many guiding assumptions of previous discussions of bilingualism, and have important consequences for the framing of educational policy for Hispanics, especially since these findings rest on an analysis of the historical and political position of Puerto Ricans in U.S. society.

A critical reading of *La Carreta Made a U-Turn*,[2] by the young "Nuyorican" poet Tato Laviera, provides corollary insights. In this volume, poetry itself poses the issue of acculturation in reference to language and verbal symbolization, the hub around which numerous aspects of Puerto Rican culture ultimately turn. Can verse written in English, and at an increasing distance from the national language and traditions, still be considered Puerto Rican literature? Is bilingual poetry, which so insistently presupposes a Hispanic and Caribbean language background, no more than an ethnic thread within the diverse fabric of contemporary North American writing? The very groping for a category in which to place a characteristic poetic language quickly lands one at the center of the assimilation controversy, and evokes the most critical consequences that arise from an interpretive description of prevailing cultural patterns.

An in-depth socio-linguistic study and the critical interpretation of emergent literary voices provide but another point of entry into the needed theoretical debate, and cannot presume to yield any ready and felicitous resolution to what will surely remain, in many ways, an inscrutable paradox. Yet such exercises signal, in dramatic form, the grave methodological and ideological impasse of much contemporary thinking about ethnicity, cultural identity and the assimilation process. The alternative approach that concludes this essay constitutes a preliminary, tentative means of transcending that impasse, and of setting future accounts of Puerto Rican experience in the United States in line with a more dynamic and variegated vision of cultural change.

The Socio-Linguistic Evidence

For language minorities in the United States, the acquisition of standard English is presumed to signal both a willingness to assimilate and an effort to take the most crucial first step to gain the knowledge and skills that enable social advance. Learn the language, it is said, and the doors of the "larger" society will swing open. There is, of course, a kernel of accuracy to such reasoning and it impels millions of Puerto Ricans, Chicanos and other Latinos to struggle daily for educational opportunity, employment and access to social services.

However persuasive it may appear, though, the language-as-lever rationale is riddled with contradictions. As it informs public opinion and policy, it is little more than a rationalization used to conceal the element of coercion that runs through the entire history of language contact under colonial conditions. The very term *bilingualism* has itself been used as a convenient cover for the long-term imposition of English in Puerto Rico. What is touted as the most desirable circumstance—trading Puerto Rican Spanish for communicative skills in English—turns out to be not so much a life-enlarging choice as an outright obligation.

Vague definitions and tenuous premises, such as the ingrained assumption that "correct language" somehow implies good behavior and intelligence, are further rationales for the adoption of the standard variety of English.[3] The insidious system of stratification identifies undesirable speech as the speech of undesirables. The consequences of this circular rationale are felt by the poor and working class of all nationalities, but the magnified disadvantage for language minorities is obvious. Rather than assessing intellectual abilities, standards of measurement—whether based on oral or written language—mainly detect deviations from a prestige dialect and the learned routines of social interaction. Clearly, the bias inherent in such hierarchical rankings complement and reinforce the elaborate tracking system at work throughout the educational process and in the society as a whole.

But the most telling case against emphasizing language choice and use is the growing evidence that points to social status as the key to educational success, and not vice versa.[4] Formal schooling and language acquisition, although held up as a ready panacea to economic and political disadvantage, have made only minor inroads into the stubborn system of class and national stratification; to a large extent, in fact, they have served to obfuscate the need for deeper social change. The tiny, often selective trickle of Puerto Ricans into higher education and the professions is the exception that proves the rule. Making it through school and gaining command of English afford little real prospect of alleviating the vast inequities and discrimination that keep the majority of Puerto Ricans on the bottom rung on the social ladder.

These sobering circumstances, however, and the cynical apologetics that support the central thrust of public policy, are no reason to relent in the battle for quality education geared to the needs of Spanish-language minorities. The main arena of struggle recently has been in the establishment of bilingual programs in the public schools. The effectiveness of these efforts has been at best uneven, the most visible impediment being reluctant and piecemeal institutional commitment. But many bilingual programs have also been hampered by the unclear, diffuse and often conflicting goals of the legislators and educators involved. Here, too, numerous issues are fraught with confusion: the choice between English proficiency and Spanish maintenance, or their potential compatibility; the meaning and content of "bicultural" curricula; and the range of language practice among the student population.

The last issue is most pertinent to this essay; the widespread ignorance and disregard for actual linguistic experience results in gravitation toward the accepted norms of Spanish or English language "standards." Only recently—and halfheartedly—has attention been paid to dialect usage as a legitimate mode of social communication compatible with broader educational objectives, rather than as a mark of deviance and retardation to be rooted out in favor of sanctioned language norms. The stigma attached to code-switching—the seemingly haphazard and uncontrolled alternation between one language and another that is characteristic of many Puerto Ricans and other bilinguals—continues to take on pathological proportions to educators of all cultural leanings and pedagogical philosophies.

It is here, in the description and assessment of how Puerto Ricans actually communicate, that a reformulation and redirection of language and educational policy must begin. The results of an intensive look at language use in a Puerto Rican community follow. To study bilingualism concretely, we sought to understand the norms of speaking in daily interaction by observing residents in a single block in New York City over a long term. We also conducted linguistic studies and an attitudinal survey to complete the description of language use and to take account of community members' own perceptions of the language problem.[5]

We chose El Barrio, or East Harlem, as our site of study because it is a large, old, stable Puerto Rican community, with three generations of U.S.-based Puerto Ricans as well as recent and circulating migrants. Except for the absolute size and ethnic density[6] of the community, the demographics of East Harlem are similar to those for the total Puerto Rican population in New York: the majority were born in the United States or have lived here for more than ten years; slightly over half were born in Puerto Rico; fifty percent are under twenty-five years of age. It is a poor neighborhood where one third of the residents live below the poverty level. No single sample, of course, is fully reliable for purposes of generalization; the richness of the present data base, however, and our diversified socio-linguistic approach ensure that the cultural and political implications to be drawn contain valid suggestions for new lines of thinking and analysis.

A person's placement within the social organization of this working-class community is determined as much by the facts of migration frequency, recency, and other particulars—as by age and sex.[7] Language use, skills, and outlook connect to these factors in rather complex and surprising ways. Language preference was not decisive among the various motives for community association, and the range of linguistic abilities, although wide, did not obstruct communication.

In contrast to the traditional immigrant pattern of transition from the foreign language to English over three generations, with grandparents and grandchildren being virtually monolingual in one or the other language, nearly all Puerto Ricans are bilingual to some degree, with second language skills acquired, for the most part, outside any formal language instruction. There seems to be a life cycle of language use in the community. The younger children learn Spanish and English simultaneously, hearing both languages from those who use them separately and from those who combine them in various ways. The older children and adolescents speak and are spoken to increasingly in English, which accords with their experience as students and as members of peer groups that include non-Hispanics. In young adulthood, as the school experience ends and employment responsibilities begin, the use of Spanish increases, both in mixed usage and in monolingual speech to older persons. At this age, then, the Spanish skills acquired in childhood but largely unused in adolescence become notably reactivated. Mature adults speak both languages. Older persons are, for the present at least, Spanish monolingual or nearly so.

The new roles associated with adulthood involve more serious relationships with family members of all ages. The familial networks, like the general community, are affected by circulating migration, making bilingualism necessary. Migration patterns not only place certain persons of all ages in the Spanish-speaking environment of Puerto Rico, but also require that those who remain in New York communicate with persons who circulate between the two places, with recent arrivals, and with persons who came as adults and who continue to speak Spanish. Although there are societal institutions that tend to reinforce one or the other language, the Spanish-maintaining counterforces become prominent as Puerto Ricans pass from adolescence to adulthood.

How, then, are we to characterize the bilingual practice of Puerto Ricans? Theorists hypothesize that without situational separation of the two languages, the bilingualism of a group is transitory. Others claim that the use of two languages simultaneously is a psychological malady, or at least "uncivilized." And the non-standard varieties and apparently low levels of literate achievement further buttress condemnation of bilingualism. Yet our research indicates a dynamic bilingualism, with several varieties of the languages remaining systemically intact. A full appreciation of such structural features, however, requires a historical framework.

Just as four centuries of Spanish colonialism have been responsible for the Caribbean variety of Spanish that Puerto Ricans speak, so, too, is U.S. colonialism crucial to the language dynamic current in the last part of this century. The colonial status of Puerto Rico underlies such social conditions as complex and circular migration patterns, economic stratification, American citizenship and monolingual language policies. Given the dialectical nature of these social factors, the same processes that instigate change also have stabilizing influences within the community, counteractive to the more obvious effects of assimilation. Bilingualism that makes use of nonstandard and class-based vernacular speech is qualitatively different from separated bilingualism comprised of literate standards. Interpretation of the sociolinguistic situation of Puerto Ricans in the United States must therefore be placed within the context of working-class culture and language practice.

Contrary to popular belief, Puerto Ricans living in the United States are bilingual. According to the linguistic arithmetic of colonialism, however, one plus one equals zero, for standard tests would probably label many Puerto

Ricans here as "alingual"—that is, lacking in written and oral competence in either language. Prevailing social and educational practices thus convert an enviable asset into a crippling handicap; facility in two languages, which multiplies the communicative and expressive horizons of a people, turns into a trap that blocks them from all access to recognized linguistic command. Rather than enjoying, combining and developing skills in the two languages, Puerto Ricans are instead caught between them.

Before treating combined usage, it must be recognized that both poles in the Puerto Rican's bilingual range are colonial dialects. Puerto Rican Spanish, with its admixture of indigenous, African and peasant qualities, is stigmatized to this day as a corruption of the pure mother tongue and its supposedly more faithful Latin American variants. The class basis of this judgment is obvious. Unfortunately, this kind of purist condescension toward Puerto Rican Spanish is very much alive among many bilingual educators intent on the maintenance and cultivation of Spanish. Thus the very idiom that Puerto Ricans bring to the bilingual arena as their own is one that has historically been viewed as inferior and associated with deviance and ignorance. Clearly, some Hispanic teachers and intellectuals have been as responsible for perpetuating this devaluation as their North American "overseers."

The acquired language—the urban varieties of American English most immediately accessible to Puerto Ricans—may also be downgraded dialects, distinct from, but sharing much with black English. The studies and struggles surrounding the recognition of that variety are most pertinent. Having learned English well enough to communicate actively with their working-class peers, Puerto Ricans—even those who speak little Spanish—enter school with the prospect of having to relearn the language to use it "properly." The transfer, within a generation, from Spanish to English is merely the first step toward social success and acceptance. Class placement then forces still another language adjustment if Puerto Ricans are to "succeed"— the transfer from the colloquial English of the neighborhood and workplace to the more formal language of educational and professional life.

Most Puerto Ricans in the United States, however, are not located at either end of the Spanish-English spectrum, but range throughout it. The resulting phenomenon is the interpenetrating usage of both languages— derogatorily called "Spanglish"—in a wide range of circumstances, especially for in-group communication. Interpenetrating usage is condemned even more vehemently than usage of either variety alone. Code-switching is viewed as the tragic convergence of two nonstandard vernaculars, and thus is assumed to epitomize the collapse of the integrity of both. It is in this context, where practical bilingualism occurs most spontaneously and expressively, that the charge of alinguality has gained its widest currency. For many observers, Puerto Rican and American alike, code-switching amounts to contamination and interference, an easy recourse to compensate for incomplete resources in either idiom. The obvious first impulse is to untangle the two and enforce language separation to restore each unit and usage to its appropriate place within monolingual discourse.

A corollary, though somewhat more sympathetic, view is that bilingual Puerto Rican speech is a phenomenon of transition. Puerto Ricans cannot and should not be expected to carry through the language transfer overnight; with time and pedagogical supervision, hangovers from Spanish will recede and English will win out. The analogy to other foreign-language immigrant groups is obvious and unquestioned. Even where the need for special educational services is acknowledged, their main function is viewed as simply to facilitate a process that the passage of generations, in any event, will take care of.

The results of our empirical and theoretical study contradict both of these assessments of Puerto Rican bilingualism. Code-switching represents neither the lack of language nor structural convergence. Rather, sentences that used both Spanish and English were found to be grammatical in both languages; switching occurs only where the structures of Spanish and English are congruent. We found that balanced bilinguals engaged in more intimate, intricate kinds of switching, while those with fluency in one language avoided syntactic risks by switching between sentences or switching only independent particles and exclamations. Rather than compensating for monolingual deficiency, code-switching often signals an expansion of communicative and expressive potential.

Many aspects of the Spanish spoken by Puerto Ricans are also mistakenly thought to be the result of English influence. The characteristic weakening of plural endings was found to be due to neither linguistic convergence nor the deterioration of the grammatical category of number. Ambiguity is never the result, because variable agreement and contextual indicators of plurality provide redundancy. In another area of structure, the proportional distribution of Spanish verb forms in East Harlem was found to be basically the same as that in the dialogue of a fifteenth-century Spanish novel. Aspects of verbs and semantic fields covered by the tenses are also similar to those in standard grammars. Claims of deformation or convergence with English, therefore, seem unfounded. The most visible aspects of language contact, the presence of loan words, also has only a superficial effect on linguistic structure, and is, after all, part of every kind of contact between cultures. It is really social prejudice that leads to the categorical condemnation of forms that occur infrequently as characteristic of Puerto Rican speech.[8]

Although structural convergence is a fallacious notion that derives from a superficial examination of language practice itself, the idea that Puerto Rican bilingualism is a transitional stage in a process of adjustment is based on misleading socio-logical and historical assumptions. Separation and loyalty in themselves cannot and have not preserved languages in contact. Demographic, institutional and political factors, among other social conditions, oppose or confirm subjective concerns about language purity. Constantly nourished by both material and ideological influences that are counteractive to smooth language shift, Puerto Rican bilingualism seems to resist both political forces and scientific readings that indicate assimilation.

The most obvious of these factors—and ones that differentiate Puerto Ricans from previous immigrants—are the proximity of the native land (allowing for frequent returns to, and visits from, the Island), the unabating influx of more Puerto Ricans into areas of high Hispanic concentration, and the increasingly circulatory character of the migratory movement. All tend to replenish the presence and influence of Spanish in all aspects of social life. At a more fundamental level, the conditions of colonial oppression have accompanied the entire process of displacement.

The linguistic impact of this pervasive, persistent subjugation is diverse and includes both implicit and overt intensive pressure to abandon Spanish altogether. But rampant inequality and prejudice also serve to isolate a people within the society, to concentrate them in designated neighborhoods, educational tracks and positions in the job market, and to leave them with nothing but their own resistance and resources. This effective ghettoization, the sinister, real-life reflex of ethnic pluralism, is a major objective factor in the seemingly enigmatic maintenance of Spanish even among third-generation and fourth-generation Puerto Ricans in the United States. It must significantly inform any socio-linguistic analysis.

There are also vital subjective factors that reveal pressures felt and exerted in the socio-linguistic situation and that condition the use of language in everyday interaction. In our language attitude survey we found a conscious and widespread connection to bilingualism, so much so that bilinguals are perceived to be most prevalent in the Puerto Rican community.[9] Most of those interviewed found no conflict between speaking English and being Puerto Rican, or speaking Spanish and being actively involved in American culture. They readily admit that many speakers mix both languages in discourse and view this positively. Both languages are valuable. English is recognized as an asset, and Spanish remains important both as a marker and a component of the culture.[10] On the other hand, none of those interviewed advocate complacency toward the preservation and development of Spanish-language skills, tasks that are viewed as a responsibility of the group itself and as a legitimate right in a democratic society. The dynamic transformation of several traditions into a creative national identity can be seen as opposed to unidirectional acculturation.

By virtual consensus, Puerto Ricans want to maintain Spanish. This is true even for young people who admit to not knowing much Spanish. The feeling is that Spanish should he audible and visible wherever Puerto Rican culture exists, an attitude that connects to both observed language use and the postulated life cycle of language competence. This is concretely manifested in the norms of etiquette in which Spanish speakers are almost always accommodated. Puerto Ricans also want to learn English; for most, a person who is more fluent in English than in Spanish is neither a paradox nor an anomaly, much less a case of deliberate or unwitting cultural betrayal. These findings reveal that both linguistic and cultural identity are changing in response to economic and social transformations, and that interpenetrating bilingualism is the idiom in which these cultural changes are expressed.

There was nearly unanimous support for the principle of bilingual education, although unfortunately this consensus also tended to be uncritical and somewhat confused. Education that both elaborates standard skills and recognizes the communicative value of community speechways, and education that begrudgingly concedes a program to remedy the lack of English, are fundamentally different. This is evident not only from the very conceptualization of the problem, but also at the concrete level of interaction with the bilingual or potentially bilingual child. A community that is composed of people in movement between Latin America and the United States and that communicates bilingually will surely want bilingualism. It misses the point to pose the problem of language choice—Spanish or English—as the simple connection between language and cultural identity.

Although these many linguistic issues seem somewhat abstract, they manifest themselves concretely in coercion and exclusion in language use, and provoke linguistic resistance in response. Concerns about the structural integrity of linguistic varieties, language distribution and attitudes about language and identity thus reflect a more encompassing cultural and political problematic.

Just as the relative subordination of Spanish is but one piece in a larger structure of hemispheric domination, so the Hispanic determination to maintain Spanish is only secondarily, and by derivation, a purely linguistic issue. Rather, this struggle is motivated by an identification with all Latin Americans and, at a deeper level, with the cause of justice in their behalf. Similarly, the drive to gain command of English reflects both economic pressures and the constraints typical of an arrogantly monolingual society. The desire to master English does not come from narrow self-interest; nor does the cultivation of Spanish or proclaimed reverence for the cultural heritage ensure either particular concern for the conditions under which Puerto Ricans live or interest in changing them for the better.

Thus a realistic understanding of the language-culture nexus calls into question both conventional linguistic approaches to Puerto Rican experience and the assimilationist or cultural nationalist orientations in which they are grounded. Rigorous linguistic description is of course indispensable in exposing the profound complexity of the language contact situation in its own right. In addition, a comprehensive conception of language as a system of interaction may help overcome the frozen dichotomy that ties English and Spanish to monolithic cultural blocks, while the analysis of verbal communication serves to illuminate some of the most distinctive qualities of contemporary artistic production and innovation. But explaining these socio-linguistic conditions and even elaborating the rules that govern their practical workings call for placing linguistic considerations in a wide-ranging context of cultural and political theory.

Culture Makes a U-Turn

La Carreta Made a U-Turn, Tato Laviera's first book of poems, clearly belongs to the so-called Nuyorican modality. Freely bilingual in style and conception, it was written by a young Puerto Rican who grew up in the streets of New York City. The poems are filled with that biting defiance and strident pride that erupted on the literary landscape in 1973 with *Puerto Rican Obituary* by Pedro Pietri.[11] Laviera's is another voice responding to the oppression and misery that have been the lot of most Puerto Ricans since their proverbial oxcart pulled up to Ma Liberty's Golden Door. Mass unemployment; inadequate and distorted education; rampant prejudice and injustice; high crime rates and drug abuse that are systematically fostered by the very society that condemns them; social isolation, whether behind bars or in depressed, run-down neighborhoods—these are and promise to remain the most evident thematic sources of Puerto Rican cultural works in the United States.

To expose and denounce such negative conditions, writers like Tato Laviera draw vital inspiration from the struggle to resist the conspiring forces of assimilation and exclusion, forced incorporation and endemic inequality. Their main recourse is the spirit of national, or "ethnic," affirmation that has been the other face of the colonial history of the Puerto Rican people, both on the Island through the centuries and over the decades as immigrants in the United States. Symbols of indigenous and slave opposition to Spanish rule are held up against the leveling effects of cultural imperialism, as is the militant courage of the Puerto Rican Nationalists, from Pedro Albizu Campos to Lolita Lebrón. These strains of the national legacy, though, most commonly appear in direct interaction with complementary expressive resources available in the immediate North American setting. Among the poets, this admixture is most evident in the bilingual technique itself, with its characteristic switching between colloquial Puerto Rican Spanish and a variety of urban American English, the latter often the dominant literary idiom. The effect is generally suggestive of contemporary black and Chicano poetry, but always with a distinctively Puerto Rican reference and expressive quality.

What makes Laviera's work particularly interesting is that in it, this Nuyorican potential finds unusually sustained realization, and that, as the title indicates, contemporary Puerto Rican experience in the United States is evoked by a direct response to the classic dramatization of the migration process in the national literature. *La carreta*, which traces the archetypal Puerto Rican journey from rural origins to the San Juan slums to the South Bronx, is a drama written in 1953 by René Marqués, one of the Island's foremost modern authors.[12] Marqués's death in 1979—the same year that Laviera's book was published—signaled the close of an era in Puerto Rican letters. In his thirty productive years, Marqués worked in a wide variety of literary forms—often with greater artistic success than in *La carreta*—and expressed a range of notions about Puerto Rican politics and culture. But it was *La carreta* that became widely familiar to Puerto Rican and international audiences and came to be extolled for over a generation as the classic literary rendition of recent Puerto Rican history.

In *La carreta*, the entire migration experience is presented as a process of abrupt moral and cultural deterioration. By the time we meet them in their dilapidated Bronx tenement, the "typical" *jíbaro* family, extended around the matriarch Doña Gabriela, has been so traumatized by their collision with a hostile, technocratic Anglo-Saxon society that their only hope for salvation is in return to the Island and the resumption of peasant life on the land. The "oxcart," guiding symbol of the play and an abiding reminiscence of abandoned national roots, must be restored to its natural place in a world uncontaminated by inhuman modernity and incompatible foreign values. The final vision of a regained life of decency on the sacred soil never fails to capture the minds and hearts of Puerto Ricans of all ages, especially the thousands who have lived through that disillusioning migration process firsthand.

Tato Laviera, who was raised as a child of *La carreta*, picks up where Marqués left off; his book, though not written in dramatic form, may be read as the "fourth act" sequel to Marqués's work. It is anything but a faithful continuation, though, since Laviera's task went beyond that of merely filling in the twenty-five years that elapsed since Marqués wrote his influential play. For Laviera, *La carreta* is not only old-fashioned but fundamentally misleading. In fact, René Marqués is considered to have steered the metaphorical Puerto Rican oxcart in the wrong direction, and *La Carreta Made a U-Turn* is an attempt to set it back on the course of real historical and cultural experience. As the "Nuyorican" corrective to an imposing national self-image, Laviera's poetry thus provides a focus for critical insights into the problems of Puerto Rican identity and assimilation in contemporary U.S. society.

The most obvious of these problems is the perennial question of return to the Island, or more generally, of the direction in which Puerto Rican migrants are headed. Laviera recognizes that, even with the substantial return migration of the past decade, going back "home" has not been the typical fate of Puerto Ricans who have come to the United States or of their offspring born here. Nor should nostalgia for the "old country" be taken uncritically as their inherent disposition or aspiration. For the most part, Puerto Ricans are here to stay, as Laviera suggests in the rather irreverent homage to his own boyhood that begins the volume:

> papote sat on the stoop
> miseducated   misinformed
> a blown-up belly of malnutrition
> papote sat on the stoop
> of an abandoned building
> he decided to go nowhere.

This is the first, most evident meaning of the "u-turn": the oxcart, rather than pointing to the long-lost byways of Puerto Rico—Marqués's own reversal of direction—is proceeding ever more deeply into the thick of North American life. Laviera titles the first part of his collection "Metropolis Dreams," a deliberate reference to the final act of *La carreta*, "La metrópoli," where the nightmarish urban reality is ultimately transcended in the dream of return to the native land. Laviera's "dreams," on the other hand, are intrinsically bound up with the metropolitan nightmare, and Puerto Rico no longer harbors any such physical or emotional release—at least not in the melodramatic, provincial, retrogressive way that Marqués suggests. The thought of return migration by now, for the likes of Laviera, hardly conjures the illusion of pastoral bliss that brought Doña Gabriela and her daughter, Juanita, to their final affirmation of life. As Laviera puts it in his bilingual poem "my graduation speech":

> i want to go back to puerto rico

> but i wonder if my kink could live
> in ponce, mayagüez and carolina
>
> tengo las venas aculturadas
> escribo en spanglish
> abraham in español
> abraham in english
> tato in spanish
> "taro" in english
> tonto in both languages

One of the many ironies about *La Carreta Made a U-Turn* is that it is, indeed, a return to Puerto Rico. The very structure of the book suggests that direction, proceeding as it does from the metropolis to "El Arrabal" (the slum), and from English to Spanish as the prevalent poetic idiom. In fact, there is throughout a closer familiarity with the Island and the Spanish language than is common in Nuyorican writing. But this is surely because Laviera spent his early boyhood in Puerto Rico, moving to New York in 1960. In that, he is different from many of his literary peers and even from such relative "old-timers" as Piri Thomas and Pedro Pietri.

But what binds this work with most others written by Puerto Ricans in the United States is that the view of Puerto Rico is conditioned by formative years lived in New York. As a result, the Puerto Rico to which the Nuyorican oxcart returns is markedly different from the Puerto Rico of the official culture. Laviera's Puerto Rican roots lead neither to the folkloric *jíbaro*, content under the Commonwealth, nor to the glorified pantheon of the national elite—two sources of patriotic pride that are so prominent in Marqués and his works. Rather, going back to Puerto Rico evokes the popular culture of an Afro-Caribbean island, the birthplace of musical and poetic forms like *la bomba, la plena, la décima*, and *el seis*. It is a culture of the slave and peasant masses, the culture of a colonial people who have known not only misery and submission—and pious "decency"—but also joy, creativity and struggle. All these strains of subordinate indigenous expression are invoked and affirmed in *La Carreta Made a U-Turn*.

Yet these expressions are also transformed, since they are in constant reciprocity with the currents and crosscurrents of cultural life in urban United States. Laviera calls his symbolical return to the Island "Nuevo Rumbón," a new path, since it clashes sharply with the dominant cultures of both societies: the elitist Hispanophile tradition of Puerto Rico and the chauvinist White Anglo-Saxon Protestant core of North American values and identity. Posed against both European legacies is the African culture base shared by Caribbean and American blacks. Thus Laviera in "the salsa of bethesda fountain" finds hostility and estrangement in North American society, as was the case in the works of earlier Island-based authors like René Marqués, José Luis González and Pedro Juan Soto. But the young Puerto Rican writers also give voice to a strong sense of cultural unity and solidarity with American blacks:

> a blackness in spanish
> a blackness in english
> mixture-met on jam session in central park,
> there were no differences in
> the sounds emerging from inside

Stylistically, this Afro-Caribbean orientation is present in the hovering influence of Luis Palés Matos, who established African rhythmic possibilities as a core element of Puerto Rican poetry. Laviera's indebtedness to Palés Matos, especially in his poems in Spanish, is conscious and explicit, though he generally adapts, rather than merely imitates, his model. The lines from "tumbao (for eddie conde)" are an example:

> pito que pita
> yuca que llama
> salsa que emprende
> llanto que llora
> última llamada sin fuego
> tumba que la tamba
> tumba que la bamba baja
> que pacheco se inspira
> que ismael la canta
> oh! y el baquiné

"el moreno puertorriqueño" is also within the Afro-Caribbean tradition. Like most of Laviera's verse, this fascinating "three-way warning poem," as he calls it, is meant to be declaimed, and it relies for its full impact on oral presentation.

Laviera's appeal to the non-European roots of colonial cultures, while sometimes veering toward a clichéd spiritualized Africanism, is by no means uncritical or merely escapist. Africa is a source and reference point, not a sacred hermitage: a sympathetic connection to Africa must also be a questioning one if it is to align with present-day realities. Laviera makes this clear in the pensive "the africa in pedro morejón":

> yes, we preserved what was originally african,
> or have we expanded it? i wonder if we have
> committed the sin of blending? but i also hear
> the AFRICANS love electric guitar clearly mis-
> understanding they are the root,
> or is it me who is primitive?
> damn it, it is complicated.

"The american dollar symbol," the poem continues, "that's african; / the british sense of royalty, that's african; / the colors in catholic celebrations, / that's african." And in the closing lines, the appealing mythologies preached by his Afro-Cuban friend seem to dash against the sobering reality of the New York ghetto:

> this high-priest, pedro, telling me all of this
> in front of an abandoned building.

No remote ideals or easy ways out can alter the immediate stage-setting of Puerto Rican life in New York. However much pride and inspiration may be gained from national origins and the Afro-Caribbean heritage, the "abandoned building" is always hauntingly there, the inevitable backdrop and immediate historical circumstance in which those counter-traditions are really at work. Here, in the land of "broken English dreams," as Pietri called it, is where the *carreta* now sits, where masses of Puerto Rican workers have come to live with little prospect of either advancement or return to Puerto Rico.

Laviera is also keenly aware of the political impetus that set the crowded exodus in motion—for him, René Marqués and the postwar migration are both products of the Muñoz Marín era in Puerto Rican history. Luis Muñoz Marín, at the helm of Island politics from 1940–68, and the father of Operation Bootstrap and Free Association Statehood (Commonwealth), kindled the false sense of freedom, mobility and progress that impelled the oxcart to the benevolent North. In "something i heard," Laviera comments bitterly on the hypocrisy of this influential political rhetoric:

> on the streets of san juan
> muñoz marín stands on top
> of an empty milk box
> and brings his land, liberty,
> bread message to a people
> robbed of their existence.
> napoleon's father attentively

> listened as muñoz said, "inde-
> pendence is just around the corner."
>
> napoleon's father took it
> literally, he went around
> the corner and found a donkey
> tied up to a pole.

He lashes out "against muñoz pamphleteering" in another poem, that "hollow sepulcher of words, / words i admired from my mother's eyes, / words that i also imbedded as my dreams." And in direct reference to the migration, "inside my ghetto i learned to understand / your short range visions of where you led us, / . . . your sense of stars landed me in a / north temperate uprooted zone." The populist promises of Muñoz Marín, his patriotism divested of the demand for independence, formed the ideological program for René Marqués and *La carreta*—"el concepto del vocablo PATRIA," as Laviera puts it, "que Luis Muñoz le dio a los carreteros."

From all of these angles and with recurrent irony, Laviera anatomizes the Puerto Rican cultural experience in New York. He reflects critically on all that would give false solace to his uprooted compatriots, as in the memorable "song of an oppressor," directed against the magnetic television novela "Simplemente María," which keeps his poor working-class mother in a state of sentimental hypnosis:

> mami, you sit so calmly
> looking at your novelas . . .
> mami, tears of sacrifice sanctify
> your delicate face, valley of tears
> in your heart
> mami, i love you
> this spirit of love gives me rancor
> and hatred, and i react to the song
> simplemente maría.

And after all, isn't *La carreta* itself like a novela par excellence, a heartrending melodrama of the Puerto Rican migration?

But perhaps Laviera's most penetrating commentary is the very linguistic range and modulation of the poetry itself. Between the English poems that begin the book and the Spanish poems that end it, bilingual switching and blending are employed with consistent dexterity. The overall impression, despite the strategic shift from one language to the other, is one of almost undetectably fluid transition, and from the standpoint of either language tradition, of a qualitative expansion of idiomatic resources. As recent studies of Chicano literature show, bilingual writing entails more than merely utilizing the aggregate of expressive possibilities in each of the vernaculars, as if the options were simply between two fixed vocabularies. More than a poetic device, code switching corresponds directly to the generalized linguistic practices of Puerto Ricans and Chicanos whose experiences gave rise to, and are in turn recaptured in, the representative works of each new generation of writers.

In *La carreta Made a U-Turn*, moreover, as in much Nuyorican writing, bilingual usage is also a matter of thematic concern in its own right, central to what is being said and not merely a device. Laviera's "my graduation speech" is an excellent example, at once an enactment of the linguistic dilemma of Puerto Ricans in the United States and a telling commentary on it. At first glance the poet-persona seems only to be confirming that the jarring clash between Spanish and English has left Puerto Ricans hopelessly inarticulate and illiterate in either language and even in their makeshift "Spanglish." The poem ends:

> hablo lo inglés matao
> hablo lo español matao
> no se leer ninguno bien
>
> so it is, spanglish to matao
> what i digo
>
> ¡ay, virgen, yo no sé hablar!

But a closer look suggests that this cynical castigation of his linguistically crippled countrymen and of the educational system responsible for such an outcome—since it is, after all, his "graduation speech"—is only its most evident intention. The entire poem, in fact, rather than degenerating into sheer nonsense or incoherent rambling, is a carefully structured argument that demonstrates a wealth of expressive potential and a rigorous logical ability. Prefacing his self-mocking "speech" with the succinct paradox, "i think in spanish i write in english," the speaker then offers possible "resolutions" to the conflict—return to Puerto Rico or deliberate gravitation toward one or the other language. Each is rejected, the second not only because his voice does not fit neatly into either exclusive idiom, but also because such a choice would only limit his linguistic virtuosity. Furthermore, the poem illustrates that the apparent contradiction between thought and language ("i think in spanish i write in english") can be and is contraverted in the course of actual conceptualization and verbalization. Thus "¡ay, virgen, yo no sé hablar!" at the close must be understood ironically: the reader is by now aware that the speaker knows what he is saying and can say what he thinks, in both languages and in a wide array of combinations of the two.

Laviera is not claiming to have ushered in a "new language," the tendency at times in the more magniloquent pronouncements of the "Nuyorican renaissance."[13]   Rather, his intention is to illustrate and assess the intricate language contact experienced by Puerto Ricans in New York, and to combat the kind of facile and defeatist conclusions that stem so often from a static, purist understanding of linguistic change. Laviera is emphasizing that the cultural decimation endured by Puerto Ricans in the United States, most glaringly evident in the bewildering, unequal clash between English and Spanish, has another side. Perhaps covertly that same process also involves an enrichment, or a shift of focus, that at the linguistic level serves to define the expressive resources available to the Puerto Rican poet in the United States.

From this critical and realistic perspective, then, Puerto Ricans in the United States are tending toward neither assimilation nor uncritical cultural preservation; they are neither becoming Americans nor continuing to be Puerto Rican in any handed-down or contrived sense. Their historical position as a colonial people at the lowest level of the North American class structure makes either option unfeasible. But what is left is not simply confusion, or cultural anomaly, or a "subculture of poverty," as a wide spectrum of commentators, including René Marqués, Eduardo Seda-Bonilla[14] and Oscar Lewis,[15] conclude. It is a delicate balance, "a tight touch," as Laviera calls a remarkable short poem. Although he casts illusions aside, he is still not disillusioned, but instead builds a new affirmation from the life he sees and feels around him:

> inside the crevice
> deeply hidden in basement land
> inside an abandoned building
> the scratching rhythm of dice
> percussion like two little bongos
> in a fast mambo.
>
> quivering inside this tiny ray
> of sun struggling to sneak in.
>
> the echo of the scent attracted
> a new freedom which said, 'we are
> beautiful anywhere, you dig?'

Despite its personal, idiosyncratic qualities, the work of Tato Laviera is representative of a contemporary cultural movement and embodies the dialectics of everyday language among present-generation Puerto Ricans in the United States. In music, literature, painting, theatre and dance, Puerto Rican artists are giving expression to the experiences of a people at the intersection of two nationalities, in settings provided quite often by important support institutions, such as Taller Boricua, Teatro 4 and Museo del Barrio. Of all the arts, contemporary Puerto Rican music surely suggests the most prolific and most widely proliferating innovations that come from the interweaving of diverse cultural traditions.

Many of these experimental fusions and crossovers, of course, strongly suggest the pluralist melting pot and, regarded partially, seem to indicate that assimilation is indeed in full swing. But because this fused expression is thoroughly conditioned by the abiding colonial relationship, Puerto Rico remains a key source of reference and collective identity, a wellspring of resistance to the arrogant workings of pervasive cultural subordination. At the same time, this artistic output is also firmly grounded in the socio-cultural experience of the larger Puerto Rican population in the United States. It is directly tied to the ongoing struggle for equality in all spheres of social life, such as the demands for bilingual and bicultural education.

But the linkage to the larger, substantially working-class community runs deeper. Most of the cultural spokesmen who make up this movement—and Tato Laviera is but one among many—were raised in working-class families and neighborhoods, and little or nothing in their subsequent social experience has induced them to forget their class origins. Frequently, of course, the lumpen and the unemployed inhabit their works, not the proletariat, because the artistic locus is usually ghetto streets and tenements, not factories or union halls. This divergence from a consistent working-class standpoint is at times severe, so much so that the predominant image remains at the level of *West Side Story* and a kind of "Rican Superfly," and the "art" consists of little more than a strained glorification of ethnic uniqueness. But this lumpen orientation demands qualification, because it is in large measure the actual position of immigrant Puerto Rican workers in the reserve and service sectors of the U.S. labor force. Thus, as the following lines from Laviera's poem to "el sonero mayor" (the musician, Ismael Rivera) make clear, the appeal to the lumpen should not be set apart too rigidly from a more explicit class perspective:

> pero creo que había un vacío
> en su alma, a veces oíamos
> sus canciones pero no lo que

él decía. solamente mi hermano
pablo y todos los compañeros
de la soledad y la ironía:

los de las cárceles ... los de fort worth ... los de lex. ky.
los de la 110 ... los de la castro viña ... los del
barrio obrero ... los de martín peña ... los de puerta
de tierra ... los lumpen pobres de la tierra

* * *

These two dimensions of Puerto Rican language and culture in the United States—national resistance and the vantage point of the have-nots—provide valuable coordinates for assessing the theoretical debate over assimilation. In general, the discussion has laid excessive stress on one or the other, depending on whether the commentator is Puerto Rican or North American. Island-based writers such as Eduardo Seda-Bonilla,[16] Manuel Maldonado-Denis[17] and Luis Nieves-Falcón[18] tend to view assimilation as the fatal assault on the national culture of a colonially oppressed people; many North American social scientists such as Oscar Handlin,[19] Joseph Fitzpatrick[20] and Oscar Lewis[21] interpret assimilation as the problematic insertion of still another ethnic subculture into the variegated current of the North American immigrant experience.

Such a "socio-demographic" approach, which aligns squarely with Milton Gordon's paradigm, fails to recognize, or take account of, the colonial nature of this interaction, and for the most part implicitly, if not forthrightly, denies that Puerto Rico has so much as a national culture. Even the "radical" critiques of this mainstream research model, as for example, in *Divided Society: The Ethnic Experience in America*,[22] attach the issue of ethnic assimilation too mechanically to factors of economic and social mobility to assist reliably in assessing the specific cultural direction of Puerto Ricans as a colonial "minority." Increased economic advantage with inevitable cultural integration—often in the supposedly egalitarian, pluralist sense—is still the abiding assumption.

Puerto Rican commentators usually steer clear of these illusions; they see assimilation as the forceful loss of the national culture in its glaringly unequal contest with imposed foreign values. There is, of course, a formidable tradition of assimilationism and cultural accommodation among colonial thinkers, couched most typically in cosmopolitan Occidentalist terms. The writings of Eugenio Fernández Méndez[23] clearly exemplify this tradition, though many of the apologists for Commonwealth status, with all their appeals to the cultural patrimony, share the same universalizing orientation.

But the Puerto Rican intellectuals who have been most vocal about the assimilation process in the United States generally depart from anti-imperialist, cultural nationalist premises. Among them, Seda-Bonilla and Nieves Falcón lean more heavily on North American sociology, while Maldonado-Denis, José Luis González[24] and Juan Angel Silén[25] attempt to ground their interpretations in a Marxist framework. They are in agreement, though, in their stress on racial and linguistic differences, which stem from the social oppression of a colonized nationality, as the essential defining element in the cultural experience of Puerto Ricans in the United States.

This political emphasis is appropriate, particularly as a means to counteract the immigrant analogy and ethnic pluralism that pervade North American analysis. Social scientists in the United States tend to reduce the national and colonial dimension, but the Puerto Rican writers fall into reductionism, too, although of a different kind. They pose the clash of national cultures as an absolute polarity, with each culture understood in static, undifferentiated and outdated terms. Thus any disappearance of Puerto Rican traits and the taking on of present U.S. cultural lifeways signifies the surrender of the Hispanic tradition to that of Anglo-Saxon—in a word, assimilation. The complex class dynamic at work in both Puerto Rican and North American history, and at the basis of the migration itself, falls from view in this assessment.

Yet both the overarching Hispanic and Anglo-Saxon traditions have been subject to constant challenge from cultural forces within their own societies, forces that are subordinate and oppositional and that may therefore converge in ways that cannot be written off as mere "assimilation." Upward mobility is not involved here, nor does such convergence necessarily indicate the abandonment of authentic national "roots." One thinks of the indigenous and Afro-Caribbean traditions in Puerto Rican culture and how they interweave with black and other Caribbean cultures in the United States. Even the elements of coercion and inequality, so central in culture contact within an imperialist framework, play no role in this kind of interaction. Rather, shared and parallel social experiences primarily influence the cultures and language practice of working people.

At the level of popular culture, as distinct from the dominant national heritage of each society, the question of assimilation must be viewed from an angle quite different from that of the opposing flanks in the theoretical debate. Popular culture not only places in question the privileged status of the elite tradition, which presumes to define the indispensable features of entire cultures, but is also in constant tension with the very tenets of "nationality" itself, to the extent that these tenets are confining and at odds with other sources of social identity. In this respect, a strong countercurrent to the assimilation process that affects Puerto Ricans in the United States entails an "internationalization" of inherited cultural experience. The works of a representative Puerto Rican writer such as Tato Laviera and the bilingual speech characteristics of the community as a whole seem to elude categorization in terms of the current intellectual controversy; both testify to a cultural transformation that would break clear of the bounds set by a narrow national reference, without submitting to the leveling effect of some catch-all multicultural pluralism.

Finally, such a unifying culture and language contact also goes beyond the notion of ethnic unity of nonwhites or Third World minorities, as expounded, for instance, by Manuel Maldonado-Denis,[26] among Puerto Rican thinkers, and by Robert Blauner[27] in the United States. The strength of this appeal to Third World solidarity lies in its insistence on a qualitative distinction between "immigrant" and "colonial" minorities, and points correctly to unity among racially oppressed groups as their first and most immediate path of political alignment. For this reason, the Third World perspective is properly regarded as a progressive, anti-imperialist position, since it undercuts the relativist understanding of ethnicity at the heart of cultural pluralist theory. Interestingly enough, in their exclusive emphasis on nonwhite as a social category, both Maldonado-Denis and Blauner (among others) allow the national dimension to collapse into another version of racial and ethnic classification, thereby extracting it, once again, from the socio-economic context.

The case against this line of interpretation is well stated by Peter Kwong in *Chinatown, N.Y.*, when he argues:

> What I am trying to get away from [in advocating a "national approach" based on political and class analysis] is the all-too-common tendency to use "racial" factors to explain the condition of minorities in this country. To assert that selection and discrimination are a result of pigmentation and physical characteristics is both unscientific and imprecise; it fails to explain the many subtle differences in the way the United States social system operates vis-a-vis each racial group, as well as to encompass within its framework class divisions within such groups . . . And although physical characteristics obviously play a part in such discrimination, the theory of "race," as opposed to a "national" approach, can only provide a superficial and generalized explanation of a national group's experience.[28]

What Peter Kwong cc   nic reductionism"—the term used by
Colin Greer in his ess   Class"[29] —is historical interpretation

grounded in an understanding of the class dynamic at work both within each group and in its particular relation to the larger society. The value of the historical method in the study of Puerto Rican culture in the United States is obvious, since most commentary on Puerto Rican acculturation, whether here or in Puerto Rico, goes back no farther than the 1950s; such commentary fails to draw on the wealth of relevant insights in such important documents about the earlier decades as *Memorias de Bernardo Vega*[30] and Jesús Colon's *A Puerto Rican in New York*.[31]

The filling in of multiple antecedents to the process in its more recent manifestations is indeed necessary, but the full historical picture must also include considerations regarding the likely tendencies for both the short-term and long-term future. Here, in addressing the need for a reliable prognosis, the question of cultural transformation can be seen to mesh inextricably with political analysis. The usual conclusion is to say that Puerto Ricans in the United States are caught up in a process of "transition." We must ask, transition to what, total incorporation or perennial national disadvantage and exclusion? Whether resolutions are primarily sought in accumulated adjustments of the existing arrangement or in more basic structural change is decisive. Depending on the magnitude and depth of such change and the role in it played by Puerto Ricans, the entire tortured scenario of accommodation versus self-maintenance could readily fade into historical oblivion.

When the dimensions of class and nationality serve as the basis for analysis, what had seemed the pitiable loss and absorption of the inherited cultural tradition appears as its extension and enrichment through a process of internationalization. From this perspective of interaction among working-class cultures of diverse nationalities—occurring against a backdrop of persistent inequality and commercialist distortion—the very range and desirability of visible historical alternatives become increasingly inclusive in scope. Just as rigorous a study of the linguistic situation of Puerto Ricans in the United States evokes an interpretation of the overall cultural experience, so the debate over the direction of Puerto Rican culture can only be assessed, and advanced, within the full span of pertinent options and horizons.

"Qué assimilated, brother, yo soy asimilao": The Structuring of Puerto Rican Identity in the U.S.

I carry	mis raices
my roots	las cargo
with me	siempre
all the time	conmigo
rolled up	enrolladas
I use them	me sirven
as my pillow	de almohada

Francisco Alarcón

A young Chicano friend, on a recent first visit to New York City, shared with me some interesting impressions of the Puerto Ricans there and made comparisons with his own people in the Southwest. Of course he was reeling with the similarities between the huge Spanish-speaking neighborhoods of New York and Los Angeles where all your senses inform you that you are in Latin America, or that some section of Latin America has been transplanted to the urban United States where it maintains itself energetically, while interacting directly and in intricate ways with the surrounding cultures. Chicanos and Puerto Ricans in the U.S., the present pillars of the so-called "Hispanic" minority, stand at the same juncture, straddling North and South America and embodying the unequal, oppressive relation between them. And Francisco, a sensitive student of Chicano culture, suddenly became even more aware of the remarkable cultural convergence and correspondences that accompany such shared historical experiences. "¡Somos Raza! ¡Somos Latinos!"

First published in *The Journal of Ethnic Studies* 13/3 (Fall 1985): 1–16. A Spanish translation appeared in *Casa de las Américas* 26/152 (Sept–Oct 1985): 54–63.

he would say, thinking of El Barrio and the Lower East Side, and of East Los and La Misión. We are bilingual and bicultural, and for both Chicanos and Nuyoricans those terms signal a complex duality of transcendence and denial, harmony and imposition, solidarity and disadvantage.

Yet, along with this suddenly heightened sense of Hispanic unity and cultural complementarity, Francisco also began to make note of differences, ways in which the Nuyorican position in U.S. society diverges from that of his fellow Chicanos. The most obvious of these, in his view, was the closeness between Puerto Ricans and Blacks. Of course Chicanos and African Americans have long shared a common cause as victims of racism and exploitation, and comprise natural allies in political and social movements. Culturally, too, there has been ample interaction, but nothing resembling the intensity and extent of influence between Black and Puerto Rican cultures in New York. El Barrio flows off imperceptibly into Harlem, Williamsburgh into Bedford-Stuyvesant, while, by contrast, sharper lines seem to separate East Los Angeles from Watts, and other Southwest barrios from their adjacent Black neighborhoods. Wherever he looked and listened, Francisco witnessed young Puerto Ricans and New York Blacks talking and walking in the same manner, singing and dancing with the same style and often seeming indistinguishable in appearance and action. He heard Nuyorican poetry and salsa, and detected more Afro-American language and rhythms than anything familiar to him in Chicano expression. He saw the Guardian Angels in the subways and Black and Puerto Rican families co-habiting the tenements and housing projects. He heard about the Black and Puerto Rican legislative caucus in Albany and the programs in Black and Puerto Rican studies in the colleges. He even took in the movie "Wild Style" and was amazed at the integral participation of both groups in forms of contemporary street art and performance, like graffiti, rap music and break dancing.

You just don't see as much of that out West, he concluded, his fascination at the phenomenon betraying both admiration and perplexity. Together, we groped for explanations, recognizing that it was important to account for this notable divergence between two groups—Nuyoricans and Chicanos—otherwise so compatible and constituent of a common "Latino" identity. We realized that underlying all the other reasons having to do with factors of social history, geographical placement, migratory patterns and even racial characteristics, the Nuyoricans' relatively closer cultural proximity to U.S. Blacks is based on their Caribbean origins and, even beyond that, with Africa. We couldn't carry the point much further, but were confident that the Afro-Caribbean traditions borne by Nuyoricans in the new setting, even light-skinned Puerto Ricans and the many who might even look like Chicanos, made for a more fluid, reciprocal relation with the culture of Black

Americans. Maybe African Americans are to Puerto Ricans, Francisco suggested, what Native Americans are to Chicanos—a kind of cultural tap root, a latent bond to ethnic sources indigenous to the United States, yet radically challenging to the prevailing cultural hierarchy.

This probing of differences led us back to a sense of the parallels between our two groups, but this time the convergences were of a deeper, more subtle kind than those indicated by our common label as "Hispanics." Beneath and beyond that officially promoted category of Spanish language minority, Chicanos and Nuyoricans are caught up in a similar spiritual dynamic, one which, in each case, meshes "outside" and "inside," Latin American background and the internal U.S. cultural context. The close, long-standing interaction between Puerto Ricans and Blacks, and between Chicanos and Native Americans, exposes the superficiality and divisiveness of the term "Hispanic" in its current bureaucratic usage. It became clear that for either group to accept that rubric at face value would mean to agree to relegating and ultimately severing a crucial nexus in its quest for collective identity. This, we felt, was an important lesson to absorb at a time when loudly publicized projections of "Hispanics" as the "fastest growing minority" are setting off waves of Anglo hysteria and some defensive jitters among leaders of other oppressed.

What the Chicano observer could only dimly appreciate on his brief visit, though, was that the striking affinity between Puerto Ricans and Blacks in New York is but one thread in a complex fabric of Third-World cultures cohabiting the inner city neighborhoods and institutions. Emigrants and refugees from many of the Caribbean and Latin American countries are now entering their second and even third generation of presence there, with Dominicans, Jamaicans and Haitians adding most substantially to the Caribbeanization of New York begun by Puerto Ricans and Cubans before them. Add the sizeable numbers of Asian and Arab peoples, and the non-European complexion of the city's multi-ethnic composite becomes still more prominent. As each group and regional culture manifests itself in the new setting, and as they increasingly coalesce and interact in everyday life, New York is visibly becoming the source of a forceful, variegated alternative to mainstream North American culture.

For this crossing and blending of transmitted colonial cultures is not to be confused with the proverbial "melting pot" of Anglo-American fantasy, nor is it a belated example of "cultural pluralism" as that phrase is commonly used in U.S. social science and public discourse. Though characterized by the plurality and integration of diverse cultures, the process here is not headed toward assimilation with the dominant "core" culture, nor even toward respectful coexistence with it. Rather, the individual and interweaving cultures involved are expressions of histories of conquest, enslavement and forced incorporation at the hands of the prevalent surrounding society. As such, the main thrust in each case is toward self-affirmation and association with other cultures caught up in comparable processes of historical recovery and strategic resistance.

The path of "assimilation in American life" has been amply charted in U.S. social science and codified in paradigmatic terms by Milton Gordon.[1] The guiding model rests firmly on analogies to the experiences of European immigrant groups. The attempts at modification, and even rejoinders to this approach pronounced with a view toward cases complicated by racial stigmatization and prolonged economic and social disadvantage, have largely gone to reinforce that familiar image of cultural shedding, adjustment and reincorporation. The theory of "internal colonialism," no doubt the most consistent rejection of the reigning ethnic ideology, nevertheless retains the vision of each minority group forming its sense of identity in its relation to, and self-differentiation from, the dominant Anglo culture. Colonial minority resistance to assimilation is still presented as occurring within the pluralist field of options and with its sight set, however resentfully, on that very ethnic mosaic from which it is being excluded. Each group manifests itself singularly in its own terms and primarily as an effort at cultural maintenance over against that which negates it.[2]

The interaction among popular colonial cultures in New York suggests a markedly different process, one which is indeed pluralist and confluent in nature and perhaps for that reason even more challenging to established thinking on ethnic relations. But if the transformation of Puerto Rican culture in the U.S. setting is something other than assimilation, what is it? How is it to be defined in terms other than loss of the old and acquisition of the new, or as the fateful confrontation between two unequal and mutually exclusive cultural monoliths? The problem is clearly more than a terminological one, for it has to do with detecting a developmental pattern leading neither to eventual accommodation nor to "cultural genocide." Beyond these two options, characteristic respectively of North American and Island-based Puerto Rican commentary on the Nuyorican experience, a more intricate structuring of ethnicity is evident.

In the following I will seek to trace some contours of this alternative dynamic. Though focussing on Nuyorican culture as expressed in its poetry, my observations may be readily generalized to apply to other colonial minorities, with samples of poetic discourse simply serving as distilled representations of other aspects of cultural life. A further qualification is that I have in mind primarily the contemporary generation of Puerto Ricans living in New York City; again it is hoped that my comments also help to clarify, with a minimum of distortion, the cultural experience of earlier generations and of Puerto Ricans in other parts of the U.S. Finally, any interpretation of cultural process presupposes a coherent analysis of the conditioning political and economic reality, in this case colonialism, labor migration, patriarchy and racial inequality. Such an analysis, as it is being advanced by fellow researchers at the Center for Puerto Rican Studies and elsewhere, forms the basis of my present reflections.[3]

* * *

One can see four definitive moments in the awakening of Nuyorican cultural consciousness which are linked by three transitional phases from one field to the other. The moments are not necessarily stages in a chronological sense, nor do the transitions follow one another in any set order. I will present them as a sequence for hypothetical purposes, understanding that what I am describing is really more a range of constantly intersecting possibilities and responses arising simultaneously at the individual and collective levels.

The first moment is the here and now, the Puerto Rican's immediate perception of the New York that surrounds the person. Prior to any cultural associations or orientations, there are the abandoned buildings, the welfare lines, the run-down streets, the frigid winter nights with no heat, in short, the conditions of hostility, disadvantage and exclusion that confront the Puerto Rican in day-to-day reality. Corresponding to the absence of economic and political opportunity is the lack of cultural access and direction of any kind: the doors to the prevailing culture are closed. One young writer aptly refers to this sense of emptiness as the "state of abandon,"[4] and another, thinking of his own boyhood, characterizes it in the following lines:

> papote sat on the stoop
> miseducated   misinformed
> a blown-up belly of malnutrition
> papote sat on the stoop
> of an abandoned building
> he decided to go nowhere.[5]

It is this very moment of the Puerto Rican experience in New York that is typically isolated and sensationalized by the dominant culture, as in entertainment packages from "West Side Story" to "Fort Apache" and in social pathologies like Oscar Lewis's *La Vida.*[6] The mass public is made to delight in this drama of sheer desperation and brutality, particularly when it is also comforted with the thought that such "subcultural" misery is, after all, self-inflicted. And, indeed, for many Puerto Ricans themselves the only recourse in the face of this estranging here and now often involves damage and jeopardy and, of course, disproportionate social recrimination.

But for a variety of reasons, often having little to do with the existing educational system, awareness turns in the direction of the second moment: Puerto Rico. The passage from the immediacy of New York to the Puerto Rican cultural background is generally less geographical than spiritual and psychological, its impetus deriving from the intimacy of family life with nostalgic reminiscences of parents and grandparents. It tends to present a romanticized, idealized image of Puerto Rico, and is only rarely informed by any political account of the migration and the colonial conditions that propelled it.[7] A memorable example of this transition from ghetto to garden, from infernal New York to edenic Puerto Rico, may be found in the opening chapters of Piri Thomas's autobiographical novel *Down These Mean Streets*. Piri remembers that as a child during the Depression years, his mother used to warm the frigid winter nights with her soothing words about the "quiet of the greenlands and the golden color of the morning sky, the grass wet from the *lluvia*." And that other Nuyorican "classic," Pedro Pietri's *Puerto Rican Obituary*, illustrates the same type of contrast; the famous title poem, in fact, is structured as a gradual passage from the deathly tedium, hopelessness and "colonial mentality" of Puerto Rican life in New York to a forceful exhortation to rise from the dead and be transported to a "beautiful place," "where beautiful people sing / and dance and work together / where the wind is a stranger / to miserable weather conditions."[8]

If the first moment is the state of abandon, the second is the state of enchantment, an almost dream-like trance at the striking contrast between the cultural barrenness of New York and the imagined luxuriance of the Island culture. This contrast, often expressed in physical terms as one of cold and warmth, darkness and light, grey and bright green, runs through the literature of the migration, one familiar example being the refrain to the popular song: "Mamá, Borinquen me llama, / este país no es el mío, / Puerto Rico es pura flama, / y aquí me muero de frío." This Puerto Rico, of course, cannot be tested for its historical or even geographical authenticity, since it is initially conjured for metaphorical, emblematic reasons.

While making no claim to realism, the evocation of Puerto Rico cannot be dismissed early as mere archaism, for even the opposition of physical environments implies an ecological and esthetic rejection of the imposed New York conditions. The "rediscovery" of Puerto Rico, however utopian, is thus a constituent in the active search for cultural guidance and meaning in a social context bereft of accessible human bearings. Sandra María Esteves, another of the young New York poets, traces this passage from disorientation to dream to reawakening in her poem entitled "Here":

I am two parts / a person
boricua / spic
past and present
alive and oppressed
given a cultural beauty
... and robbed of a cultural identity

I speak the alien tongue
in sweet borinqueño thoughts
know love mixed with pain
have tasted spit on ghetto stairways
... here, it must be changed
we must change it

I may never overcome
the theft of my isla heritage
dulce palmas de coco on Luquillo
sway in windy recesses I can only imagine
and remember how it was

But that reality now a dream
teaches me to see, and will
bring me back to me.[9]

Clearly, it is not only swaying palm-trees and sunny beaches that the New York Puerto Ricans find in their invoked homeland, as important as that ecological vision may be in the construction of a new identity. It is also "my isla heritage," by which is meant, first of all, a different, more human way of living and relating to people. Beneath the more beautiful landscape the Nuyoricans gain sight of a more appealing culture, one in which they feel included and able to participate. The validation of Spanish is an important initial impetus, even if that means, as in the phrase "my isla heritage," the inclusion of a Spanish word in an English-language context.

More than language, however, the main content of this second moment is the recovered African and indigenous foundation of Puerto Rican culture. Along with increased political awareness comes a more critical relation to the "heritage," and a growing distinction between the official, dominant version of the national culture and its popular base. The racism encountered in the U.S. impels the Nuyorican even more resolutely toward the Taíno and Afro-Caribbean background, which constitutes the major thematic reference point and expressive resource in Puerto Rican culture in the U.S. It is the colonized within the colony whom the Nuyoricans identify as their real forebears in the national tradition, a continuity which is readily evident in much of the music, poetry and art, and in many aspects of daily life.

The continuum is popular culture, the culture of poor and working-class Puerto Ricans spanning the centuries and the process of emigration and re-settlement. For at the popular level, the formation of the national culture exemplifies the very transculturation and interaction of diverse racial and language cultures which is so systematically obstructed and feared in the fa-miliar U.S. setting. It is possible for new cultures to emerge without loss or abandonment of the old, certainly a vital lesson for young Puerto Ricans be-ing pressed into a foreign mold. Recognizing that this so-called "syncretism" has occurred in Puerto Rico under conditions of colonial domination and racial and social inequality further deepens the Nuyoricans' understanding of the social dynamic and points to the class dimension of cultural change.

That which begins as and appears on the surface to be no more than the nostalgic, metaphorical evocation typical of an immigrant sensibility is in the Puerto Rican case an apprenticeship in social consciousness, the reconstructed "patria" serving as the relevant locus of cultural interaction and contention. Identification with the popular traditions within the colonial culture not only exposes the racial and class hierarchy which during the first moment, in the New York here and now, the Nuyorican could only confront at an immediate, experiential level. Popular culture also represents the current of resistance and opposition to that system and, in larger terms, a mode and function of cultural production different from that of both the dominant elite culture and the commercially packaged mass culture. In this sense, the legacy of oral traditions and artisan craft finds a direct extension in Nuyorican artistic expression. The reliance on improvisation and performance, and the abiding conception of expressive resources as tools, help counteract the pressure toward standardization and the estrangement of culture from its personal and social origins.

The third moment is located back in New York, but the passage there, the return and reentry, is infused with those new perspectives gathered in the course of cultural recovery. While previously, during the first moment, life was sheer hostility and exclusion, the New York scene now includes the Puerto Ricans, if only by force of their own deliberate self-insertion into the urban landscape. Looking at New York, the Nuyorican sees Puerto Rico, or at least the glimmering imprint of another world to which vital connections have been struck. This transposition of the cultural background finds cogent expression in the poetry of Víctor Hernández Cruz, who ends his poem "Los New Yorks" with the stanza, "I am going home now / I am settled there with my fruits / Everything tastes good today / Even the ones that are grown here / Taste like they're from outer space / Walk y suena / Do it strange / Los New

Yorks." And in a short poem entitled "BronxOmania," the poet discovers Puerto Rico while riding in the subway:

> snake horse stops at bronx clouds
> end of lines and tall windowed cement
> comes to unpaved roads and wilderness
> where the city is far
> and spanish bakeries sell hot bread
> the roar of the iron snake
> plunges at closing doorways
> down fifty blocks
> is the island of Puerto Rico.[10]

This atmospheric, visionary presence of the homeland, so pervasive in the literature of the migration, is again the outward indication of an awakened cultural consciousness. The spiritual orientation gained through recapturing the Puerto Rican background conditions this renewed encounter with New York, lending meaning and historical perspective to what had been a scene of sheer abandonment and disorientation. The predicament of bilingualism, for example, which confronted the Nuyorican in the first moment as a confining and prejudicial dilemma with no visible resolution, now becomes an issue of social contention and beyond that, a sign of potential enrichment and advantage. Though not a socially recognized asset, bilingual discourse and continued access to Spanish have been a major element in the reinforcement of Puerto Rican cultural identity and in the self-definition of a group demonstrating the full range of Spanish-English language contact.

The racial situation is also altered as a result of the imaginative passage to and from the site of cultural origins. The divisions, confusions and inescapable degradations suffered by Puerto Ricans because of the Black versus White polarities of U.S. racial classification give way to a proud identification with Afro-Caribbean cultural traditions. The influence of the Civil Rights and Black Power movements were, of course, of direct importance to the Nuyorican revival of the late 1960s, but recognizing a similar thrust in the re-interpretation of their own cultural heritage contributed greatly to this active affirmation of African roots. Furthermore, the multi-racial composition of the Puerto Rican people and the elaborate process of mixing evident in the formation of the national culture suggest a more dynamic, historically differentiated relation between race and culture than was conceivable to the Puerto Ricans in their direct, unreflected subjection to U.S. racism.

The Nuyorican also reenters New York with a heightened sense of the duality of cultural life and expression, the differences and interrelationships between official and commercially produced culture on the one hand and

popular culture on the other. Thus, in addition to the cultivation of indigenous and Afro-Puerto Rican sources such as *la bomba* and *la plena* in the
music and the Afro-Antillean rhythm and language of Luis Palés Matos in
the poetry, Nuyorican expression responds to and articulates the creative
experience of the people. Instead of the cultural vacuum characteristic of
the state of abandon, the feeling that there is and can be no culture where
the only concern is survival and coping, there is now a recognition that the
life of poor people is a legitimate and abundant source of cultural energy.
This validation of popular culture is present in the conversational and colloquial qualities of Nuyorican poetic language and in the common emphasis
on public performance and delivery. Exposure to traditional Puerto Rican
forms like the *décima, controversia* and *plena* makes clear to the Nuyorican that the cultural life of his people is one of improvisation, communal
participation and commentary on topical local events.

All of these horizons of the re-encounter with New York through Puerto
Rican eyes comprise what can most aptly be considered an awakened national consciousness, or consciousness of nationality. For taken together and
brought to bear on the U.S. context, such new and otherwise concealed perspectives on language, race and cultural dynamics constitute an assertion of
national origins. "En el fondo del nuyorican hay un puertorriqueño," one of
the poets has said, paraphrasing the title of a well-known short story by José
Luis González.[11] Despite the endless endeavor to reduce Puerto Rican cultural identity to more manageable terms of language group, race or ethnicity,
and thus to insert it into some larger aggregate, the third moment of Nuyorican awareness actually involves an introduction of the national dimension
to U.S. ethnic relations. For it is on that basis, as a lingually, racially and
culturally distinctive national group, that Nuyoricans define their identity
in the U.S. And it is on that basis that they constitute their position in the
society and their relation to other cultures.

The fourth moment is this branching-out, the selective connection to
and interaction with the surrounding North American society. Generally,
of course, this experience is considered in isolation, with the overriding
concern being the issue of Puerto Rican assimilation. The advantage of
tracing the various moments surrounding and conditioning that controversial
point of intersection is to suggest that there is a complex process involved,
which is by no means unreflected, unidirectional or limited to the options of
incorporation or self-exclusion. When account is taken of the full trajectory
and shifting geography of Nuyorican identification, it becomes clear that
something other than assimilation or cultural separation is at work.

The first path of Puerto Rican interaction with North American culture is
toward those groups to whom they stand in closest proximity, not only spa-

tially but also because of congruent cultural experience. For Puerto Ricans in New York, this means, first of all, Black Americans and other migrants from the Caribbean and Latin America. With such groups, a strong process of cultural convergence and fusion occurs, what one commentator, J.M. Blaut, has called "the partial growing-together of the cultures of ghettoized communities."[12] This "growing-together" is often mistaken for assimilation, but the difference is obvious in that it is not directed toward incorporation into the dominant culture. For that reason, the "pluralism" that results does not involve the dissolution of national backgrounds and cultural histories but their continued affirmation and enforcement even as they are transformed. Given the basis of social parity among groups with a common cultural trajectory, the very relation between unity and diversity contrasts with that operative in the established scheme of ethnic pluralism.

It is from the vantage of this coalescence with the cultures of other colonial minorities that Puerto Ricans assume collective interaction with the Anglo-American society at large. The branching-out is selective, with a gravitation toward other popular cultures with a background of social disadvantage: the Chinese, the Arabs and, more cautiously, the Irish, Italians and Jews. It is a fusion, significantly, at the popular level of shared working-class reality, and one expressive of recognized marginalization and exclusion. And because it involves the retention and extension of the inherited cultures rather than their abandonment, the process has remarkable cultural consequences, described by Blaut as "the healthy interfertilization of cultures, the efflorescence of new creative forms in painting, poetry, music, and the like, and the linking up of struggles."[13]

Even at that point, as Nuyorican modes of expression come to intermingle with others and thus distinguish themselves from those of the Island legacy, it is not accurate to speak of assimilation. Rather than being subsumed and repressed, Puerto Rican culture contributes, on its own terms and as an extension of its own traditions, to a new amalgam of human expression. It is the existing racial, national and class divisions in U.S. society which allow for, indeed necessitate, this alternative course of cultural change.[14]

*   *   *

Such, then, are four moments of Nuyorican cultural interaction with U.S. society, briefly summarized as the here-and-now, Puerto Rican background, reentry and branching out. Again, they are not necessarily to be taken as sequential stages in the manner in which I have presented them but as fields of experience joined by transitional phases of cultural awareness. How and to what extent these moments of sensibility relate to the advance of political consciousness is even another, more complicated matter. It is clear, in any case, that Puerto Rico not only serves as an imaginary realm of cultural self-discovery, but must also be recognized as a nation whose political status looms large on the agenda of international relations. The quest for Puerto Rican identity in the United States thus remains integrally tied to the prospects of national independence or continued colonial subordination to or, as the official euphemism would have it, "association" with the United States. Generally speaking, the gathering of cultural consciousness on the part of the Nuyoricans inclines them toward the first of these options.

It will also be necessary, with further study, to elaborate the correspondences between the cultural geography outlined here and the multiple spatial directions of the Puerto Rican migration. I would only suggest that the spiritual movement back and forth between New York and Puerto Rico bears some significant correlation to the migratory circulation of Puerto Ricans in the ongoing exchange of workers for capital under colonial conditions. In the Puerto Rican case, neither the migration itself nor the cultural encounter with U.S. society is a one-way, either/or, monolithic event. Rather, it is one marked by further movement and the constant interplay of two familiar yet contrasting zones of collective experience.[15]

I would conclude by acknowledging that the structure of the Puerto Rican's coming-to-consciousness which I present here as my own invention actually dawned on me as I read the work of another poet friend, Tato Laviera. For Laviera's three books of poems to date, when read in succession, take us through the entire journey, each volume giving voice to one of the passages from one moment to the next. The first, *La carreta Made a U-Turn* focuses on the contrast between the New York here-and-now and the Puerto Rico of enchantment and cultural richness.[16] The second book, entitled *En Clave* or *Enclave*,[17] transports that meaning gathered from the national culture and establishes a distinctive place for it in the re-encountered New York setting. And the third, most recent volume, *AmeRícan*, is the branching out, the striking of sympathetic chords with other cultural groups on the basis of expansive Puerto Rican sounds and rhythms. The poet ranges widely in his "ethnic tributes," as he entitles a substantial part of the book, addressing and embracing many of the adjacent peoples in the crowded New York environs. One of the heartiest of these embraces is called "jamaican":

> reaches their guts into the Caribbean
> the second africa, divided by yemaya
>
> reaches their guts into the third world,
> marley-manley emerging people
>
> reaches their guts into urban america,

reggae-reggae, modern english.

reaches their guts into ethiopia,
rastafarian celebrated deities.

reaches their guts into washington sq. park,
jamaican english, folkloric blackness,
reaches their guts into puerto ricans,
where we shared everything for free,
yeah, brother, very good, very, very
good, yeah, real good![18]

Here is the young Puerto Rican re-fashioning New York City along
Caribbean, Third World lines, or voicing resonantly his awareness that history is doing so.

Yet as is clear from the neologistic title "AmeRícan," Laviera is intent on
reaching beyond the New York enclave. He seeks to stake a claim for Puerto
Rican recognition before the whole U.S. society, especially as Puerto Ricans
are by now clustered in many cities other than New York. He is goading
the society to come to terms with the "Rican" in its midst, arguing through
puns and ironic challenges that he will not be an American until he can
say "Am-e-Rícan" ("I'm a Rican") and be proud of it. He even diagnoses,
in similar playful terms, the problem of assimilation. "Assimilated?" he
begins one poem, "qué assimilated, brother, yo soy asimilao," and ends with
a confident reference to the Black base of Puerto Rican popular culture,
"delen gracias a los prietos / que cambiaron asimilado al popular asimilao."

And in reaching across the U.S., not assimilating but growing together
with neighboring and concordant cultures, how could the Nuyorican poet
fail to embrace the Chicano? Getting to Chicago, Houston and Los Angeles,
Tato Laviera surely sensed what Francisco felt during his days in New York.
Chicanos and Nuyoricans, concentrated at opposite ends of the country,
branching out in different cultural directions, still exemplify a close cultural
affinity.

As a final note, listen to Tato Laviera, the Nuyorican, rapping to his
Chicano brothers. Here again, in "Vaya carnal," it is the poet affirming a
new language mix, "Chicano-riqueño," and at the same time forging those
deeper cultural links which unite Mexicans and Puerto Ricans beneath the
"Hispanic" surface:

Vaya, carnal
sabes, pinche, que me visto
estilo zoot suit marca de

pachuco royal chicano air
force montoyado en rojo
azul verde marrón nuevo
callejero chicano carnales
eseándome como si el ese ese
echón que se lanza en las
avenidas del inglés con
treinta millones de batos
locos hablando en secreto
con el chale-ese-no-la chingues
vacilón a los gringos americanos,
¿sabes?, simón, el sonido del este
el vaya, clave, por la maceta
que forma parte de un fuerte
lingüismo, raza, pana, borinquen,
azteca, macho, hombre, pulmones
de taíno, de indios, somos
chicano-riqueños, que curado.
simón, qué quemada mi pana,
la esperanza de un futuro
totalmente nuestro,
tú sabes, tú hueles,
el sabor, el fervor del
vaya, carnal.[19]

One of the many "casitas" found in "El Barrio" and the South Bronx, New York City, ca. 1990. Photographer Martha Cooper. Courtesy of Martha Cooper.

Living Borders / *Buscando América*: Languages of Latino Self-Formation

Latinos as a Social Movement

"My grandparents didn't get special language instruction in school. In fact they never finished high school because they had to work for a living." Latinos hear this and similar statements every time the question of bilingual education comes up. Such statements highlight an important difference— the maintenance of another language and the development of interlingual forms—between this "new" immigrant group and the "older," "ethnic" immigrants. The fact is that Latinos, that very heterogeneous medley of races and nationalities,[1] are different from both the "older" and the "new" ethnics.[2] To begin with, Latinos do not comprise even a relatively homogeneous "ethnicity." Latinos include native-born U.S. citizens (predominantly Chicanos—Mexican-Americans—and Nuyoricans—"mainland" Puerto Ricans) and Latin American immigrants of all racial and national combinations: white—including a range of different European nationalities— Native-American, Black, Arabic and Asian. It is thus a mistake to lump them all under the category "racial minority,"[3] although historically the U.S. experiences of large numbers of Mexican-Americans and Puerto Ricans are adequately described by this concept.[4] Moreover, both of these groups—unlike any of the European immigrant groups—constitute, with Native-Americans, "conquered minorities."[5]

If not outright conquered peoples, other Latin American immigrants heretofore inhabitants of the "back yard" over which the United States claims the right of manifest destiny, have migrated here for both political and economic reasons, in part because of U.S. intervention in their homelands.

Co-authored with George Yúdice. Published in *Social Text* 24 (Fall, 1990): 57–84.

From the time of José Martí, who lived in New York for over one third of his life during the 1880s and 1890s, slowly establishing the foundations for the Cuban independence movement, to the 1980s sanctuary movement for Central American refugees, U.S. actions (military incursions as well as economic sanctions) in Latin America have always generated Latin American migrations. The policies of U.S. finance institutions (supported by the U.S. government and, at times, by its military), moreover, have brought enormous foreign debt to Latin America and with it intolerable austerity programs that have induced many to seek a living in the United States.[6]

The result is a U.S. Latino population projected to be over 30 million in 1990, a minority population unprecedented in the history of the United States. Sheer numbers are in themselves influential, but the way in which the numbers increase is more important. As a result of continuous immigration over the last 30 years, as well as the historical back-and-forth migration of Mexican-Americans and Puerto Ricans and more recently of other national groups, Latinos have held on to Spanish over more generations than any other group in history. Ninety percent of U.S. Latinos speak Spanish.[7] In contrast, speakers of Italian dwindled by ninety-four percent from the second to the third generation.[8]

The civil rights movement spurred new forms of consciousness and political action among Chicanos and Nuyoricans. They and other Latinos have been able to use the language issue as a means to mediate diverse types of political enfranchisement and social empowerment: voting reform, bilingual education, employment opportunities, and so on.

In fact, the conditions for identity-formation, in all its dimensions (social, political and especially aesthetic), have been largely provided by the struggle over how to interpret language needs and the adjudication and legislation, on that basis, of civil rights directed primarily (but not exclusively) to Latinos.

In recognition of these conditions, which were not in place when the two major trends in ethnicity theory (the "melting pot" of the early twentieth century and the "new ethnicity" of the '50s and '60s) emerged, we feel that there is greater explanatory power in a "new social movement" approach to Latino identity. By "new social movements" we refer to those struggles around questions of race, gender, environment, religion and so on, which cannot be fully encompassed under the rubric of class struggle and which play out their demands on the terrains of the body, sexuality, language, etc., that is, those areas which are socially constituted as comprising the "private" sphere. This is not to say that the inequalities (and causes rooted in relations of production) referred to by class analysis have disappeared. On the contrary, from the perspective we adopt, such inequalities (and their causes) can be seen to multiply into all spheres of life. Capitalist society does not cause racism any more than it does linguistic stratification; it does, however, make all these differences functional for the benefit of hegemonic groups. A social movement approach does not so much disregard class exploitation as analyze how racism, sexism, linguistic stratification, etc. are mobilized through "both discursive positions and control of the means of production and coercion."[9] Under these circumstances, political agency is, according to Stanley Aronowitz,

> constituted in the gap between the promises of modern demo-
> cratic society and its subversion by the various right-wing states.
> Politics renews itself primarily in extra-parliamentary forms
> which, given the still potent effectivity of the modern state form,
> if not its particular manifestations of governance, draws social
> movements into its orbit. Some call this cooptation, but it is
> more accurate to understand it as a process related to the eco-
> nomic and cultural hegemony of late capitalism, which draws
> the excluded not only by its dream work, but by the political
> imaginary that still occupies its own subjects.[10]

What is particularly different about the new social movements is that they enter the political arena by "address[ing] *power itself* as an antagonist," such that they must deploy their practices in the cultural as well as economic spheres. To understand Latinos, then, we must understand the conditions under which they enter the political arena. Among these conditions, which were not in place when the "ethnic" (European) immigrants negotiated their enfranchisement in the U.S., are the welfare state (which in part brought to the fore the terrains of struggle and which neo-conservatives are currently attempting to dismantle) and the permeation of representation by the consumer market and the media.

In what follows, we explore how Latino identity is mediated and constructed through the struggle over language under such "post-modern" conditions.

The Struggle Over Language

First of all, the name, "America." Extrapolating from Edmundo O'Gorman's meditation on the "invention of America,"[11] we might say that "America" has been conceived over and over again throughout history. The name "remains the same," but it has had successive reconceptualizations (it is rewritten in the Borgesian sense that Pierre Menard rewrote *Don Quixote*) and with each one the terrain changes. The current mass migration of Latinos

to the United States engenders such a process of reconceptualization, bringing to mind F. J. Turner's notion of America as a moving frontier and giving
it another twist so as to invent a new trope: America as a "living border." If
the "discovery" of "America" transformed the ocean into a frontier on whose
other side lay a "new" world, and if that new world was subsequently defined
by the westward movement and capitalization of the margin, under-*writing*
"the record of social evolution"[12] or modernity and providing a " 'safety
valve' for the discontent of a new industrial proletariat"[13] largely comprised
of European immigrants, then the latest reconceptualization of America by
Latinos is a cultural map which is all border, like the inter-lingual speech
(or Spanglish) of Chicanos and Nuyoricans.

> I [. . .] opt for "borderness" and assume my role: My gener-
> ation, the *chilangos* [slang term for a Mexico City native], who
> came to "el norte" fleeing the imminent ecological and social
> catastrophe of Mexico City, gradually integrated itself into oth-
> erness, in search of that other Mexico grafted onto the entrails
> of the et cetera ... became Chicano-ized. We de-Mexicanized
> ourselves to Mexi-understand ourselves, some without wanting
> to, others on purpose. And one day, the border became our
> house, laboratory, and ministry of culture.[14]

Contemporary Latino artists and writers throw back the anxiety of ambivalence cast upon them as an irresolvable perplexity of naming and placing.
Gómez-Peña talks of "this troubled continent accidentally called America"
and "this troubled country mistakenly called America."[15] "AmeRícan," announces Tato Laviera in the title poem of his third book of Nuyorican poetry,
"defining myself my own way many ways Am-e-Rícan, with the big R and
the accent on the í."[16] The hallowed misnomer unleashes the art of brazen
neologism. The arrogance of political geography backfires in the boundless
defiance of cultural remapping. The imposed border emerges as the locus of
re-definition and re-signification. The cover illustration of *AmeRícan* boasts
a day-glo Statue of Liberty holding aloft a huge *pilón* of liberty, the majestic
torch of *comida criolla, ajo y plátano*. Latino taste buds water with *mofongo*
and *mole*. "English only Jamás!," "Sólo inglés, no way!"

Latino affirmation is first of all a fending off of schizophrenia, of that
pathological duality born of contending cultural worlds and, perhaps more
significantly, of the conflicting pressures toward both exclusion and forced
incorporation. Another Nuyorican poet, Sandra María Esteves, thematizes
this existential split in much of her work: "I am two parts / a person boricua /
spic past and present alive and oppressed."[17] Esteves enacts the bewilderment, darting back and forth between unreal options and stammering

tongues, "Being Puertorriqueña Americana Born in the Bronx, not really jíbara Not really hablando bien But yet, not gringa either, Pero ni portorra, pero sí portorra too Pero ni que what am I?"[18] She cannot "really" be both, she realizes, but she senses a unique beauty in her straddling position, and is confident in the assertion, which is the title of her poem, that she is "Not Neither."

Contrary to the monocultural dictates of the official public sphere, the border claims that it is "not nowhere." This first gestus of Latino cultural practice thus involves an emphatic self-legitimation, a negation of hegemonic denial articulated as the rejection of anonymity. Though no appropriate name is available in the standard language repertoires, whether English or Spanish, namelessness is decidedly not an option. Whatever the shortcomings and misconceptions of bureaucratic bilingualism, alinguality is neither the practiced reality nor a potential outcome of Latino expressive life. The interlingual, border voice characteristically summons the tonality of the relegated "private" sphere to counter the muzzling pressure of official public legitimation.

The trope of a border culture is thus not simply another expression of post-modern aesthetic indeterminacy, along the lines of Derrida's decontextualized frame or *parergon*, "the incomprehensibility of the border at the border,[19] or a Baudrillardian simulacrum (*neither* copy *nor* original).[20] The trope emerges, rather, from the ways in which Latinos *deploy* their language in everyday life. It corresponds to an ethos under formation; it is *practice* rather than *representation* of Latino identity. And it is on this terrain that Latinos wage their cultural politics as a "social movement." As such, Latino aesthetics do not pretend to be separate from everyday practices but rather an integral part of an ethos which seeks to be politicized as a means to validation and self-determination. And it is precisely the projection of this ethos into the culture at large and into the political arena which threatens the dominant "Anglo" culture with loss of control of its physical and metaphorical borders. As the shrillest voices of the English-Only movement have put it, such Latino language and cultural practices threaten national unity and security.[21] Latino disregard for "our borders" may result in the transformation of the United States into a "mongrel nation."[22]

> There are misguided persons, specifically Hispanic immigrants, who have chosen to come here to enjoy our freedoms, who would legislate another language, Spanish, as co-equal and co-legal with English … If Hispanics get their way, perhaps someday Spanish could replace English entirely … we ought to remind them, and better still educate them to the fact that the

United States is not a mongrel nation.

Language has been accurately characterized as "an automatic signaling system, second only to race in identifying targets for possible privilege or discrimination."[23] Unpack the discourse against the language of Latinos and you've got a panoply of racist and classist repudiations:

> These children of illegal aliens will remain part of that population which never learns English, and threatens to make America a bilingual country costing the American taxpayer billions of dollars.
>
> Token citizenship will not help poor, unskilled Hispanics when they find themselves in a permanent underclass, isolated by a language barrier. The hopes that brought them here in the first place will turn to despair as they become dependent upon government handouts . . .
>
> Congress has presented the indigenous population of Mexico with an open invitation to walk across our Southern Border.[24]

Language, then, is the necessary terrain on which Latinos negotiate value and attempt to reshape the institutions through which it is distributed. This is not to say that Latino identity is reduced to its linguistic dimensions. Rather, in the current socio-political structure of the United States, such matters rooted in the "private sphere," like language (for Latinos and other minorities), sexuality, body and family definition (for women and gays and lesbians), etc., become the semiotic material around which identity is deployed in the "public sphere." The purpose always seems to be to maintain hegemony or to negotiate empowerment of those groups which have been discriminated against on such bases.

The attack on the perceived linguistic practices of Latinos is a vehicle for attacks on immigration, bilingual education, inclusion of Latinos in the services of the welfare state, and above all, a repudiation of the effect that Latinos are having in reshaping U.S. culture. Furthermore, such attacks highlight the influence that the dominant groups in the U.S. expect Latinos to have on foreign policy. Their rhetoric harbors the fear that U.S. imperialism in Latin American countries is boomeranging and eroding U.S. hegemony.

The language question then is a smoke screen for the scapegoating of Latinos on account of recent economic, social and political setbacks for the United States. "Anglo insecurity" looks to the claims of Latinos and other minority constituencies for the erosion of the United States' position in world leadership, the downturn in the economy and the bleak prospects for social mobility for the next generation.[25] In fact, now that dominant

U.S. national rhetoric seems no longer able to project a global communist bogey, due to political changes in the Soviet Union and Eastern Europe, this rhetoric will increasingly consolidate its weapons against Latinos as the drug-disseminating enemy within. The War on Drugs will increasingly become a War on Latinos and Latin Americans, as the recent brutal U.S. invasion of Panama has demonstrated. Furthermore, U.S. intervention in Latin America will increase as "the Pentagon searches for new ways to help justify its spending plans."[26]

Toward a Multicultural Public Sphere (Versus Hegemonic Pluralism)

The effect of dominant U.S. reaction to the special language needs that Latinos project and the rights that they claim on that basis has been to strengthen the moves toward unity on the part of diverse Latino communities. Otherwise divided by such identity factors as race, class and national origin, there are economic, social and political reasons in post-civil-rights U.S. why Latinos can constitute a broadly defined national and trans-national federation which aspires to reconceptualize "America" in multicultural and multicentric terms that refuse the relativist fiction of cultural pluralism. It is for this reason that we have proposed to look at Latino negotiation of identity from a social movement perspective rather than a (liberal-sociological) ethnicity paradigm.

It is a commonplace among contemporary theorists of ethnicity in the U.S. that the assimilationist or "melting pot" paradigm of the first half of the century "failed to explain what it most needed and wanted to explain— the persistence of racial stratification . . . "[27] The "new ethnicity" paradigm, which emerged to remedy the failure of assimilation theory and, as we stated above, to counter the gains made by blacks and other "racial minorities" in the wake of civil rights activism, makes the basic claim that ethnicity becomes the category around which interests are negotiated when class loses its moorings in post-industrial society. The "new ethnicity" can be understood to form part of what Habermas has posited as a "neo-conservative post-modernism," that is, the rejection of "cultural modernism," because it has eroded traditional moral values and the continued espousal of infrastructural modernity or capitalism cum technical progress and rational administration.[28] The false premise of this argument, of course, is that the economy can be independent of culture; this theory thus serves the purpose of providing a cultural (or ethnic) politics in post-industrial society with no need to resort to economically based categories such as class: "In trying to account for the upsurge of ethnicity today, one can see this ethnicity as the emergent expression of primordial feelings [or "reenchantment," G.Y.

and J.F.], long suppressed but now reawakened, or as a 'strategic site' chosen by disadvantaged persons as a new mode of seeking political redress in the society."[29] The falsity of the model, of course, is that blacks and other "racial minorities" can be equated with white "ethnic" groups.[30] The result is reinforcement of existing class inequalities expressed in ethnic/racial terms.[31]

"Racial" movements could be understood to be the first of the "new social movements" or "new antagonisms" that call into question forms of subordination (bureaucratization and consumer commodification of "private" life) in the post World War II U.S. They do not, however, retreat from "cultural modernism"[32] (the erosion of traditional moral values undergirded by class, race and gender discriminations) but rather extend it to the point of questioning "infrastructural modernism." Among the challenges is the push to legitimize the adjudication and legislation of rights on the basis of group need rather that the possessive individualist terms that traditionally define rights discourse.[33] "New ethnicity" theory is only one of a panoply of strategies by which neo-conservatives have sought to contest the extension of rights on the basis of group criteria (affirmative action, headstart programs, anti-discrimination statutes, and so on). The result has been the acknowledged loss of foundations for rights and the shift to a paradigm of interpretability. Group rights must take place, then, in a surrogate terrain, like language or the family. According to Minow,

> One predictable kind of struggle in the United States arises among religious and ethnic groups. Here, the dominant legal framework of rights rhetoric is problematic, for it does not easily accommodate groups. Religious freedom, for example, typically protects individual freedom from state authority or from oppression by private groups. Ethnic groups lack even that entry point into constitutional protection, except insofar as individuals may make choices to speak or assemble in relation to a chosen group identity.[34]

If the framework of rights is an impoverished one for the struggles of the new social movements, then what has been the means to greater political participation? One alternative has been to engage in the struggle of needs interpretations. According to Nancy Fraser, "political issues concerning the interpretation of people's needs [are translated] into legal, administrative and/or therapeutic matters,"[35] *differentially* according to the identificatory features (race, class, gender, religion and so on) of the group.

Fraser goes on to argue that in each branch (juridical, administrative, therapeutic) of the late capitalist welfare state, there are gender and racially defined subsystems such that certain genders and races are positioned differently as regards possession of rights or eligibility for benefits and services.[36] The struggle around needs, then, is more typical of those groups that are socially "marked."[37]

Such "markedness" is at work in the struggle over Latino *language needs*; it was only by arguing for the legitimacy of the need for special language education that the Bilingual Education Act of 1968 was legislated as a civil right.[38] And it is around this "need" that dominant groups have launched their counter-attack. Some of the arguments for bilingual education posit a need for a positive self-image premised on the validation of the mother language and the culture of the minority student. However, based on instrumental rationality, dominant groups insist that the need of immigrant groups is to assimilate into mainstream society and thus the only special educational benefit that need be provided is special English instruction.

During the Carter administration, bilingualism and biculturalism were weakened by a new bilingual education law (1978) which limited access to bilingual programs and required teachers to know English as well as Spanish. A 1979 study "exposed" bilingual programs to be "a strategy for realizing the social, political and economic aspirations of the Hispanic peoples."[39] Carter himself said: "I want language taught—not 'ethnic' culture, etc."[40]

Arguments for and against bilingual education aside, our point is that the struggle over needs interpretations—in this case around the need for special language education—is what in the present historical conjuncture in the U.S. mediates accumulation of value politically, economically and socially. Latinos, after all, have made significant gains (they have professionalized) in the educational system because they can more easily qualify for the job requirements (Spanish language literacy) of bilingual education. Language, as we shall demonstrate below, is also the terrain on which Latino "aesthetics of existence" or affirmative self-formative practices operate.

According to Habermas, oppositional, resisting discourses emerge when the validity of legal norms is questioned from the perspective of an everyday practice that refuses to be depoliticized by the "steering mechanisms" of law, bureaucracy and consumerism.[41] Through such resistant everyday practices, Latinos have contributed to reshaping the public sphere of American society. Or perhaps it would be more exact to say they have contributed to the emergence of a contestatory "social sphere" which blurs the public/private dichotomy because needs "have broken out of the domestic and/or official economic spheres that earlier contained them as 'private matters.' "[42] Another way of conceiving this contestation is to imagine social space as networks of conflicting and allied public spheres. What is defined as "private" from the purview of one, is "public" or political from the purview of another.

The relevance of casting Latino negotiation of identity as a contribution to the creation of an alternative public sphere can be brought out by situating it within Oskar Negt and Alexander Kluge's expanded understanding of the concept. They do not limit it to 1) the institutional settings of public opinion (media, parliaments, etc.) but extend it to 2) "the ideational substance that is processed and produced within these sites," and 3) "a general horizon of social experience,"[43] or "drive toward self-formation and self-reconstruction" (in the collective sense of "self") which is limited or crippled by the first sense.[44] An alternative model can be culled from Bakhtin's writings on "behavioral ideology" and the constitution of identity through the reaccentuation of speech genres. Ideological or discursive production is institutionally bound but is generally (except in cases of outright force) open to modulation whereby persons "author themselves" or make discourse "one's own" in the media of speech and behavioral genres.[45] Our utterances are necessarily enunciated and organized within such genres, which bear institutional marks. Self-formation is simultaneously personal and social (or private and public) because the utterances and acts through which we *experience* or gain our self-images are reaccentuated in relation to how genres have institutionally been made sensitive or responsive to identity factors such as race, gender, class, religion and so on.

In post-modernity, "private" identity factors or subject positions may become unmoored from institutionally bound generic structures, turning "intimacy [. . .] the practical touchstone for the substance of the public sphere."[46] Experience, situated thus, is what fuels the utopian and contestatory potential of self-formation:

> What is even more significant is that subjective or psychological phenomena are now increasingly seen as having epistemological and even practical functions. Fantasy is no longer felt to be a private and compensatory reaction against public situations, but rather a way of reading those situations, of thinking and mapping them, of intervening in them, albeit in a very different form from the abstract reflections of traditional philosophy or politics.[47]

Alternative public spheres, with their different, situated knowledges, are for Negt and Kluge, constituted by the conflictual back and forth *crossover* of everyday experience and fantasy over the boundaries of the hegemonic public sphere.[48]

On the other hand, the hegemonic public sphere itself "tries to develop techniques to reincorporate fantasy in domesticated form."[49] This is precisely the function of "new ethnicity" theory: to co-opt the alternative public sphere of a multicultural society in such a way that ethnic difference is reduced to its superficial signs, or from Negt and Kluge's perspective, a sublimation of the "unconscious practical criticism of alienation."[50]

Bowing to Prospero: Richard Rodriguez's Reprivatization of Crossover Experiences

There is no better example of the attempt to channel the "crossover" toward an ersatz pluralism than Richard Rodriguez's "middle-class pastoral": *Hunger of Memory: The Education of Richard Rodriguez.*[51] It is the story of a now influential "public" man who traded his former identity (as oppressed working class Chicano), his former symbolic authorities (his parents), his former language (Spanish) by assimilating to the *gringo* middle class under the tutelage of new symbolic authorities (his teachers and intellectual mentors, especially Richard Hoggatt). His life reads like an advertisement against bilingual education; Spanish is the "private" language of the ethnic, English the "public" language of empowerment:

> Supporters of bilingual education today imply that students like me miss a great deal by not being taught in their family's language. What they seem not to recognize is that, as a socially disadvantaged child, I considered Spanish to be a private language. What I needed to learn in school was that I had the right—and the obligation—to speak the public language of *los gringos*. The odd truth is that my first-grade classmates could have become bilingual, in the conventional sense of that word, more easily than I. Had they been taught (as upper-middle-class children are often taught early) a second language like Spanish or French, they could have regarded it simply as that: another public language. In my case such bilingualism could not have been so quickly achieved. What I did not believe was that I could speak a single public language ...
>
> Fortunately, my teachers were unsentimental about their responsibility. What they understood was that I needed to speak a public language ... [52]

This passage conceals a romanticized projection concerning the "privacy" of Spanish, for Rodriguez clearly recognizes that Spanish could also be a "public" language. He makes this recognition only to discard it on the basis that his disadvantaged status could not let him aspire to an alternative publicity in Spanish. It is his own rejected sentimentalism toward Spanish, then, which lies at the root of the bad faith which he attributes to bilingual educators and others who seek to keep, cultivate or invent Latino culture and language as a competing, alternative public discourse. Instead, Rodriguez draws a tighter and tighter net around that which he (and the dominant culture) has defined as private until it is strangled out of existence and he emerges as his own abstracted interlocutor: "I hear an echoing voice—my own resembling another's. Silent! The reader's voice silently trails every word I put down. I reread my words, and again it is the reader's voice I hear in my mind, sounding my prose."[53] Who is this interlocutor but the symbolic Other (the law of the Anglo father or teacher) with whom he has identified after his linguistic and cultural "castration":

> I write today for a reader who exists in my mind only phan-
> tasmagorically. Someone with a face erased; someone of no
> particular race or sex or age or weather. A gray presence. Un-
> known, unfamiliar. All that I know is that he has had a long
> education and that his society, like mine, is often public (*un
> gringo*).[54]

Regarding the "castration" metaphor (which marks the moment of entry into the "public" realm of the symbolic), it should be remembered that Rodriguez has symbolically renounced his Chicanoness by attempting to shave off the darkness of his skin:

> I took my father's straight razor out of the medicine cabinet.
> Slowly, with steady deliberateness, I put the blade against my
> flesh, pressed it as close as I could without cutting, and moved it
> up and down across my skin to see if I could get out, somehow
> lessen, the dark.[55]

At the end of this same chapter ("Complexion"), his public identity has made his skin color meaningless. It is the value that he has gained as a public individual (*un gringo*) which contextualizes his complexion's meaning:

> The registration clerk in London wonders if I have just been
> to Switzerland. And the man who carries my luggage in New
> York guesses the Caribbean. My complexion becomes a mark
> of my leisure. Yet no one would regard my complexion the
> same way if I entered such hotels through the service entrance.
> That is only to say that my complexion assumes its significance
> from the context of my life. My skin, in itself, means nothing.[56]

After this thought, Rodriguez returns to consider *los pobres mexicanos* with whom he has worked during the summer. Their skin color signifies disadvantage, it speaks their "private" silence to him: "Their silence is more telling. They lack a public identity. They remain profoundly alien."

This is surely a comforting thought for conservatives who would like to see all entitlements for Latinos removed. They need not fear the blurring of boundaries between public and private. Rodriguez charges that it is the advocates of bilingual education and minority compensation who have sold their identity to bureaucratic policy makers:

> The policy of affirmative action, however, was never able to distinguish someone like me (a graduate student of English, ambitious for a college teaching career) from a slightly educated Mexican-American who lived in a barrio and worked as a menial laborer, never expecting a future improved. Worse, affirmative action made me the beneficiary of his condition. Such was the foolish logic of this program of social reform.[57]

Yet it is he who has cashed in on his legitimation of middle-class privilege. The irony is that despite his disavowal of Chicano or minority status, he is read and his book is assigned in numerous college English courses precisely because he reassures "anguished Anglos" that the "latinization of America will, in time, lead to Hispanic integration."[58] He has spoken against bilingual education and affirmative action from Reagan's White House and has done quite well on the college lecture circuit as Prospero's tamed servant (a nifty turn of events for a book that begins thus: "I have taken Caliban's advice. I have stolen their books. I will have the run of this isle.").[59]

It is no mere coincidence that Rodriguez is one of only two Latino writers (the other is Luis Valdez) cited by Werner Sollors in *Beyond Ethnicity. Consent and Descent in American Culture,*[60] for he fits the refurbished rhetoric endemic to the "ethnicity paradigm": viz. the negotiation of assimilation and cultural pluralism. "The language of consent and descent has been flexibly adapted to create a sense of Americanness among the heterogeneous inhabitants of this country."[61] Both Sollors and Rodriguez coincide in deriving this dynamic of consent and descent from the Puritans to the most recent immigrants. Sollors quotes Timothy Smith to the effect that the process of immigration (uprooting, migration, resettlement, community-building) constituted for the Puritans a transcendent experience that laid the basis of American ethnicization. This process, according to Smith and Sollors, even includes Afro-American *immigrants!*[62] And the literature that it, the ethnicization process, provides, functions as a "handbook" or a "grammar" for "socialization into the codes of Americanness."[63]

Rodriguez, in a recent *The New York Times* supplement, *A World of Difference*, appeals first to the grammar school and then to consumerism for the "handbook" that can harmonize the diversity that constitutes the United States:

> Language is the lesson of the *grammar* school. And from the schoolmarm's achievement came the possibility of a shared history and a shared future ... At the bank or behind the counter at McDonald's, or in the switch room of the telephone company, people from different parts of town and different parts of the country, and different countries of the world learn that they have one thing or another in common. Initially, a punch clock. A supervisor. A paycheck. A shared irony. A takeout lunch. Some nachos, some bagels, a pizza. And here's a fortune cookie for you: Two in their meeting are changed.[64]

Crossing over the Contradictions of Latino Market and Media

Rodriguez is not entirely correct, however, about the integrative force of consumerism for producing assimilated "Americans." Diverse Latino communities are also partially united by market and media courting of the 100+ billions of dollars that the 30+ millions of Latinos offer. One advertising agency's pitch to businesses reads: "[O]ur market is very young and very very sensitive. You don't have the clutter of the Anglo market."[65]

Language, again, is the terrain on which the heterogeneous constituencies of Latinos are rallied not only as consumers but also as cultural subjects. This is certainly a major factor which was not in place when theories of ethnicity were devised to account for the incorporation of the "older" immigrants into U.S. society. Language is the major cultural glue provided by Spanish Television. Two of the major networks, Univisión and Telemundo, highlight the transnational and unifying character of their programming. Indeed, Telemundo's slogan is: *"Telemundo: uniendo a los hispanos."*

Strategists of marketing and the commercial media have not joined the English Only movement, nor do they seem to share the anxieties over cultural balkanization or contamination which propel it. Rather, the corporate "publicity sphere" has availed itself of the multicultural reality as a way of targeting consumer markets and taste cultures. Although for their own interested motives, advertisers reach out to the "Hispanic" market with campaigns custom-made for the culture, with special attention to holidays, family and religious life, and to the up-beat, success-story side of Latino experience.

Citibank, for example, makes an effort to salute prominent Hispanic businessmen, especially those who "got help along the way from Citibank. One owns a chain of travel agencies; another runs six McDonald's franchises." They claim with pride that, worldwide, Citibank "employs more Hispanics and does more business with Hispanics than any other bank."[66] Pan Am has even adapted its jingles—"it is a very musical market"—to appeal to its "Hispanic" customers, "so we retained the theme but added a Latin feel with percussion and woodwind instruments."[67]

The Spanish language, of course, figures prominently in this ethnically tailored publicity. While many campaigns are rendered simultaneously in Spanish, advertisers recognize that translation is not enough. Here again the "Latin feel" plays a key role. Pepsi Cola, for instance, took pains, and advice from their "Hispanic" marketing agency, to adapt their slogan "Catch that Pepsi spirit":

> If we had put that straight away into Spanish, viewers would have considered it voodoo, something about a spirit flying through the air. So we changed it to read, 'Vive el sentir de Pepsi.' That means, Live that Pepsi feeling. That's what the English slogan intends to say, but you have to know the idiosyncrasies of the market to put it across.[68]

Citibank goes even further; beyond capturing in Spanish the spirit of the English copy, they resort to the bilingual pun to catch the sympathetic giggle of potential customers and make them feel included. "We're going to play on the language here," their spokesman at Castor Spanish International says, "telling them that 'We always say sí at Citibank' (pronounced see-tee-bank in Spanish)."[69]

Ironically, this practice of linguistic and cultural adaptation on the part of commercial publicity is more suggestive than the traditional public sphere of Latino expression, especially those dimensions of it that go beyond mere responses to hegemonic negation. As publicity agents suggest, "When translation isn't enough, try 'trans-creation.' " The idea of "trans-creation," for the advertisers, a gimmicky term aimed at maximizing specificity in targeting differentiated consumer publics, is appealing and apt as a characterization of border culture expression and self-definition. As one "Hispanic" media executive puts it, the "proper execution" calls for a sense of "the familiar Spanish patois of the community, reflecting not only different words and meanings, but also differences of rhythm of speech and inflection." Latino artists and poets also need to "trans-create" in this sense, at least at a tactical level, as does the wider Chicano and Nuyorican community in its everyday speech and expressive practices. In order to vocalize the border, traversing it is not enough; we must be positioned there, with ready and simultaneous access to both sides.

Perhaps the commonality between these two otherwise divergent worlds is the issue of needs. The advertiser bent on "reaching" and "selling" the Hispanic market, and the Latino cultural agent who would voice and envision the people's life-world, both inhabit a public sphere conceived of as the arena for the articulation and satisfaction of collective needs. Beyond the contention over rights and policies, the force of consumption, understood in its broadest sense, holds sway in the culture of experience. Here the private sphere, rather than being categorically autonomized, informs the public and even fuels the drive for social legitimation. "Trans-creation," whether from commercial or expressive and representational motives, serves to counteract the reduction of social experience to the dominion of laws and consensual ethical norms.

Such "crossovers" are a reality today, rooted in the bilingualism and bi-culturalism of Latinos. Many critics have correctly pointed to the erosion and misrepresentation by the mass media of traditional cultural forms and experience. But the market and the media are not the only forces in society and their interaction with other factors such as state bureaucratic appara-tuses, law and social institutions, can have consequences that go beyond the simplistic "colonization" of the Latino lifeworld. For example, the con-tradiction created in the dominant classes by divergent treatment of Latino language practices (opposition in the "social" sphere and enthusiastic ac-ceptance and application in the commercial sphere) has opened up a space in which Latinos negotiate new cultural forms that impact upon the culture at large.

Compromised as it is, even Coors turns to Spanish-language advertising to undo the negative effects of its hiring policies with regard to Latinos[70] demonstrates the extent to which consumerism blurs the cultural boundaries which so threaten dominant non-Latino groups. Those dominant groups which fear the "threat" of Latinization of U.S. culture, if also owners of businesses or directors of social and political institutions that could profit from Latino patronage, often find themselves having to cater to the needs interpretations of Latinos. The hysterical objections made against the pub-lic reach of Latino ethos through market and media, objections similar to those against bilingual education, only testify to the pervasiveness of Latino influence:

Freedom of speech is not unlimited. As Justice Brandeis has pointed out, no one is free to shout "fire" in a crowded theater. Speech and information are often curtailed in matters relating to

national security, for example. Cutting off American citizens
from sources of information in the language of their country,
fostering language segregation via the airwaves, these are major
problems that warrant the steps we propose [i.e., limiting the
growth of Spanish-language radio stations].[71]

Latino experience in the U.S. has been a continual crossover, not only
across geo-political borders but across all kinds of cultural and political
boundaries. Political organization, for example, is necessarily coalitional;
in order to have an impact Latinos have formed alliances to elect officials
who will represent their interests. Throughout the sixties and seventies,
Latinos formed or reformed dozens of national lobbying organizations. Up-
permost in their lobbying efforts are counterarguments against discriminatory practices in immigration, hiring and educational policies, opposition to
government intervention in Latin America, especially Central America and,
of course, promotion of language issues. It should be added that Latinos of
all backgrounds (with only the partial exception of Cuban Americans) are
assiduous supporters and participants in the solidarity and sanctuary movements. These forums are very important because they exert a progressive
influence, especially as regards women's issues like abortion, on groups
that have a conservative cultural heritage. Furthermore, the political and
cultural crossover involved in these activities contributes to the creation of
alternative public spheres in the United States.

Crossover does not mean that Latinos seek willy nilly to "make it" in
the political and commercial spheres of the general culture. These spheres
are vehicles which Latinos use to create new cultural forms that cross over
in both directions. The music of Willie Colón, Rubén Blades, and other
U.S.-based Latino and Latin American musicians is a new pan-Latino fusion of Latin-American forms (Cuban *guaguancós*, Puerto Rican *plenas*,
Dominican *merengues*, Mexican *rancheras*, Argentine *tangos*, Colombian
cumbias, barrio drumming) and U.S. pop, jazz, rock, even do-wop, around a
salsa base of Caribbean rhythms, particularly Cuban *son*. Salsa cuts across
all social classes and Latino groups who reside in New York, home ground
of this fusion music. Originating in the barrios, it made its way to "down-
town" clubs and across borders to the diverse audience of the Latin American
subcontinent. The crossovers have resulted in a convergence phenomenon
which does not represent anything other than its malleability and openness
to incorporation.[72]

Salsa, perhaps better than any other cultural form, expresses the Latino
ethos of multiculturalism and crossing borders. Willy Colón, for example,
became a *salsero* precisely to forge a new "American" identity:

> Now look at my case; I'm Puerto Rican and I consider myself
> Puerto Rican. But when I go to the island I'm something else
> to them. And in New York, when I had to get documents, I
> was always asked: "Where are you from?" "I'm American."
> "Yeah, but from where?" They led me to believe that I wasn't
> from America, even though I have an American birth certificate
> and citizenship ... I live between both worlds but I also had to
> find my roots and that's why I got into salsa.[73]

Finding one's "roots" in salsa means creating them more from the hetero-geneous sounds that traverse the barrio than going back to some place that guarantees authenticity. Salsa is the *salsero*'s homeland and the means to self-validation.[74]

Despite its popularity and certain minor breakthroughs, salsa has not (yet?) "made it" in mainstream U.S. culture. Latino artists and entrepeneurs have had to form their own labels, an alternative recording industry. Only in recent years, especially with the impetus of Rubén Blades's thematization of "crossing over" in the film "Crossover Dreams," has the dominant record-ing industry not only taken on *salseros* on national labels (Blades's *Agua de Luna*, based on the stories of García Márquez, is on Elektra) but also marketed them nationally. Furthermore, the alternative public spheres of contemporary rock, such as "Rock Against Racism," have been opened up by the collaborations of such "mainstream" musicians as the Rolling Stones, David Byrne and Paul Simon with *salseros*, Chicano rockers such as Los Lobos and Latin American stars such as Milton Nascimento and Caetano Veloso.[75] Hip Hop has also brought together Afro-Americans, Latinos and Afro-Latin Americans.[76]

Trans-creating a Multicultural America

Rubén Blades has insisted that a culturally effective crossover, which he prefers to call "convergence," is not about "abandonment or sneaking into someone else's territory. I propose, rather, convergence. Let's meet half way, and then we can walk either way together."[77] At the end of the interview he adds that he does "not need a visa" for the musical fusion which he seeks. He does not want "to be in America" but rather participate in the creation of a new America.

Latinos, then, do not aspire to enter an already given America but to participate in the construction of a new hegemony dependent upon their cul-tural practices and discourses. As argued above, the struggle over language signals this desire and the opposition to it by dominant groups. This view of language, and its strategic operationality in achieving a sense of self-worth, is the organizing focus of Gloria Anzaldúa's *Borderlands/La Frontera. The New Mestiza*.[78] "Ethnic identity is twin skin to linguistic identity—I am my language. Until I take pride in my language, I cannot take pride in myself."[79] Like Rondón's arguments about salsa,[80] the language of the new mestiza is the migratory homeland in which "continual creative motion [...] keeps breaking down the unitary aspect of each new paradigm."[81] Anzaldúa acknowledges that her projection of a "new mestiza consciousness" may seem cultureless from the perspective of "male-derived beliefs of Indo-Hispanics and Anglos;" for her, on the contrary, she is

> participating in the creation of yet another culture, a new story to explain the world and our participation in it, a new value system with images and symbols that connect us to each other and to the planet.[82]

Another way of constructing Anzaldúa's mestiza poetics is as an articulation of the premise that all cultural groups need a sense of worth in order to survive. Self-determination, which in this case focuses on linguistic self-determination, is the category around which such a need should be adjudicated and/or legislated as a civil right. In order for this right to be effective, however, it would have to alter the nature (or, to be more exact, the social relations) of civil society.

Such a claim, constructed in this way, only makes sense in a social structure that has shifted the grounds for enfranchisement from one of rights discourse to the interpretations that underpin such discourse. What is the justification, however, for needs interpretation? Our claim is that group ethos, the very stuff (or the "ethical substance," in Foucault's terminology)[83] of self-formation, is what contingently grounds the interpretation of a need as legitimate so that it can be adjudicated or legislated as a right. Another claim is that group ethos is constituted by everyday aesthetic practices such as the creative linguistic practices of Latinos which in the current historical conjuncture do not amount to subalternity, but rather to a way of prying open the larger culture, by making its physical, institutional and metaphorical borders indeterminate, precisely what we have seen that the dominant culture fears.

Latino self-formation as trans-creation—to "trans-create" the term beyond its strictly commercialist coinage—is more than a culture of resistance, or it is "resistance" in more than the sense of standing up against concerted hegemonic domination. It confronts the prevailing ethos by congregating an ethos of its own, not necessarily an outright adversarial but certainly an alternative ethos. The Latino border trans-creates the impinging dominant cultures by constituting the space for their free intermingling—free because it is dependent on neither, nor on the reaction of one to the other, for its own legitimacy. Dialogue and confrontation with the "monocultural other" persists, but on the basis of what Foucault has called "the idea of governmentality," "the totality of practices, by which one can constitute, define, organize, instrumentalize the strategies which individuals in their liberty can have in regard to each other."[84]

It is in these terms that the positing of a relatively self-referential cultural ethos for oppressed groups can evade the attendant essentialist or exceptionalist pitfalls. For this ethos is eminently practical, not an alternative to resistance but an alternative form of resistance, not a deliberate ignorance of multicultural realities but a different and potentially more democratic way of apprehending them. The strategic value of this "relationship of self to self" is of utmost importance, since it defines the position from which to negotiate the existing relations of power as domination. For rather than aiming at some maximally transparent communication among hierarchically divergent subject positions, in Habermas' sense, the goal of this cultural-ethical self-formation is the adequate constitution and definition of the subject position itself. As Foucault explains in his critique of Habermas:

> I don't believe there can be a society without relations of power, if you understand them as means by which individuals try to conduct, to determine the behavior of others. The problem is not of trying to dissolve them in the utopia of a perfectly transparent communication, but to give one's self the rules of law, the techniques of management, and also the ethics, the ethos, the practice of self, which would allow these games of power to be played with a minimum of domination.[85]

"Practice of self" is understood here to refer to individuals, but is readily transferable to collective self-conducts; the relations of power are called strategic "games," but the re-writing of the rules, or the playing out of other games with other rules, clearly interfaces with the dynamics of political and cultural struggle. And the utopian horizon, which Foucault discards in its Habermasian version, is still present in this strategy of minimizing domination, especially when the view is toward the process of collective self-formation among oppressed and "other" groups. Gómez-Peña, that reliable voice of the border perspective, addresses this futuristic dimension in terms which also suggest the content and tactics of the new ethos, the alternative, multicultural "practice of self":

> The U.S. suffers from a severe case of amnesia. In its obses-
> sive quest to 'construct the future,' it tends to forget or erase
> the past. Fortunately, the so-called disenfrachised groups who
> don't feel part of this national project have been meticulously
> documenting their histories. Latinos, blacks, Asians, women,
> gays, experimental artists and non-aligned intellectuals have
> used inventive languages to record the other history from a
> multicentric perspective. Our art functions both as collective
> memory and alternative chronicle, says Amalia Mesa-Bains. In
> this sense, multicultural art, if nurtured, can become a powerful
> tool to recapture the desired historical self. The great paradox
> is the fact that without this historical self, no meaningful future
> can ever be constructed.[86]

Ethnicity-as-practice is primordially genealogical, intent as it invariably is on a recapturing and re-constituting of the past. It relies, as Michael M.J. Fischer terms it, on the "post-modern arts of memory," the collective power of recall which is only a power if it functions actively and constitu-tively. This retrospective, testimonial search is for Fischer "a (re)invention and discovery of a vision, both ethical and future-oriented. Whereas the search for coherence is grounded in a connection to the past, the meaning abstracted from that past, an important criterion of coherence, is an ethic workable for the future."[87] The "alternative chronicle" is more than merely recuperative: it is eminently functional in present self-formative practice and anticipatory of potential historical self-hood. Sandra María Esteves, in a poem cited earlier ("I am two parts / a person boricua / spic"), bemoans the forcible, physical loss of her antecedence: "I may never overcome the theft of my isla heritage ... I can only imagine and remember how it was." But that imagination and remembrance enliven her dream-work, which in turn "realizes" that lost reality in a way that leads to eventual and profound self-realization. Her poem ends, "But that reality now a dream teaches me to see, and will bring me back to me."[88]

In the post-modern context, the mnemonic "arts" of border expression are conducted in "inventive languages," a key phrase of Gómez-Peña sig-naling the characteristic expressive tactic of this process. Language itself, of course, is the most obvious site of Latino inventiveness. Whether the wildest extravagance of the bilingual poet or the most mundane comment of everyday life, Latino usage tends necessarily toward interlingual innova-tion. The interfacing of multiple codes serves to de-canonize all of them, at least in their presumed discrete authority, thus allowing ample space for spontaneous experimentation and punning. Even for the most monolingual of Latinos, the "other" language looms constantly as a potential resource, and the option to vary according to different speech contexts is used far more often than not. "Trans-creation," understood in this sense of intercultural variability and transferability, is the hallmark of border language practice.

The irreverence implicit in trans-creative expression need not be deliberately defiant in motive; it reflects rather a largely unspoken disregard for conventionally bounded usage insofar as such circumscription obstructs the need for optimal specificity of communicative and cultural context. The guiding impulse, articulated or not, is one of play, freedom and even empowerment in the sense that access to individual and collective referentiality cannot ultimately be blocked. Interlingual puns, multi-directional mixing and switching, and the seemingly limitless stock of borrowings and adaptations attest to a delight not only in excluding and eluding the dominant and exclusionary, but in the very act of inclusion within a newly constituted expressive terrain. Rather than rejecting a language because of its association with a repressive other, or adopting it wholesale in order to facilitate passage, Latino expression typically "uses" official discourse by adapting it and thereby showing up its practical malleability.

Nuyorican vernacular includes the verb "gufear," from which has derived the noun "el gufeo." The colloquial American word "goof" is clearly visible and audible, and certainly the "Spanglish" usage has its closest equivalent in the phrase "goofing on" someone or something. But as a cultural practice, "el gufeo" clearly harkens to "el vacilón," that longstanding Puerto Rican tradition of funning and funning on, fun-making and making fun. Popular culture and everyday life among Puerto Ricans abound in the spirit of "el vacilón," that enjoyment in ribbing at someone's or one's own expense, for which a wider though overlapping term is "el relajo." We might even speak, in fact, of a Puerto Rican ethos of "el relajo" which, in its interplay with "el respeto," serves to mark off consensual guidelines for interpersonal behavior.[89] Setting limits of "respectability" and testing them, "relaxing" them, conditions the dynamic of Puerto Rican culture at the level of behavioral expression. The role of "el relajo," often practiced of course by the subaltern classes in their interaction with their masters, is not derivative of or conditioned by "el respeto"; rather, the delineation of individual and group dignity draws its power from the ability to "relax (on)" the prevalent codes of "respect."

Terms and practices like "el vacilón" and "el relajo" are the Puerto Rican version of the Cuban "choteo," perhaps the most widely understood usage among the Latino nationalities and having its particular variants in the diverse national cultures. In all cases, "el choteo" involves irony, parody and many of those elements which Henry Louis Gates, Jr. has identified as constitutive of "signifyin(g)" in the African-American tradition: repetition, double-talk and semantic reversals and, most generally, gestural imitation for the sake of refiguring.[90] Colonial and elite cultures in Latin America have been constant prey to "el choteo," which also operates within and among the group to bolster or deflate spirits, whichever seems appropriate. The "signifying monkey" might instead be a dog, or a mule or a pig, or even "un bobo," a town fool or simpleton. But like "signifyin(g)," "el choteo" does have its agent, some unsuspected, improbable master of the trope who embodies the arts of memory and (re-)invention.

"El gufeo" takes the process even one step further: Latino "signifyin(g)" in the multicultural U.S. context adds to the fascination of its home-country or African-American counterparts because of its interlinguality. Double-talk in this case is sustained not merely by the interplay of "standard" and vernacular significations but by the crossing of entire language repertoires. Border vernacular in fact harbors a plurality of vernaculars comprised of their multiple interminglings and possible permutations. The result is not simply an extended range of choices and juxtapositions, the kind of "splitting of tongues" exemplified by border poet Gina Valdés at the end of her poem "Where You From?":

> soy de aquí
> y soy de allá
> I didn't build
>   this border
> that halts me
> the word fron
> tera splits
> on my tongue.[91]

The real "signifyin(g)" potential of this discourse resides in the actual interpenetration of semantic and syntactic fields, when meanings and structures become destabilized and their referential uniformity discarded. The poetry of bilingual practitioners like Alurista and Tato Laviera abounds in this kind of doubling, another striking example being the play on the words "sunrise"-"sonrisa" (smile) which occurs in the writings of both Victor Hernández Cruz and Louis Reyes Rivera. Hernández Cruz ends his often cited poem "You gotta have your tips on fire" with the lines,

> You never will be in the wrong place
> For the universe will feel your heat
> And arrange its dance on your head
> There will be a Sun/Risa

on your lips
But
You gotta have your tips on fire
Carnal[92]

In "Problems in Translation" Reyes Rivera takes up the same interlingual pun to dramatize his "discovery" of a connotative richness in his effort to adopt a new-found Spanish vocabulary:

Esa sonrisa
is not just a smile
but a brilliance you lend
from the life in your eyes
the width of your mouth
as they both
give rise to the meaning of sunfilled
    spread
across
    your
high
    boned
gentle
    face.[93]

Poetic and colloquial language use is of course only the most obvious and readily illustrated case of re-figuration in Latino cultural expression. Examples are multiplied when account is taken of the traditions of musical "signifyin(g)" in salsa, Latin jazz, *Tejano* and Latin rock, or the characteristic interplay of Caribbean or Mexican visual worlds with North American settings among Nuyorican and Chicano artists. One thinks of Jorge Soto and his "signifyin(g)" on that classical work of a Puerto Rican painting, Francisco Oller's "El Velorio" (1893). Soto reenacts and transfigures the *jíbaro* wake of the original by populating the scene with the trappings of New York tenement life. A particularly suggestive example from recent years is provided by the "casitas," the small wooden houses which have proliferated in the vacant lots of the South Bronx, El Barrio and other Puerto Rican neighborhoods. Though modeled after working class dwellings on the Island of the earlier decades, before the industrialization process overran the neighborhoods with concrete boxes, the "casitas" are typically decorated and furnished with objects pertinent to the immediate New York setting: billboards, shopping cans, plastic milk canons and the like. The effect is a remarkable pastiche in which otherwise disparate visual and sculptural worlds cohabit and collapse into one another in accordance with the inter-generational historical experience of the Puerto Rican migrant community. Perhaps most impressive cultural "signifyin(g)" occurs as the contrasting of urban spatial languages, as the tropical "casita" with its strong rural reminiscences in the form of open porches, truck gardens and domestic animals jars with and yet strangely complements the surrounding scene of strewn lots and gutted buildings. Nostalgia and immediacy parody each other in the "invention" of a tradition which captures, in striking and cogent ways, the texture of "multiculturalism" in contemporary "America."[94]

For, as Gómez-Peña suggests, in order for the "multicultural paradigm" to amount to more than still another warmed-over version of cultural pluralism, the entire culture and national project need to be conceived from a "multicentric perspective." It is at the border, where diversity is concentrated, that diversity as a fact of cultural life may be most readily and profoundly perceived and expressed. It is there, as Gloria Anzaldúa describes it in her work *Borderlands/La Frontera,* that the mestiza "learns to juggle cultures. She has a plural personality, she operates in a pluralistic mode ... Not only does she sustain contradictions, she turns the ambivalence into something else."[95] Renato Rosaldo sees in Anzaldúa's Chicana lesbian vision a celebration of "the potential of borders in opening new forms of human understanding": "She argues that because Chicanos have long practiced the art of cultural blending, 'we' now stand in a position to become leaders in developing new forms of polyglot cultural creativity. In her view, the rear guard will become the vanguard."[96]

Understood in this sense, multiculturalism signals a paradigmatic shift in ethnicity theory, a radically changed optic concerning center and margins of cultural possibility. The presumed "subcultural" tributaries feel emboldened to lay claim to the "mainstream," that tired metaphor now assuming a totally new interpretation. Tato Laviera once again is playing a pioneering role in this act of resignifying: in his new book, entitled *Mainstream Ethics,* Laviera demonstrates that it is the very concurrence of multiple and diverse voices, tones and linguistic resources that impels the flow of the whole culture of "America." The challenge is obviously aesthetic and political in intent, but it is also, as the title indicates, an eminently ethical one. "It is not our role," the book's introduction announces, "to follow the dictates of a shadowy norm, an illusive *main* stream, but to remain faithful to our collective and individual personalities. Our ethic is and shall always be current." Appropriately, the Spanish subtitle of the volume, "*ética corriente,*"[97] is more than a translation; it is a "trans-creation" in the full sense, since "current" or "common," with its rootedness in the cultural ethos of everyday life, stands in blatant contrast to the fabricated, apologetic implications of "mainstream" in its conventional usage.

The Chicano poet Juan Felipe Herrera has an intriguing *gufeo* fantasy. "What if suddenly the continent turned upside-down?" he muses.

> What if the U.S. was Mexico?
> What if 200,000 Anglosaxicans
> were to cross the border each month
> to work as gardeners, waiters,
> 3rd chair musicians, movie extras,
> bouncers, babysitters, chauffers,
> syndicated cartoons, feather-weight
> boxers, fruit-pickers & anonymous poets?
> What if they were called waspanos,
> waspitos, wasperos or wasbacks?
> What if we were the top dogs?
> What if literature was life, eh?[98]

The border houses the power of the outrageous, the imagination needed to turn the historical and cultural tables. The view from the border enables us to apprehend the ultimate arbitrariness of the border itself, of forced separations and inferiorizations. Latino expression forces the issue which tops the agenda of American culture, the issue of geography and nomenclature.

> Let's get it straight: American is a continent not a country. Latin America encompasses more than half of America. Quechuas, Mixtecos and Iroquois are American (not U.S. citizens). Chicano, Nuyorrican, Cajun, Afro-Caribbean and Quebequois cultures are American as well. Mexicans and Canadians are also North Americans. Newly arrived Vietnamese and Laotians will soon become Americans. U.S. Anglo-European culture is but a mere component of a much larger cultural complex in constant metamorphosis.[99]

For the search for "America," the inclusive, multicultural society of the continent has to do with nothing less than an imaginative ethos of re-mapping and renaming in the service not only of Latinos but all claimants.

Notes

The Insular Vision: Pedreira and the Puerto Rican Misère

[1] Some of the most influential of these statements—such as those of Eduardo Seda Bonilla and José Luis González—are included, and criticized, in the *Cuadernos de cultura* published by the *Centro de Estudios Puertorriqueños* (City University of New York) in 1976. A more recent approach to Puerto Rican culture in the United States is the chapter by Manuel Maldonado-Denis, "Cultura y Educación: el problema de la asimilación cultural" in his *Puerto Rico y Estados Unidos: Emigración y colonialismo* (México: Siglo XXI, 1976), pp. 125–154.

The present essay is intended as a continuation of the work of the *Cuaderno*. Full acknowledgement is due to the Culture Task Force of the *Centro* for its indispensable participation in the collective development of the ideas in this paper.

[2] The most immediate background for the present critique of Pedreira was a series of weekly study and discussion sessions with a group of artists, musicians and writers active in the Puerto Rican community in New York. Those sessions were held at the *Centro* and the *Taller Boricua* from October, 1976 through May, 1977 at the initiative of the Culture Task Force. Though the cultural workers involved are not to be considered responsible for the positions assumed here, the viewpoints, experiences and artistic work of Luis Aponte, Petra Barreras del Río, Jacki Biaggi, Roy Brown, Aida del Valle, Sandra María Esteves, Joe Falcón, Víctor Fragoso, José Rubén Gatzambide, René López, Jorge Pérez, Alan Siegel, Jorge Soto, Sekou Sundiata and José Valdez have provided an invaluable resource for an understanding of many aspects of Puerto Rican culture.

[3] Pedreira, *Insularismo* (San Juan: Biblioteca de Autores Puertorriqueños, 1957), p. 160. Page references in the text are to this edition. Translations are by the author.

[4] "Visión y revisión de *Insularismo*," in Maldonado-Denis, *Puerto Rico: mito y realidad* (Barcelona: Península, 1969), pp. 355–366. (Quote is from p. 355.)

[5] For a detailed account of his life and work, see Cándida Maldonado Ortiz, *Antonio S. Pedreira: Vida y obra* (Madrid: Editorial Universitaria, 1974).

[6] René Marqués, *Ensayos (1953–1971)* (Barcelona: Editorial Antillana, 1972), pp. 151–215. It is of some importance to note that in his psychological reflections on the Puerto Rican national character Marqués takes as his point of departure and frequent source of reference the observations about Puerto Ricans by the United States literary critic Alfred Kazin. Kazin recorded these remarks, gathered during a year teaching American literature at the University of Puerto Rico (1959–60), in his article "In Puerto Rico," *Commentary* XXIX/2 (February, 1960), pp. 108–114. See also the responses to Kazin by Stan Silver and Keith Botsford in "Controversy: On Puerto Rico," *Commentary* XXIX/5 (May 1960), pp. 430–436. The comments by Botsford, who spent some time with Kazin during his visit, seem appropriate; Botsford found in his article "a blend of conceit and truculent provincialism, a proportion I had observed in the man before seeing it demonstrated in the article." In fact, Kazin is following directly, though probably unknowingly, in Pedreira's line of thinking in *Insularismo* when he says, "the Puerto Ricans live on an island in every sense of the word: they are here, and their minds don't roam around much." The familiar tones of the "Ugly American" ring through, as when he illustrates his theories by observing

his students' "refusal to visualize a New England landscape or wintry weather." "It's not simply that they have not seen snow," he continues, for "neither had the young heroine of Carson McCuller's novel, who so longed to see some. It's that they are here and cannot easily imagine anything too different from their island, their town." Did it ever occur to Kazin that the imagination is sometimes "limited" by what a people see fit to imagine?

[7] There is a sizeable and rapidly growing literature on Antillean Indian societies. A helpful glossary of indigenous terms, which includes a bibliography of the major relevant work, is Luis Hernández Aquino's *Diccionario de voces indígenas de Puerto Rico* (Bilbao: Editorial Vasco Americana, 1969). Aside from the very early work by Jesse Walter Fewkes and the significant contributions by the authors mentioned, there have also been some initial attempts at a more philosophical approach; see, for example, Jalil Sued Badillo, "Ideology and History: The Theme of Our Indigenous Roots," *Cuaderno de cultura* (New York: Centro de Estudios Puertorriqueños, 1976), unit 2, pp. 1–27. The *Cuaderno* also contains a critique of Sued Badillo's essay, "Puerto Rican History and the Theme of Our Indigenous Roots," *Ibid.*, pp. 178–186. For a first example of a Marxist analysis, see Francisco Moscoso, "Tributo y formación de las clases en la sociedad de los taínos de las Antillas," paper delivered at the 7th "Congreso Internacional para el Estudio de las Culturas Pre-Colombinas de las Antillas Menores," Caracas, Venezuela, 1977.

[8] A forceful recent repudiation by a Latin American writer of this typical Hispanophilia may be found in Roberto Fernández Retamar, "Contra la leyenda negra," *Casa de las Américas* XVI/99 (November-December, 1976), 28–41.

[9] For a critique of Pedreira's dismissal of the early centuries of colonial rule, see the unpublished Master's dissertation by José Manuel Torres Santiago, *Una interpretación social y política de los antecedentes de la poesía puertorriqueña en los siglos 16, 17 y 18* (State University of New York at Buffalo, n.d.), esp. pp. 1–19. See also José Luis González, *Literatura y sociedad en Puerto Rico: De los cronistas de Indias a la generación del '98* (México: Fondo de Cultura Económica, 1976), pp. 15–16.

[10] *The America of José Martí: Selected Writings*, ed. and trans. Juan de Onís (New York: Minerva, 1954), p. 141. Ibid., p. 147.

[11] *Ibid.*, p. 147.

[12] Pedreira, *Obras completas* (San Juan: Instituto de Cultura Puertorriqueña, 1970), II, pp. 7–552. See especially the first chapter, "La introducción de la imprenta en Puerto Rico," pp 27–38. See also note 20 below.

[13] Manrique Cabrera, *Historia de la literatura puertorriqueña* (Rio Piedras: Editorial Cultural, 1971); Josefine González, op. cit., note 9 above.

[14] Lucien Febvre and Henri-Jean Martin, *The Coming of the Book* (London: New Left Books, 1976), p. 207.

[15] Franco, "Dependency Theory and Literary History: The Case of Latin America," *Minnesota Review*, 5 (1975), 65–80 (quote from p. 68).

[16] *Ibid.*, 69.

[17] (New York: Knopf, 1965); see especially "Alienation as the Key to Mannerism," pp. 94–114.

[18] Tapia y Rivera, *Mis memorias* (San Juan: Editorial San Juan, 1973), p. 10. The most scrupulous account of the various conflicting theories as to the precise date and nature of the arrival of the press to Puerto Rico appears in the first chapter of Pedreira's *El periodismo en Puerto Rico*. The version of Tapia y Rivera (which is

based, in turn, on José Julián Acosta's notes to the first history of the colony, Iñigo Abbad's *Historia geográfica de Puerto Rico*) asserts that the first press was brought to the Island by Juan Rodríguez Calderón in 1808. Later historians, however, such as Eduardo Neumann, Cayetano Coll y Toste and Salvador Brau, contend that it was not even a Spaniard but a Frenchman named Delarue who introduced the press in the year of 1806.

[19] *La peregrinación de Bayoán* (San Juan: Instituto de Cultura Puertorriqueña, 1970), p. 42.

[20] Mariátegui, *Siete ensayos de interpretación de la realidad peruana* (Santiago, Chile: Editorial Universitaria, 1955), pp. 28–9. Translation mine. It might be noted that one need not even turn to the revolutionary criticism of Mariátegui to recognize the leading role of Peruvian writers—from Garcilaso de la Vega to Manuel González Prada to César Vallejo—in the integration of Indian experience and expression into the modern cultural struggle.

The leading intellectual and pedagogical thinker of early twentieth-century Perú, Manuel Vicente Villarán, also upheld a very powerful and unflinching demand for justice toward the Indian people and heritage. See the excellent summary of Villarán's position in Leopoldo Zea, *Dos etapas del pensamiento en Hispanoamérica: del positivismo al romanticismo* (México: Colegio de México, 1949), pp. 249–52.

[21] The evidence provided by Francisco Moscoso, op. cit. (note 7 above) of the emergence of class relations in Taíno society does not contradict the basic lines of this argument.

[22] This and the following passages from the chronicles are quoted in the first chapter ("The Discovery of the New Wold in the Imagination of Europe") of Pedro Henríquez Ureña's *Literary Currents in Hispanic America* (Cambridge: Harvard University Press, 1945), pp. 6, 11 and 13 respectively. See also Bartolomé de las Casas, *The Devastation of the Indies* (New York: Seabury, 1974), especially the introduction by Hans Magnus Enzensberger, "Las Casas, of A Look Back into the Future," pp. 3–34. Another relevant recent essay is Julio Le Riverend, "Problemas históricos de la conquista; Las Casas y su tiempo," *Casa de las Américas*, XV/85 (July-August, 1974), 4–15.

[23] Franco, op. cit. (note 15), p. 70.

[24] See, for example, Pedro C. Escabí and Elsa M. Escabí, *La décima: estudio etnográfico de la cultura popular de Puerto Rico* (Río Piedras, Puerto Rico: Editorial Universitaria, 1976), which includes an extensive bibliography. Other relevant references include María Cadilla de Martínez, *La poesía popular en Puerto Rico* (Madrid: Cuenca: 1933); Marcelino Canino Salgado, *El cantar folklórico de Puerto Rico* (Río Piedras, Puerto Rico: Editorial Universitaria, 1975); and *La copla y el romance en la tradición oral de Puerto Rico* (San Juan: Instituto de Cultura Puertorriqueña, 1968); Eloísa Rivera Rivera, *La poesía en Puerto Rico antes de 1843* (San Juan: Instituto de Cultura Puertorriqueña, 1965); Cesáreo Rosa-Nieves, ed., *Antología de décimas cultas de Puerto Rico* (San Juan: Editorial Cordillera, 1975), II, pp. 1002–1008; and *Guajana*, II/10 (April-June, 1968).

[25] Tomás Blanco, "Elogio de 'la plena,'" *Revista del Ateneo Puertorriqueño*, I (1935), 97–106 (quote from p. 103). Also included in *Antología del pensamiento puertorriqueño*, ed. Eugenio Fernández Méndez (Río Piedras, Editorial Universitaria, 1975), II, pp. 1002–1008.

[26] On the beginnings of Puerto Rican working-class organization and literary expression, see the paper by Ricardo Campos Orta, "Apuntes sobre la expresión cul-

tural obrera en Puerto Rico," presented at the "Conferencia de historiografía puer-torriqueña" held in April, 1974 under the sponsorship of the Centro de Estudios Puertorriqueños.

[27] For a summary of racial theorizing in Latin American writing, see Jean Franco, *The Modern Culture of Latin America: Society and the Artist* (Middlesex: Penguin, 1970), pp. 55–61. See also César Graña, "Cultural Nationalism: The Idea of Histor-ical Destiny in Spanish America," *Social Research*, XXIX (Winter, 1962), 395–418. On race relations and racial thinking in Puerto Rican history, see Luis M. Díaz Soler, *Historia de la esclavitud en Puerto Rico (1493–1890)* (Rio Piedras: Editorial Uni-versitaria, 1970), and Isabelo Zenón Cruz, *Narciso descubre su trasero: el negro en la cultura puertorriqueña* (Humacao: Editorial Furidi, 1874).

[28] For an extensive critique of Sarmiento's racist ideas, both in *Conflictos y armonías* and in his early masterpiece *Vida de Juan Facundo Quiroga: Civilización y barbarie* (1845), see Roberto Fernández Retamar, "Algunos usos de la civilización y la barbarie," *Casa de las Américas*, XVII/102 (May-June, 1977), 29–52. See also Ezequiel Martínez Estrada, *Sarmiento* (Buenos Aires: Biblioteca Argos, 1946).

[29] Manrique Cabrera, op. cit. (note 11), p. 175. Significantly, Pedreira's geo-graphic and "atmospheric" determinism also has its forebears in Puerto Rican liter-ature, notably in the famous stanza of Gautier Benítez in his "Canto a Puerto Rico" (1873):

> Todo es en ti voluptuoso y leve,
> dulce, apacible, halagador y tierno,
> y tu mundo moral su encanto debe
> al dulce influjo de tu mundo externo.

Here again, recent Puerto Rican criticism has accepted favorably this manner of "nat-ural" attribution. In mounting a defense of the verisimilitude and exact faithfulness of Gautier Benítez' evocations of the Puerto Rican landscape, José Luis González cites these very lines when he contends, "if there is anything that unequivocally distinguishes the tropical Puerto Rican landscape from others of the same latitude it is precisely what Gautier indicates with insuperable exactitude, in a quatrain of the 'Canto a Puerto Rico' ... " (*Literatura y sociedad*, p. 121). It seems the writer was so enchanted by the seductive beauty of the romantic poet's verse that he failed to take account of the apology for colonial domination which make up the immedi-ate context within the poem. The entire "Canto a Puerto Rico" appears in Gautier Benítez, *Vida y obra poética* (Río Piedras: Editorial Edil, 1970), pp. 213–219. An English translation is available in *Borinquen: An Anthology of Puerto Rican Liter-ature*, ed. María Teresa Babín (New York: Knopf, 1974) pp. 89–92. The lines cited are translated,

> All is sensual and gentle in you,
> sweet, peaceful, flattering, tender,
> and your enchanted moral world
> is born of the sweet influence
> of your external island world.

[30] Zeno Gandía, *La charca* (San Juan: Instituto de Cultura Puertorriqueña, 1975), p. 24.

[31] Quoted in Michael Benton and Jonathan Harwood, *The Concept of Race* (New York: Praeger, 1975), p. 41. For the background of racial thinking in the United States during the nineteenth century, see John S. Haller, Jr., *Outcasts from Evolution: Scientific Attitudes of Racial Inferiority, 1859–1900* (Chicago: University of Illinois, 1971).

[32] *The America of José Martí*, p. 150. See also Martí's articles on the "race question" ("la cuestión racial") in Martí, *Obras completas*, (Caracas, 1964), II, pp. 484–496. See also the speech delivered by Fernando Ortiz in 1941, *Martí y las razas* (Havana: Publicaciones de la Comisión Nacional Organizadora de los Actos y Ediciones del Centenario y del Monumento de Martí, 1953).

[33] Blanco, op. cit., p. 100. Emphasis should also be placed in this context on the outstanding role played by the eminent Cuban intellectual Fernando Ortiz, whose polemical work *El engaño de las razas* (Havana, 1946) is a testament to his contribution to the battle against racism in his time.

[34] Hostos, *Obras completas* (San Juan: Editorial Coquí, 1969), VII, pp. 152–155.

[35] Rodó, *Ariel*, ed. Gordon Brotherston (Cambridge, 1967) pp. 25–26.

[36] Sánchez, *Balance y liquidación del novecientos: ¿Tuvimos maestros en Nuestra América?* (Lima, 1968), p. 107. Other writings on Rodó and "Arielismo" include Martin S. Stabb, *In Quest of Identity: Patterns in the Spanish-American Essay of Ideas* (Chapel Hill, 1967), pp. 35–46; Hugo Torrans, *Rodó: Acción y libertad* (Montevideo, 1973); and Víctor Pérez Petit, *Rodó: Su vida-Su obra* (Montevideo, 1937).

[37] On Rodó's background for the "Ariel" myth, see Roberto Fernández Retamar, "Caliban: Notes Towards a Discussion of Culture in Our America," *The Massachusetts Review*, XV, 1–2 (Winter-Spring, 1974), pp. 7–72. That essay, translated here by Lynn Garafola, David Arthur McMurray and Roberto Márquez, originally appeared as "Calibán: Apuntes sobre la cultura en Nuestra América" in *Casa de las Américas*, XII, 68 (September-October, 1971), 124–151. See also Gordon Brotherston's introduction to *Ariel*, op. cit., pp. 1–19.

[38] Brotherston, p. 15. For this historical assessment of Rodó, see Fernández Retamar, pp. 31–34, and Mario Benedetti, *Genio y figura de José Enrique Rodó* (Buenos Aires, 1966).

[39] Quoted by Fernández Retamar, "Caliban," p. 18. The evidence of Rodó's explicit debt to Groussac is cited by Brotherston, p. 13.

[40] *Ariel*, pp. 68–9.

[41] Quoted in Stabb, op. cit. (note 39), pp. 42–43.

[42] Vasconcelos, *Obras completas* (México: Libreros Mexicanos, 1958), II, p. 941.

[43] Fernández Retamar, "Caliban," p. 24. For a further elaboration of the analysis in "Caliban," see Fernández Retamar's subsequent recent essays, "Algunos usos de civilización y barbarie," loc. cit. (note 31 above) and "Nuestra América y Occidente," *Casa de las Américas*, XVI/98 (September-October, 1976), 36–57. An important, and hitherto unnoticed, anticipation of Fernández Retamar's partisanship with Caliban may be found in Jean Guéhenno's *Caliban parle* (Paris: Grasset, 1928). An empassioned, working-class response to Renan and the reactionary French elite, *Caliban Speaks* constitutes a valuable link between the cultural and ideological perspective of the European proletariat and that of the anti-imperialist liberation movement. For an early (1929) recognition of the book's pertinence to the Latin American revolutionary struggle, see the review by José Carlos Mariátegui, "Caliban parle."

[44] See, for example, Jean Franco, *The Modern Culture of Latin America*, pp. 225–6.

[45] Quoted Franco, *ibid.*, p. 226.

[46] See, for example, Manuel Maldonado-Denis, "Ortega y Gasset and the Theory of the Masses," *Western Political Quarterly*, XIV/3 (September-December, 1961), 676–690. Another example of an uncritical presentation of Ortega's ideas by an influential Puerto Rican intellectual is Jaime Benítez, *Political and Philosophical Theories of José Ortega y Gasset* (Chicago: University of Chicago Press, 1965). More critical assessments may be found, for example in Michael Harrington, *The Accidental Century* (New York: Macmillan, 1965), pp. 213–10 and Raúl Roa, "Dichos y hechos de Ortega y Gasset," *Cuadernos Americanos*, LXXXV/1 (January-April, 1956), 130–1.

[47] Maldonado Denis, "Ortega y Gasset and the Theory of the Masses," 680.

[48] The two statements by Ortega y Gasset are quoted in Robert McClintock, *Man and His Circumstances: Ortega as Educator* (New York: Columbia, 1971), pp. 199 and 201 respectively.

[49] Ortega y Gasset, *The Revolt of the Masses* (New York: Norton, 1957), p. 82.

[50] *Ibid.*, p. 52.

[51] *Ibid.*, p. 82.

[52] Spengler, *The Decline of the West* (New York: Knopf, 1962), p. 97.

[53] Lloréns Torres, *Obras completas* (San Juan: Instituto de Cultura Puertorriqueña, 1975), I, pp. 290–1.

[54] Géigel-Polanco, "La nacionalidad puertorriqueña," *Ateneo puertorriqueño*, II/2 (1936), 87–93.

[55] Spengler, *The Decline of the West*, p. 74.

[56] *Ibid.*, p. 73.

[57] *Ibid.*, p. 25.

[58] *Ibid.*, pp. 25–6.

[59] Herbert Maruse, *Negations: Essays in Critical Theory* (Boston: Beacon, 1968), p. 107.

[60] *Ibid.*, p. 108.

[61] *Ibid.*, p. 95.

[62] Lenin, *Collected Works*, (Moscow: Progress, 1964), XXXIII, pp. 349–50. Lenin, it might be noted, was quick to point out the apologetic content of *The Decline of the West* when, on the occasion of the tenth anniversary of *Pravda* (May 2, 1922), he proclaimed: "The old bourgeois and imperialist Europe, which was accustomed to look upon itself as the centre of the universe, rotted and burst like a putrid ulcer in the first imperialist holocaust. No matter how the Spenglers, and all the enlightened philistines who are capable of admiring (or even studying) Spengler may lament it, this decline of the old Europe is but an episode in the history of the downfall of the world bourgeoisie, oversatiated by imperialist rapine and oppression of the majority of the world's population."

[63] This claim is upheld, for example, in the balanced study by H. Stuart Hughes, *Oswald Spengler: A Critical Estimate* (New York: Scribner's, 1952), pp. 132–3. See also Fritz Stern, *The Politics of Cultural Despair: A Study in the Rise of the Germanic Ideology* (Garden City: Anchor, 1965), pp. 246 and 293–4.

[64] Spengler, *Selected Essays* (Chicago, 1967), pp. 206–7.

[65] Lukács, *Von Nietzsche zu Hitler oder Der Irrationalismus und die deutsche Politik* (Frankfurt: Fischer, 1966), esp. "Kriegsund Nachkriegszeit (Spengler),"

pp. 149–161.

[66] See among the growing literature on the history of the class struggle in Puerto Rico, the writings of Angel C. Quintero Rivera: *Lucha obrera en Puerto Rico: Antología de grandes documentos en la historia obrera puertorriqueña* (C.E.R.E.P., 1971); "La clase obrera y el proceso político en Puerto Rico," *Revista de Ciencias Sociales*, XVII/1–2 (March-June, 1974), 145–198; "El Partido Socialista y la lucha política triangular de las primeras décadas bajo la dominación norteamericana," *Revista de Ciencias Sociales*, XIX/1 (March, 1975), 47–100. See also Ricardo Campos and Frank Bonilla, "Industrialization and Migration: Some Effects on the Puerto Rican Working Class," *Latin American Perspectives*, III/3 (Summer, 1976), 66–108. For a first study of the cultural expression of the Puerto Rican working class in the formative years (1890–1930), reference is again made to the essay by Ricardo Campos Orta (note 28 above).

[67] The attempt by Gordon K. Lewis, for example, to ground a strategy for Puerto Rican revolution in *The Second Discourse, Emile* and the *Social Contract* can only mislead and mystify the realities of the modern-day class struggle; see *Notes on the Puerto Rican Revolution: An Essay on American Dominance and Caribbean Resistance* (New York: Monthly Review, 1974), pp. 227–30.

[68] The relation between Rousseau and the tradition of Marxist theory is most cogently discussed in Lucio Colletti, *From Rousseau to Lenin* (New York: Monthly Review, 1973). Rousseau's importance within a broad revolutionary anthropological framework is presented in Stanley Diamond, *In Search of Primitive* (New Brunswick, NJ, 1974).

[69] Maldonado-Denis, loc. cit. (note 4 above), 363–4. It must be recognized that Maldonado-Denis has gone a long way toward repudiating this class position in more recent writings; see for example, his "Aproximación crítica al fenómeno nacionalista en Puerto Rico," *Casa de las Américas*, XVII/102 (May-June, 1977), 13–28).

[70] Quoted in *Marx and Engels on Literature and Arts*, ed. Lee Baxandall and Stefan Morawski (New York: International General, 1974), pp. 84–5.

[71] Such is the tendency in the only other critical discussion of *Insularismo* to date, aside from that of Maldonado-Denis: Juan Angel Silén's chapter, "The Literature of Docility," in his *We, the Puerto Rican People* (New York, Monthly Review, 1971).

[72] In reference to this theme, the work of Gervasio Luis García is outstanding on the origins of the Puerto Rican working-class movement. See also the Master's thesis by Amílcar Tirado Avilés, "Las ideas y la acción de Ramón Romero Rosa, obrero tipográfico 1896–1907" (State University of New York, Buffalo, 1976), and Juan Flores and Ricardo Campos, "National Culture and Migration: Perspectives from the Puerto Rican Working Class," in this volume. A critique of conventional folklore study may be found in Rogelio Martínez Furé, "Folklore: Another Revolutionary Struggle," *Canto Libre*, 11/2 (1975), 3–34.

The Puerto Rico that José Luis González Built

Acosta-Belén, Edna (ed.)
   1979 *The Puerto Rican Women*. New York: Praeger.
   1980 *La mujer en la sociedad puertorriqueña*. Río Piedras: Huracán.
Blanco, Tomás
   1935 "Elogio de 'la plena,' " *Revista del Ateneo Puertorriqueño* I: 97–106.

1950 *Sobre Palés Matos*. San Juan: Biblioteca de Autores Puertorriqueños.

Bourdieu, Pierre
1977 *Outline of a Theory of Practice*. Cambridge: Cambridge University Press.

Díaz Quiñones, Arcadio
1982 *El almuerzo en la hierba*. Río Piedras: Huracán.

Fromm, Georg H.
1977 *César Andreu Iglesias*. Río Piedras: Huracán.

García Candini, Nestor.
1977 *Arte popular y sociedad en América Latina*. Mexico: Grijalbo.
1979 *La producción simbólica*. Mexico: Siglo XXI.
1982 *Las culturas populares en el capitalismo*. Havana: Casa de las Américas and México: Nueva Imagen.

González, José Luis
1973a *En Nueva York y otras desgracias*. México: Siglo XXI.
1973b *Veinte cuentos y Paisa*. Río Piedras: Cultural.
1976a *Conversación con José Luis González*, Arcadio Díaz Quiñones (ed.). Río Piedras: Huracán.
1976b *Literatura y sociedad en Puerto Rico*. México: Fondo de Cultura Económica.
1977 "Bernardo Vega: El luchador y su pueblo." pp. 9–25 in *Memorias de Bernardo Vega*. Río Piedras: Huracán.
1979 "Literatura e identidad nacional en Puerto Rico" in Quintero Rivera et al. *Puerto Rico: Identidad nacional y clases sociales*. Río Piedras: Huracán.
1980a *El país de cuatro pisos y otros ensayos*. Río Piedras: Huracán.
1980b *La llegada*. Río Piedras: Huracán.

Maldonado Denis, Manuel
1982 "En torno a *El país de cuatro pisos*." *Casa de las Américas* 135 (November-December), 151–159.

Marqués, René
1962 *El puertorriqueño dócil y otros ensayos*. Barcelona: Editorial Antillana. (Originally published in 1977).

Méndez Ballester, Manuel
1980 "Un ataque brutal." *El Nuevo Día* (May 12).

Méndez, José Luis
1982 "La arquitectura intelectual de *El país de cuatro pisos*." *Claridad*, 16 (April 22) and 23 (April 29).

Moscoso, Francisco
1981 "The Development of Tribal Society in the Caribbean." Ph.D. dissertation, SUNY, Binghamton.

Pedreira, Antonio S.
1934 *Insularismo*. Río Piedras: Edil (1973).

Picó, Fernando
1981 *Amargo café*. Río Piedras: Huracán.
1984 *Los gallos peleados*. Río Piedras: Huracán.

Quintero Rivera, Angel G.
1972 *Lucha obrera*. Río Piedras: CEREP.
1976a *Workers Struggle in Puerto Rico*. New York: Monthly Review Press.
1976b *Conflictos de clase y política en Puerto Rico*. Río Piedras: Huracán.

1980 "Clases sociales y cultura nacional en Puerto Rico." *El Nuevo Día* (December 16).

1983 *Historia de unas clases sin historia (Comentarios críticos a* El país de cuatro pisos). Río Piedras: Cuadernos CEREP.

Quintero Rivera et al.

1979 *Puerto Rico: Identidad nacional y clases sociales.* Río Piedras: Huracán.

Rodríguez Juliá, Edgardo

1983 *El entierro de Cortijo.* Río Piedras: Huracán.

Romero Rosa, Ramón

1982 "A los negros puertorriqueños," in *Sources for the Study of the Puerto Rican Migration.* New York: Centro de Estudios Puertorriqueños. (Originally 1899, 1901).

Sued Badillo, Jalil

1978 *Los caribes: realidad o fábula.* Río Antillana.

1979 *La mujer indígena y su sociedad.* Río Piedras: Antillana.

Williams, Raymond

1977 *Marxism and Literature.* London: Oxford University Press.

1982 *The Sociology of Culture.* New York: Schocken.

"Bumbún" and the Beginnings of Plena *Music*

[1] The main source for information on early *plena* is the book by Félix Echevarría Alvarado, *La plena: origen, sentido y desarrollo en el folklore puertorriqueño* (Santurce: Express, 1984). Based on interviews with many of the surviving pioneers of the *plena* and their families, and containing photographs and song texts, this unassuming work provides crucial new insights into the history of the form and sets the record straight on many counts. The most valuable historical and political analysis of the *bomba* and *plena* tradition to date is Jorge Pérez, "La bomba y la plena puertorriqueña: ¿Sincretismo racial o transformación histórico-musical?" *Anales* (Havana, Centro de Estudios del Caribe, 1988). Pérez's essay is a first effort to set forth a periodization of the *plena* tradition and also takes issue with many methodological and theoretical assumptions underlying the treatment of the *plena* in the standard writings on Puerto Rican popular music: María Luisa Muñoz, *La música en Puerto Rico* (Sharon, CT: Troutman, 1966); Francisco López Cruz, *La música folklórica de Puerto Rico* (Sharon, CT: Troutman, 1967); and Héctor Campos Parsi, *La gran enciclopedia de Puerto Rico: Música,* vol. 7 (Madrid: Ediciones R, 1976).

Plena has become the topic of broad cultural and sociological interest among Puerto Rican writers over the past decade or so. In his *Literatura y sociedad en Puerto Rico* (1976), José Luis González signaled the key importance of the *plena*, "the most representative genre of modern Puerto Rican folklore," for the study of Puerto Rican literature and culture in the twentieth century, and announced plans for a book on the subject. More recently, Edgardo Rodríguez Juliá's excellent testimonial, *El entierro de Cortijo* (Río Piedras: Huracán, 1983), has done much to kindle interest and understanding among a wide readership, while the ongoing research by such scholars as Angel Quintero Rivera and Rafael Aponte-Ledée promises to add significant new knowledge and approaches.

The present sketch on *plena* beginnings was intended as part of a longer essay to accompany the film on *plena* produced by Pedro Angel Rivera and Susan

Zeig. Collaboration on the film project and conversations with my generous and knowledgeable friends René López and Jorge Pérez guided this effort.

Cortijo's Revenge: New Mappings of Puerto Rican Culture

[1] *El Mundo*, August 9, 1988, p. 33.

[2] *El Mundo*, August 13, 1988, p. 23.

[3] *El Mundo*, September 5, 1988, p. 5.

[4] Cited in *El Mundo*, December 11, 1988, p. 39.

[5] *El Mundo*, August 10, 1988, p. 35.

[6] *El Nuevo Día*, June 6, 1988, p. 53.

[7] *El Mundo*, December 11, 1988, p. 39.

[8] Edgardo Rodríguez Juliá. *El entierro de Cortijo* (Río Piedras: Huracán, 1983), p. 37. Page references in text are to this edition.

[9] *El Mundo*, August 9, 1988.

[10] Ramón Romero Rosa. "El negro puertorriqueño," in *Sources for the Study of the Puerto Rican Migration* (New York: Center for Puerto Rican Studies, History Task Force), c1982.

[11] A.G. Quintero Rivera. "Ponce, the Danza and the National Question: Notes Toward a Sociology of Puerto Rican Music," *Cimarron.* 1(Winter 1986):49–65.

[12] Antonio S. Pedreira. *Insularismo* (Río Piedras: Edil, 1973), p. 94.

[13] *Ibid.*

[14] See the previous chapter of this book.

[15] Tato Laviera. *AmeRícan* (Houston: Arte Público Press, 1985).

[16] *Insularismo*, p. 110.

[17] Philip Brookman and Guillermo Gómez-Peña, eds. *Made in Aztlán.* Centro Cultural de Raza (San Diego, CA: Tolteca Pubs., 1987).

[18] Gloria Anzaldúa. *Borderlands / La Frontera: The New Mestiza* (San Francisco, Spinsters/Aunt Lute, 1987), p. 80.

[19] "The Flying Bus," trans. Elpidio Laguna-Díaz, in *Images and Identities: The Puerto Ricans in Two World Contexts* (New Bruswick: Transaction, 1987), pp. 17–25. Original text in Spanish, "La guagua aérea," in *Imágenes e identidades: el puertorriqueño en la literatura* (Río Piedras: Huracán, 1985), pp. 23–30.

[20] Sandra María Esteves. *Yerba Buena* (New York: Greenfield Review Press, 1980).

[21] Tato Laviera.

[22] *Insularismo*, p. 157.

[23] *Ibid.*, pp. 136–137.

[24] Tato Laviera, "rafa," *Enclave* (Houston: Arte Público Press, 1981).

National Culture and Migration: Perspectives from the Puerto Rican Working Class

[1] The text of the debate on House Bill 14 is reprinted in Amílcar Tirado Avilés, *Las ideas y la acción de Ramón Romero Rosa, obrero tipógrafo* (unpublished Master's thesis, State University of New York at Buffalo, 1976), pp. 174–6. De Diego: "Yo creo que el trabajo en el hombre no debe regularse, pues esto es atentatorio a la

libertad de contratación. Un hombre puede trabajar y echar sobre sus hombros la carga que pueda resistir con arreglo a su constitución y energías. Y hacer una ley en ese sentido equivaldría a obligar a las casas mercantiles y factorías a envasar sus artículos o productos con arreglo a una determinada cantidad de peso, cosa que sería irrealizable . . . El obrero no debe esperarlo todo del Estado; él puede y debe elevarse por su propio esfuerzo y subir si es necesario con uno, con dos, con tres quintales a cuestas hasta escalar como Sísifo a la altura de la roca. En Alemania, en Inglaterra, en los Estados Unidos los obreros han laborado propiamente su dignificación y han logrado hacer asociaciones respetables, sin que hayan concurrido otros factores que sus propias iniciativas y sus honrados esfuerzos."

[2] Romero Rosa, *Ibid.*: " . . . nosotros sabemos que la mayoría de la clase de trabajadores agrícolas permanece en un estado de analfabetismo tal, que casi puede comparársela a la bestia. Negada de todas las luces de la instrucción, escasa del pan del estómago, como cohibida del pan del cerebro, yo entendía que nosotros, representantes del pueblo de Puerto Rico, debíamos acudir en auxilio de ella . . . Bien es cierto que la miseria ha existido siempre; pero la miseria antigua era de orden natural, promovida por acidentes; la miseria de ahora es de orden artificial, promovida por la sobreproducción del maquinismo . . . nosotros que a cada instante hablamos a nombre de la patria puertorriqueña, estamos en el deber de acudir a favor de la clase preferida. Si queremos hacer patria, acudamos con nuestra inteligencia y nuestros esfuerzos posibles, a levantar la clase campesina, abeja laboriosa, que por ella empieza la patria puertorriqueña. Acudamos a favor de la clase campesina para que mañana podamos decir, que hemos hecho una patria digna, honrada, inteligente y laboriosa."

[3] Concha Meléndez, *José de Diego en mi memoria* (San Juan: Instituto de Cultura Puertorriqueña, 1966).

[4] José de Diego, "Cuestiones obreras: Discurso del autor, como presidente de la Cámara de Delegados, en la sesión del 28 de enero de 1913," *Obras completas* (San Juan: Instituto de Cultura Puertorriqueña, 1966), II, pp. 191–214.

[5] De Diego, *Obras Completas*, II, pp. 547–8: "Somos ciudadanos de los Estados Unidos, vivimos y veinte mil soldados nuestros irán a pelear y morir bajo su gloriosa bandera . . . debemos esperar a que la sangre puertorriqueña avive el resplandor de la bandera de los Estados Unidos, para que esa sangre derramada por ella enriquezca de un nuevo título nuestro derecho y hable por nosotros al pueblo americano en los jubilosos días triunfantes de la paz del Mundo, cuando los grandes con la ayuda de los pequeños hayan afirmado sobre bases inconmovibles la libertad de todos los pueblos de la Tierra."

[6] Rosendo Matienzo Cintrón, "Alí Biberón, Califa de la Isla de Pasmos, Tigelino su consejero y unos jóvenes turcos," *Rosendo Matienzo Cintrón: Orientador y guardián de una cultura*, ed. Luis M. Diaz Soler (San Juan: Instituto de Literatura Puertorriqueña, 1960), II, pp. 17–20.

[7] See Díaz Solar, "El Partido de la Independencia, experimento que fracasó," *ibid.*, I, pp. 522–547.

[8] Rafael López Landrón, "Los Ideales Socialistas," in Santiago Iglesias, *Gobierno propio . . . ¿Para quién?* (San Juan: Federación Libe de Trabajadores, 1907).

[9] Romero Rosa, "La cuestión social y Puerto Rico," in *Lucha obrera en Puerto Rico*, ed. A.G. Quintero Rivera (Río Piedras: CEREP, 1971), pp. 16–32. The Romero Rosa manifesto of 1899 was entitled "El Criterio Libre"; the quote reads: "Siempre sostendré con interesado afán el sagrado axioma del inmortal Carlos Marx, que dice:

'La emancipación de los trabajadores, obra ha de ser de los trabajadores mismos.' "

[10] Romero Rosa, *Ibid*.: "Jamás seré regionalista en el sentido de creerme que sea esta hermosa porción de tierra mi único y exclusivo centro de vida, por más que encierro en mi alma profundas impresiones de amor y cariño para Puerto Rico, y un mundo de poesías que entonar en holocausto de su bellezas naturales. Para mi entera convicción, en donde quiera que el hombre mueva los brazos en la fecunda labor productiva, y tenga por galardón y orgullo el destrazar sus carnes en las faenas cotidianas, allí está su patria, su honor y su vida ... "

[11] The text of "Pachín" Marín's "El Trapo" reads:

Cuando un pueblo no tiene una bandera,
bandera libre que enarbole ufano,
en pos de su derecho soberano
y el patriotismo, la gentil quimera;

si al timbre faltan de su gloria entera
bríos de combate en contra del tirano,
la altiva dignidad del ciudadano
o el valor instintivo de la fiera;

con fe gigante y singular arrojo
láncese al campo del honor fecundo
tome un lienzo, al azar, pálido o rojo,

y, al teñirlo con sangre el iracundo,
verá cambiarse el mísero despojo
en un trapo que asombre a todo el mundo.

[12] The full text of "Bandera antillana" is in De Diego, *Obras completas*, I, pp. 343–4.

[13] Romero Rosa, "El Criterio Libre": " ... el obrero no debe ser patriota en el sentido místico de la expresión ni tampoco dejarse arrastrar por los fanatismos que las religiones envuelven ... inventadas por los acaparadores, para ... llenar de fantasías y sueños de mentidos paraísos el cerebro de los infelices productores, y prepararles para la sumisión, la mansedumbre y la obediencia ciega, con el objeto de que nunca puedan rebelarse contra las injusticias de los patronos y los gobiernos y las ingratitudes de los dominadores ... desde el instante en que se establece en el obrero la regionalidad, entra a germinar en él los odios de razas y naciones para dejar sin efecto la fraternidad universal y la paz del orbe entero."

[14] Eduardo Conde, "Los Reyes Magos," *Unión Obrera* (8 enero 1905): "Basta que un niño de padres ricos ponga una pequeña cajita (y algunas veces hasta sin ponerla) con muy poca hierba en el balcón o bajo de la cama, para que al siguiente día aparezcan infinidad de regalos y golosinas, pero ... los niños pobres. ¡Ah! los que son muy pobres, los que andan descalzos y desnudos, los que no comen, los que duermen en el duro suelo de un zaguán, a la intemperie en paseos y plazuelas, los que son abandonados por sus mismos padres, porque no pueden mantenerlos, esos, ¡esos! ... ya pueden poner toda la hierba que quieran, que seguramente nada encontrarán porque los Reyes no pasan por los zaguanes, ni por paseos ni plazuelas, ellos caminan *por todo lo alto*, viajan por las azoteas para dejar los regalos a los hijos

de los satisfechos, a los que en dos minutos destrozan un juguete de diez dollars; diez dollars que han podido servir para comprar (aunque pobremente) ropa y calzado para diez niños que necesitan de ello porque no lo tienen." "Respuesta terrible tiene eso ¿por qué? Porque el infeliz obrero es explotado por el patrono de una manera abusiva y cruel; porque lo que se gasta en lujo superfino no deja para atender en ese día a esa aspiración justa de los niños pobres; porque los que tienen sus escaparates llenos de chucherías las necesitan para sacar el quiniento por cien según sus cálculos ... "

[15] "Los niños ricos, bien pueden cantar:
'Ya se van los Reyes
Bendito sea Dios
Ellos van y vuelven'
...
Sí, que vuelvan, porque ellos os quieren mucho;
que vuelvan para que os traigan más y más pitos,
tambores y carretas.
Los niños pobres también cantarán:
'Ya se van los Reyes ... '
...
Que se vayan, y ¡ojalá no vuelvan más!"

[16] Manuel F. Rojas, quoted in *Lucha obrera en Puerto Rico*, p. 73: "La independencia económica no puede ser obtenida luchando solamente en el campo económico. Mientras el capitalista reciba el poder que dimana del pueblo, convertido en ley, ley adulterada, ley confeccionada en una forma que el capitalismo es el único beneficiado, no es posible, camaradas, pensar en la independencia económica sin ley que facilite su consecución ... Aquí, en esta primera Convención del partido que representamos, debemos resolver que las fuerzas todas del pueblo se unan para luchar por la emancipación social, económica y *política* del pueblo mismo."

[17] *Memorias de Bernardo Vega*, ed. César Andreu Iglesias (Río Piedras: Ediciones Huracán, 1977).

[18] De Diego, "El Desplazamiento," *Obras completas*, II, pp. 23–26; p. 24: "sin precedentes en ningún gobierno civilizado; y es que alguien ha concebido la idea de impulsar la emigración, de ¡negociar! la emigración de puertorriqueños ... ¡El desplazamiento, el lanzamiento, la proscripción de los nativos, con carácter oficial, por medio de una ley o de un tratado o de algo que no se ha visto ni oído nunca en el derecho de gentes, en la historia de la colonización ni aun por el sistema cruel de los conquistadores asiáticos!"

[19] *Ibid.*, p. 25–6: "¡El desplazamiento! El desplazamiento en todas sus formas, hasta en aquella flamante del arreglo diplomático con países extranjeros: del lenguaje castellano por el inglés, de los jíbaros por los yankis ... ¿No se nos podría también desplazar la latitud geográfica, la Isla entera, con montañas, llanuras, ríos, árboles, para largarnos con el viento a otra parte menos perseguida por los ciclones y los gobiernos coloniales? ... Ningún puertorriqueño debe irse de Puerto Rico, ningún patriota debe abandonar a su Patria, para que su puesto sea ocupado por un invasor ... ¡todos aquí, aquí adentro, firmes, encerrados por el hambre y la protesta, sin negar a la tierra madre nuestra resistencia en la vida y nuestros huesos en la muerte!"

[20] Eduardo Conde, *Unión Obrera* (5 noviembre 1906): "En lo que a la organización de los obreros se refiere, De Diego dijo en un meeting unionista dado en

San Juan: 'Para que los obreros puedan organizarse primero tienen que curarse la anemia ... El trabajador debe ganar para su sustento y nada más'."

[21] De Diego, *Obras completas*, II, pp. 534–5: "... hace algunos años me di por entero al examen de la escuela antropológica del derecho penal y recorrí la copiosa literatura de los jurisconsultos y sociólogos italiano en la materia: me sorprendí de que Lombroso, si mal no recuerdo en *L'Uomo Delinquente* encontrase en el tipo del norteamericano el super hombre de la edad moderna, de cuello prolongado, largas piernas, ancho tórax, fisiológicamente dotado de una voluntad agresiva y tenaz en la lucha por el progreso ... estimé aún más altamente el valor moral de los Estados Unidos, de este pueblo oriundo ya de una de las razas superiores de Europa, fortalecido por el cruzamiento con otras razas de análogo origen, situado en una colosal porción del Mundo, ante los prolíficos dones del suelo, del subsuelo y del cielo, ampliáronse así mi admiración y mi simpatía hacia el pueblo americano ... porque mi fe también crecía en la justicia que ha de otorgar al pueblo puertorriqueño y la eficacia de la insistencia de nuestra demanda por el bien y la libertad de nuestro pueblo."

[22] *Memorias de Bernardo Vega*, p. 38: "Todos se dolieron de mi decisión de partir, por la pérdida, según dijeron, que significaba para nuestro naciente movimiento obrero, pero no se esforzaron por disuadirme. Como socialistas, nuestra trinchera estaba en cualquier lugar del mundo."

[23] *Ibid.*, pp. 37–38: "Era yo para entonces un hombre de estatura mayor que la corriente entre los puertorriqueños. Jíbaro de la montaña, era blanco, y en mi rostro había un matiz de cera, característico de los hombres del corazón de nuestra patria. La cara redonda, de pómulos salientes; la nariz, aventada y chata; los ojos pequeños, de pupilas azules; la boca, pues diré que tenía labios de un cierto aire sensual; buena dentadura, con bien formados dientes. Tenía abundante cabellera de color castaño claro, y en contraste con la redondez de la cara, se me figura que tenía las quijadas cuadradas. En conjunto, me sentía bastante feo, aunque nunca faltaron mujeres que me tuvieron por lo contrario."

[24] *Ibid.*, p. 38: "No inspiraba mucha simpatía a primera vista, estoy seguro. No he sido nunca un hombre de fáciles amistades. Sin duda, mi físico ha tenido mucho que ver en esto. A poco de vivir en Nueva York, me di cuenta de lo difícil que se le hacía a la gente adivinar mi procedencia. En infinidad de ocasiones se me tomó por judío polaco, por tártaro, y aún por japonés ... ¡Dios perdone a mis padres por esta humanidad, que en fin de cuentas fue lo único que me legaron!"

[25] *Ibid.*, p. 244 (about Schomburgh): "Llegó aquí como emigrante y legó una rica obra a nuestros paisanos y a los norteamericanos negros: ¡magnífico ejemplo de identidad de pueblos oprimidos!"

[26] *Ibid.*, p. 40: "No quería perder ni un hálito de los últimos minutos en mi patria, últimos para mi, quizás."

[27] *Ibid.*, p. 40: "Yo no. Yo permanecí en cubierta, y estuve allí hasta que se perdió la isla en las primeras sombras de la noche." "Del compartimiento de primera comenzaron a bajar hombres de negocios, familias pudientes y estudiantes. De segunda, en la que yo me encontraba, bajábamos los emigrantes, tabaqueros en mayoría." "Con los primeros ahorros, se mandaría a buscar al familiar más cercano. Luego, al cabo de unos años, se regresaría a la patria con buenas economías. Quien más quien menos, tenía vista la finca que compraría o concebido el negocito que montaría en su pueblo ... Todos llevábamos nuestro castillito en el aire."

[28] *Ibid.*, P. 41: "Todos los recién llegados estábamos muy bien vestidos. Quiero

decir, llevábamos nuestro ajuar dominguero. Por mi parte, vestía yo un flus—como decían en mi pueblo—de cheviot azul marino. Llevaba sombrero borsalino de pajilla italiana. Calzaba zapatos negros de punto a la vista. Lucía chaleco blanco y corbata roja. Debí haber llegado con un flamante reloj pulsera, pero un compañero de viaje me aseguró que esa prenda la usaban sólo los afeminados en Nueva York. Ya a la vista de la ciudad, cuando el barco penetraba en la bahía, arrojé el reloj al mar . . . ¡Y pensar que poco más tarde esos relojes-pulsera se hicieron moda y acabaron por imponerse! Llegué, pues, a Nueva York sin reloj."

[29] *Ibid.*, p. 39: "El alba me sorprendió en la Plaza de Armas, sentado en unos de los bancos, mirando de vez en cuando el reloj del Ayuntamiento."

[30] In Spanish, the leaflet read: "Gran conferencia a cargo de d. Luis Muñoz Marín . . . Sensacionales declaraciones políticas serán hechas por este inteligente joven sobre el manifiesto hecho últimamente en Puerto Rico por los señores Tous Soto y Antonio Barceló, en nuestro empeño de no dejar huérfana de información a la colonia puertorriqueña residente en Nueva York . . . "

[31] Muñoz Marín, quoted in *El Mundo* (7 octubre 1920): "En nombre del país, de Puerto Rico y del criollismo puro, yo pido a la convención que vote unánimamente en contra del pacto con los republicanos, que es también un partido burgués, un partido de ínfima y de desvergüenza, ya que figura en el don José Tous Soto, su Presidente, que es abogado de la Guánica Central, la corporación más poderosa de Puerto Rico y una de las que explotan miserablemente el proletariado del país. Estamos viviendo aquí una hora decisiva en la historia del socialismo puertorriqueño. Todo hombre que se encuentre en este local y que siente cuales son sus ideales socialistas, cuales son sus principios y cual es su base, yo creo que ningún hombre de esta clase puede sancionar un pacto con cualquier partido burgués que haya en el mundo."

[32] Muñoz Marín, *El Mundo* (8 octubre 1920): "Algunos camaradas me han observado que en distintas ocasiones han ocurrido alianzas entre el partido socialista y el partido de orden burgués. A esto contestaba yo que ese ejemplo no se aplica al presente caso, pues aunque alianzas de esa índole las insinuó Marx en su *Manifiesto Comunista*, y hasta se han efectuado varias veces, siempre ha sido en países despóticos, militaristas, etc. y en los cuales el partido burgués tenía tantos ardores revolucionarios como el partido proletario. He dicho muchas veces que el capitalismo es un gran cuervo, del cual es el ala derecha el partido unionista y el ala izquierda el partido republicano. No veo ninguna utilidad en unirse a ésta para cortar la otra."

[33] L. Muñoz Marín, Evaristo Ribera Chevremont and Antonio Coll Vidal, *Madre haraposa: Páginas rojas* (San Juan: Cantero, Barros, 1918).

[34] Muñoz Marín, "The Pamphlet," appears in English translation (no original available) in *Borinquen: An Anthology of Puerto Rican Literature*, ed. María Teresa Babín and Stan Steiner (New York: Random House, 1974), p. 199.

[35] Proceedings of the fourth Convention of the Socialist Party, held in May, 1919, appear in *Lucha obrera en Puerto Rico*, pp. 73–94.

[36] Muñoz Marín, "La personalidad puertorriqueña en el Estado Libre Asociado," December 29, 1953: "Sabemos que la cultura puertorriqueña, lo mismo que la de Estados Unidos es y ha de ser parte de la gran cultura occidental. Pero no hay tal cosa como un hombre occidental que no sea hombre de algún sitio de Occidente. Si no somos occidentales con raíces puertorriqueñas, seremos occidentales sin raíces. Y la vitalidad de los pueblos tiene gran necesidad de raíces. Somos gente occidental a la manera de nuestas raíces. Somos americanos de Estados Unidos y americanos de América y occidentales de Occidente. Y los somos como puertorriqueños de Puerto

Rico."

[37] Muñoz Marín, "Declaraciones de Gobernador de Puerto Rico ante la Junta de Aeronáutica Civil" (31 enero 1949), *Los gobernadores electos de Puerto Rico* (Río Piedras: COSEBI, 1973), I, p. 15: "Y los puertorriqueños tienen tanto derecho como los ciudadanos de cualquier estado de la Unión a poder trasladarse a los sitios donde haya nuevas oportunidades de trabajo."

[38] Muñoz Marín, "Mensaje a la decimoséptima Asamblea Legislativa en su tercera Legislatura Ordinaria; (14 marzo 1951), *ibid.*, p. 198: "De no haber sido por la migración—con la cual podemos sin embargo contar como normal en el flujo de ciudadanos dentro de la Unión—el número de desempleados hubiera aumentado en vez de hacerse ligeramente reducido ... "

[39] Muñoz Marín, "La personalidad puertorriqueña en el Estado Libre Asociado": "De gente como él se hicieron los Estados Unidos. Gente que individualmente se fueron adaptando a la cultura que encontraron allí y contribuyendo a ella y enriqueciéndola. El puertorriqueño que establezca residencia en Estados Unidos debe adaptarse a su nueva comunidad como lo hicieron antes que él irlandeses, polacos, italianos y escandinavos."

[40] María Teresa Babín, "Introduction: The Path and the Voice," *Borinquen*, pp. xi–xxvi.

[41] Pedro Pietri, *Puerto Rican Obituary* (New York: Monthly Review, 1973).

[42] Jorge Soto's drawings which refer to the Puerto Rican cultural tradition appear in *Taller de cultura: Cuaderno* (New York: Centro de Estudios Puertorriqueños, 1976).

[43] *Nuyorican Poetry: An Anthology of Words and Feelings*, ed. Miguel Algarín and Miguel Piñero (New York: Morrow, 1975), p. 9.

[44] Jesús Colón, *A Puerto Rican in New York and Other Sketches* (New York: Arno Press, 1975), pp. 201–2.

[45] Louis Reyes Rivera, "For Tom and Judy," *Poets in Motion*, ed. L. Reyes Rivera (New York: Shamal, 1976), pp. 62–68.

[46] L. Reyes Rivera, *Who Pays the Cost.* (New York: Shamal, 1977).

[47] The poem "Grito de Lares" appears in *Sunbury*, 5 (1976), pp. 62–68.

[48] Eugenio Sánchez López, "Cuestión palpitante," *Unión Obrera* (10 diciembre 1906): "¿No alcanzais a ver el elemento profesional, a la Banca, el Comercio y los industriales tratando de unirse y uniéndose a sus iguales en la Nación? Seguramente que sí, y esto no es más que estos elementos interesados en salvar lo que llaman su patrimonio, no han de aferrarse á la terquedad de un regionalismo enervante. Aun cuando viviéramos la vida de 'República independiente' era inocente no poner de acuerdo nuestra organización con los camaradas de América, porque a pesar de nuestra independencia política tendríamos delante de sí como una amenaza el Coloso americano, con su Trust más temible aún. Y si por el contrario, económicamente hablando, nuestra suerte o destino industrial es idéntico al del pueblo obrero americano, y aun podemos decir más grave, porque no unimos nuestros destinos a los de aquellos compañeros. ¿Vamos a negar lo innegable, esto es, que á mayor suma de fuerzas más resistencia? ¿Seremos tan Quijotes que nuestra 'lanza' será más fuerte y mejor que la del soñador de la Dulcinea del Toboso?"

[49] Lenin, "The Nationalist Bogey of Assimilaton," chapter 3 of "Critical Remarks on the National Question" (1913), *Collected Works*, XX, pp. 17–51.

[50] The term "ethnic cysts" is used by Eugenio Fernández Méndez, "Los puertorriqueños en Nueva York," *La identidad y la cultura* (San Juan: Instituto de Cultura

Puertorriqueña, 1970), pp. 259–263; p. 263: "Deberá evitarse a todo trance la tendencia marcadísima de los puertorriqueños a formar en Nueva York un *quiste étnico* inasimilado, que será siempre motivo de discordia y fricciones."

Puerto Rican Literature in the United States: Stages and Perspectives

Works Cited

Binder, Wolfgang, "Anglos are weird people for me": Interviews with Chicanos and Puerto Ricans (Berlin: John F. Kennedy Institut für Nordamerikastudien at Freie Universität, 1979).

————, *Puerto Ricaner in New York: Volk Zwischen Zwei Kulturen* (Erlangen: Städtische Galerie, 1978).

Carrero, Jaime, *Jet neorriqueño: Neo-Rican Jet Liner* (San Germán: Universidad Interamericana, 1964).

————, *Pipo subway no sabe reír* (Río Piedras: Ediciones Puerto, 1973).

————, *Raquelo tiene un mensaje* (San Juan: Manuel Pareja, 1970).

Colón, Jesús, *A Puerto Rican in New York and Other Sketches* (New York: Mainstream, 1961).

Cotto-Thorner, Guillermo, *Trópico en Manhattan* (San Juan: Editorial Cordillera, 1960).

Díaz Valcárcel, Emilio, *Harlem todos los días* (México: Editorial Nueva Imagen, 1978).

Duany, Jorge, "Popular Music in Puerto Rico: Toward an Anthropology of Salsa," *Latin American Music Review* 5.2 (1984): 186–216.

Esteves, Sandra María, *Yerba Buena* (Greenfield: Greenfield Review, 1980).

Gelfant, Blanche H., "Mingling and Sharing in American Literature: Teaching Ethnic Fiction," *College English* 43 (1981): 763–72.

González, José Luis, "La noche que volvimos a ser gente," *Mambrú se fue a la guerra* (México: Joaquín Mortiz, 1972): 117–34.

Lewis, Oscar, *La vida: A Puerto Rican Family in the Culture of Poverty* (New York: Random, 1965).

Marín, Pachín, "Nueva York por dentro: Una faz de su vida bohemia," *La gaceta del pueblo* (1892?).

Mohr, Eugene, *The Nuyorican Experience: Literature of the Puerto Rican Minority*, (Westport: Greenwood, 1982).

Mohr, Nicholasa, *Nilda* (New York: Harper, 1973).

————, *Rituals of Survival: A Woman's Portfolio* (Houston: Arte Público Press, 1985).

Padró, José de Diego, *En Babia* (México: El Manuscrito de un Braquicéfalo, 1961).

Pietri, Pedro, *Puerto Rican Obituary* (New York: Monthly Review Press, 1973).

Rivera, Edward, *Family Installments* (New York: Penguin, 1983).

Rodríguez, Emilio Jorge, "Apuntes sobre la visión del emigrante en la narrativa puertorriqueña," *Primer seminario sobre la situación de las comunidades negra, chicana, cubana, india y puertorriqueña en Estados Unidos* (Havana: Editora Política, 1984): 445–85.

Sierra Berdecía, Fernando, *Esta noche juega el jóker* (San Juan: Biblioteca de Autores Puertorriqueños, 1939 and San Juan: Instituto de Cultura Puertorriqueña, 1960).

Thomas, Piri, *Down These Mean Streets* (New York: Knopf, 1967).

Vega, Bernardo, *Memoirs of Bernardo Vega* ed. César Andreu Iglesias, trans. Juan Flores (New York: Monthly Review Press, 1984).

Zeno Gandía, Manuel, *La charca*, trans. Kal Wagenheim (Maplewood: Waterfront, 1984).

_____, *El negocio* (Río Piedras: Editorial Edil, 1973).

_____, *Los redentores. Obras completas,* Vol. 2 (Río Piedras: Instituto de Cultura Puertorriqueña, 1973).

"La Carreta Made a U-Turn": Puerto Rican Language and Culture in the United States

[1] Milton Gordon, *Assimilation in American Life* (New York: Oxford University Press, 1963).

[2] Tato Laviera, *La Carreta Made a U-Turn* (Houston: Arte Público Press, 1979). All Laviera's poems in this essay are from this book. The term *Nuyorican* derives from a combination of New York and Puerto Rican.

[3] Standard language is widely assumed to be evidence of clear thought and more elaborated ideas. Basil Bernstein in "A Sociolinguistic Approach to Social Learning" (*Penguin Survey of the Social Sciences*, J. Gould [ed., Hammondsworth, England: Penguin Books, 1965], pp. 144–68) asserts this linkage; in *Class Codes and Control* (New York: Wiley, 1972) he argues that social control is exercised through the hegemony of such ideas (a virtual withdrawal from the controversies spawned by his work). Louis Althusser's insights on the ideological aspects of language standardization and social behavior are pertinent here ("Ideology and Ideological State Apparatuses," *Lenin and Philosophy* [New York: Monthly Review Press, Modern Reader, 1971], pp. 132–33).

[4] J.S. Coleman, *Equality of Educational Opportunity*, Department of Health, Education and Welfare (Washington, DC: U.S. Government Printing Office, 1966); and R. de Lone (for the Carnegie Council on Children), *Small Futures: Children, Inequality and the Limits of Liberal Reform* (New York: Harcourt, Brace, Jovanovich, 1979).

[5] The linguistic evidence reported in this section derives from an interdisciplinary study by the Language Policy Task Force, which includes co-authors Pedro Pedraza and John Attinasi, and Shana Poplack and Alicia Pousada. The work was sponsored by the Ford Foundation, the National Institute of Education and the Center for Puerto Rican Studies, City University of New York. Mention of specific studies is appropriate here. Pedraza was responsible for most of the fieldwork and the ethnographic description of speech, "Ethnographic Observation of Language Usage in East Harlem" (Centro de Estudios Puertorriqueños, CUNY).

The main socio-linguistic conclusions in the present article are treated at greater length by LPTF in "Social Dimensions of Language Use in East Harlem" (Centro de Estudios Puertorriqueños Working Paper no. 7, 1980) and are contextualized in "Language Policy and the Puerto Rican Community," *The Bilingual Review*, 5/1–2 (January-August, 1978): 1–40; and (Centro de Estudios Puertorriqueños Working

Paper no. 1, Language Policy Task Force). Specific studies concerning the types of code-switching and their relation to bilingual ability may be found in Shana Poplack, "Syntactic and Social Constraints on Code-switching," *Latino Language and Communicative Behavior,* Ricardo Durán, ed. (Norwood, NJ: Ablex, Language Policy Task Force Working Paper no. 2, 1978); and Shana Poplack, " 'Sometime I'll Start a Sentence in English y termino en Español': Toward a Typology of Code-switching" (Language Policy Task Force Working Paper no. 4, 1979); and David Sankoff and Shana Poplack, "A Formal Grammar for Code-Switching" (Language Pclicy Task Force Working Paper no. 8, 1980). Regarding linguistic structure, the analysis of the verbal system appears in Alicia Pousada and Shana Poplack, "No Case for Convergence: The Puerto Rican Spanish Verb System in a Language Contact Situation" (Language Policy Task Force Working Paper no. 5, 1979); and plural marking is examined in detail by Shana Poplack, "Deletion and Disambiguation in Puerto Rican Spanish: A Study of Verbal (n) (Language Policy Task Force Working Paper no. 3, 1978; expanded version in *Language,* 56/2 [Summer 1980]), and Poplack, "Variable Concord in Sentential Plural Marking" (Language Policy Task Force Working Paper no. 6, 1980). The attitudinal report appears in greater detail in John Attinasi, "Language Attitudes in a New York Puerto Rican Community," in *Ethnoperspectives in Bilingual Education Research: Bilingual Education and Public Policy in the United States*, R. Padilla, ed. (Ypsilanti: Eastern Michigan University, 1979), pp. 408–61.

[6] The block we studied is ninety percent Puerto Rican, greater in ethnic density than most Puerto Rican communities, great even in comparison with the rest of El Barrio. Actually, only twenty percent of Puerto Ricans in the United States live in neighborhoods where they are in the majority, with the average density at twenty-five percent. U.S. Department of Commerce, Bureau of the Census, New York Tract no. 166. (Washington, DC: Census of Population, U.S. Government Printing Office, 1970); U.S. Department of Labor, *A Socio-Economic Profile of Puerto Rican New Yorkers* (New York: Bureau of Labor Statistics 1975); D. Waggoner, "Geographic Distribution, Nativity and Age Distribution of Language Minorities in the United States," Spring 1976, and "Place of Birth and Language Characteristics of Persons of Hispanic Origins in the United States: Spring 1976," National Center for Educational Statistics Bulletins 78 B-S, 78 B-6. (Washington, DC, U.S. Department of Health, Education and Welfare, Education Division, U.S. Government Printing Office, 1978).

[7] In all, we discovered nine major networks of social interaction at this research site, with subgroupings in each. These were all informal associations of men, or women with or without children, or mixed adults, or adolescents, that shared leisure-time activities. Some were heterogeneous, centered upon a locale or institution; others were defined more by similar characteristics of age, sex or family. If a network consisted mainly of members of similar age and sex, the subgroupings were divided according to migration experience; if a network was defined by similar migration history, subgroupings were delineated by age and sex. All the networks interconnected in the neighborhood through friendship and familial ties. We did not follow the extensions of these networks outside the community, and we focused our observations principally on public and semipublic settings.

[8] Only balanced bilinguals and mainly Spanish-speaking persons were used in these studies, with characterization of competence derived from observed usage, self-report of the language that "feels most comfortable," and of language choice in various settings. Influence from English may of course be expected to be most apparent in the Spanish of those who almost exclusively use English. Such speak-

ers, however, were not included for analysis, because they did not produce enough Spanish to compare quantitatively with the others.

⁹ A language attitude survey was conducted through personal tape-recorded interviews using a questionnaire of over one hundred seventy-five items. The sample included ninety-one persons chosen as representative by Pedraza in the course of the ethnographic observation.

¹⁰ A *New York Times* survey conducted May 11–14, 1980, showed similar results.

¹¹ Pedro Pietri, *Puerto Rican Obituary* (New York: Monthly Review Press, 1973).

¹² René Marqués, *La carreta* (Río Piedras: Editorial Cultural, 1963).

¹³ See especially the Introduction to *Nuyorican Poetry: An Anthology of Puerto Rican Words and Feelings*, Miguel Algarín and Miguel Piñero, eds. (New York: William Morrow, 1975).

¹⁴ Eduardo Seda-Bonilla, *Requiem por una cultura* (Río Piedras: Ediciones Bayoán, 1972).

¹⁵ Oscar Lewis, *La Vida: A Puerto Rican Family in the Culture of Poverty—San Juan and New York* (New York: Random House, 1965). See also, Lewis, *A Study of Slum Culture: Backgrounds for La Vida* (New York: Random House, 1968).

¹⁶ Seda-Bonilla, *Requiem por una cultura.*

¹⁷ Manuel Maldonado-Denis, "Cultura y educación: el problema de la asimilación cultural," in *Puerto Rico y Estados Unidos: Emigración y Colonialismo* (Mexico: Siglo XXI, 1976).

¹⁸ Luis Nieves-Falcón, *El emigrante puertorriqueño* (Río Piedras: Edil, 1975).

¹⁹ Oscar Handlin, *The Uprooted: The Epic Story of the Great Migrations that Made the American People* (New York: Grosset and Dunlap, 1951); also Handlin, *The Newcomers: Negroes and Puerto Ricans in a Changing Metropolis* (Cambridge, MA: Harvard University Press, 1959).

²⁰ Joseph P. Fitzpatrick, *Puerto Rican Americans: The Meaning of Migration to the Mainland* (Englewood Cliffs, NJ: Prentice-Hall, 1971).

²¹ Lewis, *La Vida.*

²² Colin Greer (ed.) *Divided Society: The Ethnic Experience in America* (New York: Basic Books, 1974).

²³ Eugenio Fernández Méndez, "¿Asimilación o enquistamiento?: dos polos del problema de la emigración transcultural puertorriqueño," in *La identidad y la cultura* (San Juan: Instituto de Cultura Puertorriqueño, 1970), pp. 245–58.

²⁴ See *Conversación con José Luis Gonzáles*, Arcadio Díaz Quiñones, ed. (Río Piedras: Ediciones Huracán, 1976).

²⁵ Juan Ángel Silén, "Aspectos sobresalientes del problema nacional puertorriqueño y la nueva lucha de independencia," *The Rican*, 2/2–3 (1974): 14–20.

²⁶ Maldonado-Denis, "Cultura y educación," pp. 123–54.

²⁷ Robert Blauner, *Racial Oppression in America* (New York: Harper & Row, 1972).

²⁸ Peter Kwong, *Chinatown, N.Y. Labor and Politics, 1930–1950* (New York: Monthly Review Press, 1979), pp. 12–13.

²⁹ Colin Green, "Remembering Class," in *Divided Society.*

³⁰ Bernardo Vega, *Memorias de Bernardo Vega*, Cesar Andreu Iglesias ed. (Río Piedras: Ediciones Huracán, 1975).

[31] Jesús Colón, *A Puerto Rican in New York and Other Sketches* (New York: Mainstream, 1961).

"Qué assimilated, brother, yo soy asimilao": The Structuring of Puerto Rican Identity

[1] Milton M. Gordon, *Assimilation in American Life* (Oxford, 1964).

[2] See, for example, Robert Blauner, *Racial Oppression in America* (New York: Harper and Row, 1972); Tomás Almaguer, "Class, Race and Chicano Oppression," *Socialist Revolution*, 5 (1975), 71–99; J.M. Blaut, "The Ghetto as an Internal Neo-colony," *Antipode*, 6/1 (1974), 37–42.

[3] See Frank Bonilla and Ricardo Campos, "A Wealth of Poor: Puerto Ricans in the New Economic Order," *Daedalus*, 110/2 (1981), 133–176; and "Imperialist Initiatives and the Puerto Rican Worker," *Contemporary Marxism*, 5 (1982), 1–18.

[4] José Rodríguez, "Abre el Ojo: A Study of the Current State of Abandon and the Role of the Artist," Unpublished Project Report, 1981.

[5] Tato Laviera, *La Carreta Made a U-Turn* (Houston: Arte Público Press, 1979).

[6] Oscar Lewis, *La Vida: A Puerto Rican Family in the Culture of Poverty* (New York: Random House, 1965.)

[7] A discussion of this mythical imagery in Nuyorican poetry may be found in: Efraín Barradas, " 'De lejos en sueños vería . . . '; Visión mística de Puerto Rico en la poesía neoyorrican," *Revista Chicano-Riqueña*, 7 (1979), 46–56. For a more critical approach, see Felix Cortés, Joe Falcón and Juan Flores, "The Cultural Expression of Puerto Ricans in New York," *Latin American Perspectives*, 3 (1976), 117–150.

[8] Piri Thomas, *Down These Mean Streets* (New York: Knopf, 1967); Pedro Pietri, *Puerto Rican Obituary* (New York: Monthly Review, 1973).

[9] Sandra María Esteves, *Yerba Buena* (New York: Greenfield Review, 1980).

[10] Victor Hernández Cruz, *Mainland* (New York: Random House, 1973). See also his *Snaps* (New York: Random House, 1969).

[11] Tato Laviera, *AmeRícan* (Arte Público Press, 1985). The González story is entitled "En el fondo del caño hay un negrito."

[12] J.M. Blaut, "Assimilation vs. Ghettoization," *Antipode*, 15/1 (1983), 35–41.

[13] *Ibid.*

[14] Though the argument presented here concurs in general with that in Blaut, 1983, I would object to the term "ghettoization" as a way of characterizing the alternative to assimilation. Blaut's account of the convergence of Black and Puerto Rican cultures tends to reduce that process to impinging socio-economic and geographical factors, with no emphasis on cultural historical compatibilities and parallels.

[15] For a valuable recent discussion of cultural geography, see Denis E. Cosgrove, "Towards a Radical Cultural Geography," *Antipode*, 15/1 (1983), 1–11. An initial consideration of Puerto Rican migration in terms of cultural geography may be found in Frank Bonilla, "Ethnic Orbits: The Circulation of Capitals and Peoples." Conference paper: "Ethnicity and Race in the Last Quarter of the 20th Century" (SUNY-Albany, 1984).

[16] See the preceeding chapter of this book.

[17] *Enclave* (Houston: Arte Público Press, 1981).

[18] Laviera, *AmeRícan* (Houston: Arte Público Press, 1985).

[19] *Ibid.*

Living Borders / Buscando América: Languages of Latino Self-Formation

[1] We agree with Guillermo Gómez-Peña that "[t]erms like 'Hispanic,' 'Latino,' 'Ethnic,' 'minority,' 'marginal,' 'alternative' and 'Third World,' among others, are inaccurate and loaded with ideological implications ... In the absence of a more enlightened terminology, we have no choice but to utilize them with extreme care." "The Multicultural Paradigm: An Open Letter to the National Arts community," *High Performance* (Fall 1989): 20.

[2] We have decided to emphasize "Latino" for, unlike "Hispanic," it is not an identity label imposed by the politicized statistics of the Census Bureau and the market who seek to target particular constituencies for political and economic manipulation. As for the shortcomings of "Latino," we hope that this article contributes to their critique. In a nutshell, the term "older immigrants" refers to the way in which assimilationist or "melting pot" sociologists (from Robert Park to Milton Gordon) constructed the experiences of late nineteenth and early twentieth-century immigrants according to a dynamic of contact, accommodation and assimilation that eventually amalgamated them into the dominant culture. The term "new ethnics" refers to the period of (white) ethnic revival, largely coinciding with civil rights struggles and their aftermath, in which "racial minorities and white ethnics became polarized on a series of issues relating to schools, housing, local government and control over federal programs." This revival has also been understood as the dying flash of white ethnicity in a longer historical process of acculturation. Cf. Stephen Steinberg, *The Ethnic Myth. Race, Ethnicity, and Class in America* (Boston: Beacon Press, 1982), pp. 48–51.

See also Richard H. Thompson, *Theories of Ethnicity. A Critical Appraisal* (Westport, CT: Greenwood Press, 1989), for whom the "rediscovery of ethnicity [by its American observers] is largely a response to the black protest movement of the 1960s, the state's subsequent definition and legitimation of that movement as an ethnic (but not primarily a class) movement, and the resulting increase in the United States of other ethnically defined movements by Hispanics, Asian-Americans and "white ethnics," who, observing the 'success' of black organization and the state's receptivity to it, have quite unmysteriously followed a similar track" (93).

[3] "Racial minority" is a term used to distinguish the historical experiences (enslavement and/or institutional exclusion from political economic and especially social enfranchisement) of certain groups (viz. African-American, Latinos, Asian-Americans and Native-Americans) from those of European immigrant groups for whom the dynamics described by ethnicity theories made possible the enfranchisements denied to the former. Cf. Michael Omi and Howard Winant, *Racial Formation in the United States. From the 1960s to the 1980s* (New York: Routledge & Kegan Paul, 1986).

[4] The historical discrimination against Mexican-Americans and Puerto Ricans is an experience which cannot be permitted to disappear by projecting Latinos as an overarching group. Such discrimination involves a complex of racial, class and "otherness" factors which often make middle-class sectors of other Latino groups anxious and seek to dissociate themselves. On the other hand, the fact that discrimination has been directed to all Latino groups contributes to a pan-Latino rejection of discrimination aimed at any particular group.

[5] Cf. Steinberg, pp. 24, 40 *et passim.*

[6] The increase in the Latin American population in the United States can be

more accurately compared with the *overall* European influx rather than with the numbers of any one particular group. If Latin American immigration, in conjunction with the high birth rate of U.S. Latinos, continues into the next century (which is likely), then proportionately the number of Latinos will rival or supersede that of the European immigrants since the turn of the nineteenth century. From 1820 to 1930, the estimated "net immigration of various European nationalities" is as follows: Germans, 5,900,000; Italians, 4,600,000; Irish, 4,500,00; Poles, 3,000,000; Canadians, 2,800,000; Jews, 2,500,000; English, 2,500,000; Swedes, 1,200,000; Scots and Scots-Irish, 1,000,000. Cf. Steinberg, ibid., p. 41.

[7] Cf. Michael Lev, "Tracking the Hispanic TV Audience," *The New York Times* (December 13, 1989): D 17. Lev's figures are taken from a Nielsen Hispanic Television survey funded by two of the largest Spanish TV networks, Univisión and Telemundo Group, Inc.

[8] Such decreases are comparable for other European immigrant populations in the United States. Cf. Joshua Fishman, et al., *Language Loyalty in the United States* (The Hague: Mouton, 1966), pp 42–44.

[9] Stanley Aronowitz, "Post-modernism and Politics," *Social Text*, 18 (Winter 1987/88): 108. Reprinted in Andrew Ross, ed., *Universal Abandon? The Politics of Post-modernism* (Minneapolis: University of Minnesota Press, 1988), pp. 46–62.

[10] *Ibid.*

[11] Edmundo O'Gorman, *The Invention of America. An Inquiry into the historical nature of the New World and the meaning of its history* (Bloomington: Indiana University Press, 1961).

[12] Frederick Jackson Turner, "The Significance of the Frontier in American History," *The Frontier in American History* (New York: Holt, 1920), p. 11.

[13] Richard Slotkin, *The Fatal Environment. the Myth of the Frontier in the Age of Industrialization, 1800–1890* (New York: Atheneum, 1985), p. 40.

In the case of African-Americans, of course, it was not such a "safety valve" but the racist state which contained their discontent.

[14] Guillermo Gómez-Peña, "Documented/Undocumented," in *Multi-Cultural Literacy. Opening the American Mind,* eds. Rick Simonson and Scott Walker (Saint Paul, MN: Graywolf Press, 1988), p. 127 challenges.

[15] "The Multicultural Paradigm," p. 20.

[16] Tato Laviera, *AmeRícan* (Houston: Arte Público, 1984), p. 95.

[17] Sandra María Esteves, *Yerba Buena* (Greenfield Center, NY: Greenfield Review, 1980).

[18] Sandra María Esteves, *Tropical Rains* (New York: African Caribbean Poetry Theater, 1984).

[19] Jacques Derridá, "The Parergon," *October*, 9 (Summer 1979): 20.

[20] Cf. Jean Baudrillard, *De la Séduction* (Paris: Galilée, 1979). Apropos of the simulacrum, Latin Americans have dealt with problems of cultural identity in terms of the "neither-nor" since the conquest. The difference between "neither-not" (or "not nowhere") is that the former is usually expressed by elites who feel in an ambivalent position vis-à-vis metropolitan cultural valuation while the latter is situated in the struggles of subordinated groups against a cultural "nonexistence" which elites are too often willing to exploit.

Enrique Lihn has parodied the *ninguneísta* discourse in *El arte de la palabra* (Barcelona: Pomaire, 1979). "We are nothing: imitations, copies, phantoms: repeaters of what we understand badly, that is, hardly at all: dead organ grinders: the animated fossils of a prehistory what we have lived *neither here nor there,* consequently, anywhere, for we are aboriginal foreigners, transplanted from birth in our respective countries of origin" (p. 82; our emphasis). This is a parody of the anxious discourse of those elites who seek to define the nation. Roberto Schwarz has written an in-depth critique of this kind of "national problem." "Brazilian Culture: Nationalism by Elimination," *New Left Review,* 167 (January/February 1988): 77–90.

[21] Cf. R. Butler, "On Creating a Hispanic America: A Nation within a Nation?" quoted in Antonio J. Califa, "Declaring English the Official Language: Prejudice Spoken Here," *Harvard Civil Rights-Civil Liberties Law Review,* 24 (1989): 321.

[22] Terry Robbins, Presentation at Florida International University (October 8, 1987), quoted in Califa, p. 321. Terry Robbins is a former head of U.S. English operations in Florida.

[23] Deutsch, "The Political Significance of Linguistic Conflicts," in *Les Etats Multilingues* (1975).

[24] An English First analysis of Immigration Reform and Control Act of 1986, Pub. Law No. 99–603, 1986 U.S. Cong. Code & Admin. News (100 Stat.) 3359, quoted in Califa, p. 313. Calif, "Declaring English the Official Language: Prejudice Spoken Here," *Harvard Civil Rights-Civil Liberties Law Review,* 24 (1989): 328.

[25] Cf. Joshua Fishman, " 'English Only': Its Ghosts, Myths and Dangers," *International Journal of the Sociology of Language,* 125, 132 (1988), quoted in Califa, p. 329.

[26] "Government and private experts agree that the threat of war with the Soviet Union is diminishing. As a result, the nation's military services argue that a portion of the Pentagon budget in the 1990's must be devoted to combating drugs and being prepared to bring American military power to bear in the third world." Stephen Engelberg, "In Search of Missions to Justify Outlays," *The New York Times* (January 9, 1990): A14.

[27] Thompson, p. 90.

[28] Cf. Jürgen Habermas, "Modernity—An Incomplete Project," in *The Anti-Aesthetic. Essays on Post-modern Culture.* ed. Hal Foster (Port Townsend, WA: Bay Press, 1983), p. 14

[29] Daniel Bell, "Ethnicity and Social Change," in Nathan Glazer and Daniel P. Moynihan, eds., *Ethnicity: Theory and Experience* (Cambridge: Harvard University Press, 1975), p. 169, as quoted in Thompson, op. cit., p. 99.

[30] According to Michael Omi and Howard Winant, the formation of the concept of ethnicity in the United States is rooted in a different historical conjuncture than ours and, thus, occludes this difference if invoked to account for the negotiation of value by non-European immigrants: "But both assimilationist and cultural pluralism had largely emphasized European, white immigrants, what Kallen called 'the Atlantic migration.' The origins of the concepts of 'ethnicity' and 'ethnic group' in the U.S., then, lay outside the experience of those identified (not only today but already in Park's and Kallen's time), as *racial* minorities: Afro-Americans, Latin Americans, Native Americans and Asian Americans (blacks, browns, reds and yellows). The continuity of experience embodied in the application of the terms of ethnicity theory to both groups—to European immigrants and racial minorities—was not established; indeed it tended to rest on what we have labelled the *immigrant analogy." Racial Formation in the United States,* pp. 16–17.

[31] As Stephen Steinberg argues, "Kallen's model of a 'democracy of nationalities'

is workable only in a society where there is a basic parity among constituent ethnic groups. Only then would ethnic boundaries be secure from encroachment, and only then would pluralism be innocent of class bias and consistent with democratic principles." *The Ethic Myth,* pp. 260–261. The reference is to Horace Kallen, "Democracy Versus the Melting Pot," in *Culture and Democracy in the United States* (New York: Boni and Liveright, 1924). This critique extends to later studies like Nathan Glazer, *Affirmative Discrimination* (New York: Basic Books, 1975).

[32] "[N]umerous new struggles have expressed resistance.

[33] Laclau and Mouffe, p. 184. See also Martha Minow, "We, the Family: Constitutional Rights and American Families," in *The Constitution and American Life,* ed. David Thelen (Ithaca: Cornell University Press, 1988), p. 319. "Against the new forms of subordination, and this from the very heart of the new society. Thus it is that the waste of natural resources, the pollution and destruction of the environment, the consequences of productivism have given birth to the ecology movement. Other struggles, which Manuel Castells terms 'urban,' express diverse forms of resistance to the capitalist occupation of social space. The general urbanization which has accompanied economic growth, the transfer of the popular classes to the urban periphery or their relegation to the decaying inner cities, and the general lack of collective goods and services have caused a series of new problems which affect the organization of the whole of social life outside work. Hence the multiplicity of social relations [not subordinatable to "class"] from which antagonisms and struggles may originate: habitat, consumption, various services, can all constitute terrains for the struggle against inequalities and the claiming of new rights." Ernesto Laclau and chantal Mouffe, *Hegemony and Socialist Strategy. Towards a Radical Democratic Politics* (London: Verso, 1985), p. 161.

Given that these new forms of subordination and terrains of struggle were not in place before World War II, the conditions of possibility for group self-understanding are no longer those which made prior theories of ethnicity socially and politically operational.

[34] "We, the Family," p. 322.

[35] Nancy Fraser, "Women, Welfare, and Politics," in *Unruly Practices. Power, Discourse and Gender in Contemporary Social Theory* (Minneapolis: University of Minnesota Press, 1989), p. 154.

[36] For example, "[I]n the 'masculine' subsystem . . . claimants must prove their 'cases' meet administratively defined criteria of entitlement; in the 'feminine' sybsystem, on the other hand, claimants must prove conformity to administratively defined criteria of need." *Ibid.*

[37] "[I]n a given context the presence of a particular unit is in contrast with its absence. When this situation holds it is usually the case that the unmarked form is more general in sense or has a wider distribution than the marked form." John Lyons, *Introduction to Theoretical Linguistics* (Cambridge: Cambridge University Press, 1969), p. 79. The example chosen by Lyons demonstrates that markedness is directly related to socially instituted norms of "generality." One can say "Is the dog a he or a she?" but one would not ask the same if referring to a "bitch," whose gender is necessarily female. Markedness relies on already instituted norms of generality; the theory, however, does not question the grounds on which such a generality is instituted. As regards ethnicity, "WASP"s are taken to be the unmarked form, while other groups are understood as "unmarked." And yet, nearly 90% of U.S. citizens are not WASPs.

[38] In an April 1988 study—"New Voices: Immigrant Students in the U.S. Public Schools," financed by the Ford Foundation, it was argued that "schools were doing a poor job of meeting the immigrant students' *needs*" (our emphasis). Cf. Associated Press, "Study Finds Obstacles Exist for Immigrant Schoolchildren," *The New York Times* (May 10, 1988). Both this and another study advocated increasing the number of Hispanic teachers to meet the cultural needs of students and thus ease the increasing dropout rate and other apparent education dysfunctionalities. Cf. Peter Applebome, "Educators Alarmed by Growing Rate of Dropouts Among Hispanic Youth," *The New York Times* (March 15, 1987): 22.

[39] Quoted in Thomas Weyr, *Hispanic U.S.A. Breaking the Melting Pot* (New York: Harper & Row, 1988), pp. 62–63.

[40] *Ibid.*

[41] Jürgen Habermas, *The Theory of Communicative Action. Vol. II. Lifeworld and System: A Critique of Functionalist Reason*, trans. Thomas McCarthy (Boston: Beacon Press, 1987), p. 365.

[42] Fraser, p. 156.

[43] Oskar Negt and Alexander Kluge, "The Public Sphere and Experience: Selections," trans. Peter Labanyi, *October*, 46 (Fall 1988), p. 60, translator's note.

[44] Fredric Jameson, "On Negt and Kluge," *October*, 46 (Fall 1988): 159.

[45] Cf. V.N. Voloshinov, *Marxism and the Philosophy of Language*, trans. Ladislav Matejka and I.R. Titunik (New York: Seminar Press, 1973), pp. 91–97 and M.M. Bakhtin, "The Problem of Speech Genres," in *Speech Genres and Other Late Essays*, trans. Vern W. McGee (Austin: University of Texas Press, 1986), pp. 61–102.

[46] Oskar Negt and Alexander Kluge, *Geschichte und Eigensinn* (Frankfurt: Zweitausendeins, 1981), p. 944, quoted in Jameson, p. 172.

[47] Jameson, p. 171.

[48] *Ibid.*, p. 78.

[49] *Ibid.*, p. 79.

[50] *Ibid.*, p. 76.

[51] (Boston: David R. Godine, 1982).

[52] *Ibid.*, p. 19.

[53] *Ibid.*, p. 187.

[54] *Ibid.*, p. 182.

[55] *Ibid.*, p. 124.

[56] *Ibid.*, p. 137.

[57] *Ibid.*, p. 151.

[58] Thomas B. Morgan, "The Latinization of America," *Esquire* (May 1983): 56.

[59] *Ibid.*, p. 3.

[60] (New York: Oxford University Press, 1986), pp. 46, 153, and 241.

[61] *Ibid.*, p. 259.

[62] *Ibid.*, pp. 54–55.

[63] *Ibid.*, p. 7.

[64] (April 18, 1989), p. 16.

[65] Patrick Barry, "When translation isn't enough, try 'trans-creation'," Special supplement on "The Hispanic Market," *Advertising Age* (February 14, 1983): M–21.

[66] *Ibid.*, p. M 26.

[67] *Ibid.*

[68] Susan Dentzer, "Learning the Hispanic Hustle," *Newsweek* (May 17, 1982): 84.

[69] Barry, p. M 26.

[70] "[A] show of disregard can cost a firm heavily in lost sales, as the Adolph Coors Co. discovered several years ago. Charged by Hispanic groups with discriminatory hiring practices that led to a boycott of its products, the brewer has fought to rebuild its image, in part by making donations to Hispanic causes." Dentzer, p. 86.

[71] Letter from Gerda Bikales, executive director of U.S. English, to the Secretary of the Federal Communications Commission (September 26, 1985), quoted in Califa, pp. 319–20. Cf. also Associated Press, "Group Wants to Stop Ads in Spanish," *San Jose Mercury News* (December 23, 1985).

[72] "[E]l barrio es el hilo conductor"; "[la salsa] representa plenamente la convergencia del barrio urbano de hoy [porque asume] la totalidad de ritmos que acuden a esa convergencia"; "La salsa no es un ritmo, y tampoco es un simple estilo para enfrentar un ritmo definido. La salsa es una forma abierta capaz de representar la totalidad de tendencias que se reúnen en la circunstancia del Caribe urbano [incluyendo Nueva York] de hoy; el barrio sigue siendo la única marca definitiva." Cf. César Miguel Rondón, *El libro de la salsa. Crónica de la música del caribe urbano* (Caracas: Editorial Arte, 1980), pp. 32–64 *et passim.* "We object to Philip Morris or any other companies who are advertising in languages other than English," said Stanley Diamond, head of the California chapter of U.S. English, an advocacy group. "What they are doing tends to separate out citizens and our people by language." " ... This fall Diamond ... chapter launched a coupon mail-in protest against a Spanish-language Yellow Pages ... " "We certainly would feel that the corporations, the telephone company with the Spanish Yellow Pages should change ... We will do everything we can to put this advertising in English only ... and in no other language," said Diamond. In Florida, U.S. English spokeswoman Terry Robbins ... has written as a private citizen to McDonald's and Burger King protesting Spanish in fast-food menus. "Why does poor Juan or Maria have a problem ordering a Whopper?" she asked. "It isn't that they aren't able to, they don't want to."

[73] Humberto Márquez, "Willie Colón inventa cosas para que la vida no duela," *El Diario de Caracas* (February 23, 1982): 14–15.

[74] *Ibid.*

[75] Cf. Jon Pareles, "Dancing Along with David Byrne," *The New York Times* (November 1, 1989): C 1. George Lipsitz makes a similar argument about Los Lobos' networking with other groups to create a new mass audience, a new public sphere: "For [drummer] Pérez, the world of rock-and-roll music is not a place that obliterates local cultures by rendering them invisible; rather it is an arena where diverse groups find common ground while still acknowledging important differences. The prefigurative counter-hegemony fashioned by Los Lobos has indeed won the allegiance of musicians from other marginalized cultures. Their songs have been recorded by country and western star Waylon Jennings as well as by polka artist Frankie Yankovic. The Cajun accordion player and singer Jo-El Sonnier views Los Lobos as artists whose cultural struggles parallel his own." "Cruising Around the Historical Bloc—Post-modernism and Popular Music in East Los Angeles," *Cultural Critique*, 5 (Winter 1986–87), p. 175.

[76] Cf. Juan Flores, "Rappin', Writin', and Breakin': Black and Puerto Rican Culture in New York, *Dissent* (Fall 1987): 580–84.

[77] *Chicago Sunday Times* (January 26, 1987).

[78] (San Francisco: Spinsters/Aunt Lute, 1987).

[79] *Ibid.*, p. 59.

[80] See note 71.

[81] *Ibid.*, p. 80.

[82] *Ibid.*, p. 81.

[83] The "ethical substance" is one of the four dimensions that comprise "ethics." It delimits what moral action will apply to: for example, the pleasures among the Greeks, the flesh among the early Christians, sexuality in Western modernity, and, we argue, group ethos—ethnic, feminist, gay, lesbian, etc.—in multi-cultural societies. Cf. Michel Foucault, *The Use of Pleasure* (New York: Vintage, 1986), pp. 26–28.

[84] Michel Foucault, "The Ethic of Care for the Self as a Practice of Freedom," in *The Final Foucault*, eds. James Bernauer and David Rasmussen (Cambridge: MIT Press, 1988), p. 19.

[85] *Ibid.*, p. 18.

[86] Gómez-Peña, "The Multicultural Paradigm," p. 22.

[87] Michael J. Fischer, "Ethnicity and the Post-Modern Arts of Memory," in James Clifford and George E. Marcus, eds. *Writing Culture: The Poetics and Politics of Ethnography* (Berkeley: University of California Press, 1986), p. 196.

[88] Esteves, *Yerba Buena.*

[89] Cf. Antonio Lauria, " 'Respeto,' 'Relajo' and Interpersonal Relations in Puerto Rico," *Anthropological Quarterly*, 37, 2 (1964): 53–67.

[90] Henry Louis Gates, Jr., *The Signifying Monkey: A Theory of Afro-American Literary Criticism* (New York: Oxford University Press, 1988).

[91] Gina Valdés, "Where You From?" *The Broken Line / La Línea Quebrada*, 1, 1 (May 1986).

[92] Victor Hernández Cruz, *Snaps.*

[93] Louis Reyes Rivera, *This One For You* (New York: Shamal, 1983).

[94] For discussions of *casitas* see the planned volume sponsored by the Bronx Council on the Arts, especially Luis Aponte, "*Casitas* as Place and Metaphor" and Joseph Sciorra, " 'We're not just here to plant. We have culture': A Case Study of the South Bronx *Casita, Rincón Criollo*." Cf. the discussion of Sciorra's work in Dinita Smith, "Secret Lives of New York: Exploring the City's Unexamined Worlds," *New York* (December 11, 1989): 34–41.

[95] Anzaldúa, p. 79.

[96] Renato Rosaldo, *Truth in Culture: The Remaking of Social Analysis* (Boston: Beacon, 1989), p. 216.

[97] Tato Laviera, *Mainstream Ethics* (Houston: Arte Público Press, 1988).

[98] Juan Felipe Herrera, "Border Drunkie at 'Cabaret Babylon-Aztlán,' " *The Broken Line / La Línea Quebrada.*

[99] Gómez-Peña, "The Multicultural Paradigm," p. 20.